DEAR POLLY

Letters to a Victorian Lady's Maid

Ed. MERIEL HAYES

Dedicated to my grandparents:
Alfred and Mary (Polly) Hayes
Harry and Ellen Guise

DEAR POLLY

Letters to a Victorian Lady's Maid

Ed. MERIEL HAYES

To Linda Blackburn
on this day
Saturday 29ᵗʰ march 2003

Best Wishes
Meriel Hayes

BREWIN BOOKS

First Published in October 2002 by
Brewin Books, Studley, Warwickshire B80 7LG
www.brewinbooks.com

British Library Cataloguing in Publication Data
A catalogue record for this book is available from
The British Library

ISBN 1 85858 221 0

Typeset in Times.
Made and printed in Great Britain by
Warwick Printing Company Limited,
Theatre Street, Warwick, Warwickshire CV34 4DR.

CONTENTS

INTRODUCTION

I was born in Redditch in the house built for my grandfather, Alfred Hayes, on land bought from the Earl of Plymouth. When I moved, I discovered a battered box containing over one hundred and fifty letters written in the eighteen-seventies to my future grandmother Mary (Polly) Weaver. A few were written by her close friend Mary Douglas, daughter of the Rector of Hanbury, a small village in Worcestershire. The majority were written by my grandfather. They tell a story of love, disappointment, hope and determination set against a background of Victorian Britain above and below stairs.

When Alf was twelve years old he went to work as a jobbing boy for Captain and Mrs Bourne at Grafton Manor, the "big house" near Bromsgrove in Worcestershire where Alf's family lived. Four years later in 1872, Polly joined the staff as a lady's maid. They fell in love but Polly's contract was temporary and soon they found themselves hundreds of miles apart. These letters were almost their only contact as Alf tried to find a steady job and a home for himself and Polly. While Polly moved around the country becoming increasingly frail, Alf became a station porter, a gardener, an Orderly at the Royal Military College, Sandhurst and a gamekeeper. He described his day to day life vividly and commented on local and national events of the times including several trials and an inquest.

It was seven years and after many problems that Alf finally found the job and home they wanted and they were able to marry. Both grandparents died before I was born and it is through this legacy that I have got to know them and to develop an interest in Victorian social life.

Meriel Hayes

Polly

Alf

ACKNOWLEDGEMENTS

The letters were in no particular order and most were partly dated. It was only by matching events with newspapers and developing a sequence that the letters gradually revealed their story.

I am particularly indebted to:

The editor of the Bromsgrove Messenger

Staff at: Bromsgrove Library,

          Kendal Library,

          Redditch Library,

          Stockport Library and Information Service

          Windsor Library

          Kendal Record Office,

          Worcester Record Office

          Regional H.Q. of Ancient Order of Foresters

Mr. Bernard Poultney, Hanbury

Mr. Morris, Grafton Manor

Mrs. Wheatley, Hanbury

Thameslink Publishing, Windsor

P.R.O.

Inhabitants of Hanbury and Much Cowarne

Friends and relatives for their invaluable help, especially:

Mr. Ian Cash

Miss Glenys Hall

Mr. Ian Hayes

Note: Spellings are as original and not always correct.

Copy of the flyleaf of the Family Bible

John Weaver, his book: December 1795

His children:

Nancy Weaver, was born August 7th 1790, about 2 o'clock in the day.

Mary Weaver, was born July 27th 1792, about 3 o'clock

Ann Weaver, was born July 18th 1795, about 10 o'clock

Dinah (Diana) Weaver was born in the year 1798, October 8th

Elizabeth Weaver, was born in the year 1801, 25th Feby.

William Weaver, was born in the year 1803, May 14th

> (William married twice, first to Charlotte Griffiths and second to Eleanor Barley)

All born at Hanbury, Worcestershire

John Weaver died February 23rd 1818 aged 50 years

Mary, his wife, died June 4th 1841 aged 78 years

Grandchildren:

Mary, daughter of Robert and Ann Cowley, born December 14th 1816

Elizabeth, daughter of Robert and Ann Cowley, born December 25th 1818

John, son of William and Charlotte Weaver, born May 8th 1833

Ann, daughter of William and Eleanor Weaver, born Aug. 11th 1852

MARY (POLLY), daughter of William and Eleanor Weaver, born Nov. 1st 1854

died July 5th 1930

There are many friends of summer
Who are kind while flowers bloom,
But when winter chills the blossom,
They depart with the perfume.
On the dread highway of action,
Friends of worth are far and few,
So when one has proved his friendship,
Cling to him who clings to you.

Do not harshly judge your neighbour.
Do not think his life untrue,
 If he makes no great pretensions.
Deeds are great though words are few.
Those who stand amid the tempest,
Firm as when the skies are blue,
Will be friends while life withereth.
Cling to those who cling to you.

When you see a worthy brother,
Buffeting the stormy main,
Lend a helping hand fraternal,
Till he reach the shore again.
Don't desert the old and tried friend,
When misfortune comes in view,
For he then needs friendship's comfort.
Cling to those who cling to you.

A.H.

For Miss Weaver, Birchwood.

FAMILY TREE

HAYES-WEAVER

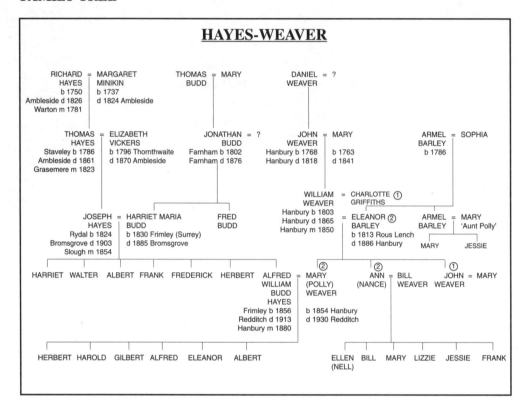

MAP OF HANBURY

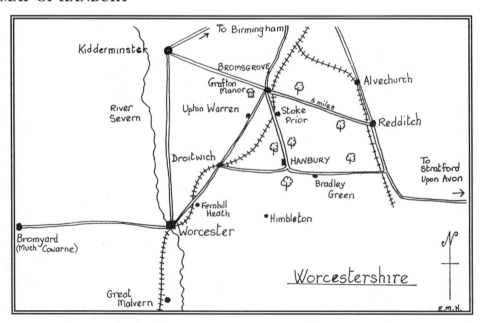

1872 - 1873

Letters written to Polly Weaver by her close friend Mary Douglas, daughter of the Rector of Hanbury - Polly's home village in Worcestershire. Polly is eighteen years old, Mary about fifteen. Polly has just gone to work as a servant for Captain and Mrs Bourne at nearby Grafton Manor. It is here that she meets Alfred Hayes who has written most of the letters in this book.

E.M.H.

The Old Rectory
Hanbury

Hanbury
1872

My dear Polly,

I was very glad to get your letter the other day. It is quite jolly to get an answer so soon. I am glad you have got a nice Church. It is a great pity they don't have the Holy Sacrament oftener.

There is a new curate come; his name is Mr Vevers. Are the children good? I must confess I should rather you took care of them than that I should. Our mowing grass will soon be long enough to cut. The bell has just begun for the half past 8 o'clock prayers. I did not know it was so late. This is beastly paper. It is so thin.

Father is in London now. He is coming back this week. He went the Monday before last. What heavy storms we have had the last few days. It has been raining this morning but the sun is shining at present. All our good folks are very well. My Aunt at the Hall has, as I daresay you know, been ill for some time. I wrote to Fanny Weaver the other day. I hope she will see fit to answer it at some future time, but she is a bad one to write.

Do you remember little duck Mike? He is quite well and he is growing very big. Jessie Barber was here on Sunday week. We were very jolly, that is we walked and talked, picked flowers and sang hymns. I have no more to say at present.

I am, dear Polly, your affectionate friend,

MARY DOUGLAS

Hanbury Rectory, Bromsgrove.
July 2nd 1872

My dear Polly,

Very many thanks for your nice letter which I was very glad to get. I dare say you have heard from someone else of the alterations which are taking place in our church. The vestry is being enlarged and the organ is going to be put back through the wall of the vestry and that large monument has been moved to another part of the church. I think it will be a great improvement but it is uncomfortable enough just now.

Leah is gone; she went last Monday. I am very sorry. She is going to learn the dressmaking which she seems to have a fancy for. I wish her joy of it. I don't know the person you spoke of when you wrote, Elizabeth Nash, but I heard she wanted a place. It rained very fast last night and this morning. Mr Carter is in the place now. I believe he is at Mrs Steels. Mr Bodwell is also here with his wife. He was married last week near Birmingham and came to Bromsgrove the same day and he walked over here in the afternoon. They are at William Phillips at the Bell.

We have also got a new curate, Mr Vevers. He says curious things sometimes. One Sunday he told us in his sermon that we were "not to drink voraciously of the pleasures of this world but only to lap off the surface." Dear Polly, I hope you are happy and getting on well and all the rest of it. I have not heard from Fanny since the beginning of April but I heard from someone that she was gone to the seaside. I suppose she will soon be coming home for a bit.

Dear Polly, we have a nice lot of hay this time. We have one field up and another that is only just beginning to be cut. Theresa sends you her love and says you must write to her first. There is an account of a Gipsy Wedding in the Bromsgrove Paper but it is nothing to brag of.

With much love, I remain, dear Polly, your affectionate.

MARY DOUGLAS

Hanbury

Well dear Polly, I am afraid you will think I am a long time answering your letter but I have very little time for writing. I have to write at nights or when I can. The church is about finished. The little new church at Burleigh is getting on nicely. They are roofing it in. I am trying to get up a subscription to buy a harmonium for it. Will you join. I am very grateful for anything however little. If you will give me anything please send stamps.

I suppose you will want to hear all about the Harvest Home which was last Thursday week. It was a nice fine day, not so cold as it had been. The church was beautifully decorated. On the important day the services were as follows: Holy Communion 8.30, Morning Prayer with Sermon 12. The Preacher was the Rev.J.Edwards of Prestbury, Gloucestershire. We had hymns 223, 224, 226, 359, 360. The text was St. James I.17. After Service the whole parish walked in procession down the road to the Hall, that is to say the band went first and we all followed as we liked. There was as usual a famous hot dinner of capital beef and plum pudding followed of course by speeches: Mr Vernon, my father, Mr Edwards, Mr.E.Bearcroft, Sir.J.Packington, Mr Amphlett and Mr.J.Wilson all spoke, and splendid speeches some of them were.

After dinner there was both dancing and games for those who liked them. Among other things there were hurdle races, football, throwing cricket balls for prizes etc. I didn't dance at all which I was sorry for I was playing Drop Glove and French Tig with a jolly set more. We had famous fun. At about 4.45 tea was ready in the tent for those who had tickets.

Bertha Greenhill and I, not having those useful little pieces of card, thought we would go and wait on the other more favoured mortals as by so doing we should get tea afterwards by so making ourselves useful without the aforesaid tickets. Accordingly with some trouble by reason of the crush at the door we got in and set to work and I can assure you it was no light job, but it all contributed to the fun. After tea we went back to games again till dark and rounded a most pleasant day. I believe about 450 people had dinner and 570 tea. Poor Walter was so unwell as to be unable to take any share in the day's pleasure. Mother was not well either but she was able to go to the ground. I wish you could have been there dear Polly.

Last Monday I went to Malvern for the day. It was very nice. How is your little boy now. We are in much the same boat as you as concerns small children. One of my uncles who has a large family happens to be changing his living so he has sent some of the kids here for the present under the care of two nurses. The eldest who is here is just 6 years, the younger is 10 months - don't you pity me. They only arrived this afternoon. Theresa and all the other folks are quite well, at least dear Mother was not at all well the earlier part of the evening but I hope she is better now. I think she overtaxed herself trying to make things comfortable for those children today.

Please write soon. I really must go to bed. Good night from

Yours affectionately

MARY DOUGLAS

P.S. Does your mistress spell her name with or without an 'e' as I always put one at the end.

Hanbury
Oct 1872

My Dear Polly,

Many thanks for the stamps you sent, also for your letter. Both were very welcome. I have got about £11.3.2 at present and more promised. Let me wish you many happy returns of the day with all blessings and I hope that each birthday as it comes round may find you so much further on the road to Heaven. I hope you don't mind bad writing. I am afraid this will be difficult to read.

I had rather you had to deal with the baby you spoke of than that I had. These we have got in the house are bad enough. They make such a row and they worry me nearly out of my life to read to them, sing to them or play with them. And their nurses expect me to supply them with books, which is next to impossible to do, as they read very fast and will not touch anything they are pleased to consider dry. They have refused to have anything to do with these books I lent them for the following reasons - one they said was dry, another was a novel and they did not care for the looks of it, the third made them feel melancholy - I don't know if I've spelt that right, it looks funny.

Mr Vevers brought his wife home the other day, she seems a nice person. Mrs George Hunt of Woolmer Green died the other day. She was quite well on Monday and died on Friday. She was buried last Monday. I have heard nothing of Fanny Weaver for ages.

I wrote to her the other day but have had no answer yet. A large blue bottlefly has just flown into my candle and has burnt off one wing and a half and is kicking up a most unconscionable row close to me.

I expect I shall go to Worcester on Saturday. If I do I shall try and get some better paper. Have you heard that smallpox is very bad in Worcester. Last Sunday we had a new tune to "Hark, hark my soul" It was such a beastly thing. A most mournful tune it was. It may have been very suitable if the hymn in question had been "Go to dark Gethsemane" or any other of that description. I hope we shall never have it again. The chestnuts on the Common are ripe. I wish I could send you some. I must now conclude.

With all good wishes. From your affectionate friend,

MARY DOUGLAS

Hanbury
Wednesday night, Dec. 1872

My dear Polly,

I'm afraid you will think me a very long time answering your letter, however I will try to send this tomorrow. You will be glad to hear that the Harmonium is come. It only arrived today. It is a second hand one, but they all say that it is the sweetest tone they ever heard - more like an organ than a harmonium. It cost £13.00. When it was new it cost £22.2.0. I wish you could see it. It has 8 stops.

As I do not suppose I shall write again before Christmas you must let me wish you now a very happy Christmas and New Year with all the blessings of the same and many of them. You will be sorry to hear that Theresa is going to leave for good on January 2nd 1873. I think everyone at Hanbury is very well. There was a wedding the other day. The young man was Clement Best but I forget who he married. There was a man drowned at Upton Warren, Monday, as he was coming home from work. I believe there is a ford across the road always but the floods were so deep that he was drowned. The little chapel is getting on pretty well. Father came home from London last night. He says there are miles and miles of country flooded between us and London.

The other night Mr Vevers had gone to see Hannah Grazier and when he came out of her house it was dark and he stepped on the top of the well which was only covered with rotten boards and in he fell. He got out again somehow, considerably bruised but otherwise none the worse. Mrs Vevers is a very nice person indeed. We all like her. She goes about the parish with her husband seeing the people and she teaches a class in the Sunday School.

James Stanton has left us and Walter is going away for good in a few days. I cannot think of any more at present.

I am affectionately yours

MARY DOUGLAS

Remember me kindly to Jessie Barber and tell her if ever she likes to write to me, I shall be very glad to receive and answer her letters. MD

Hanbury
Thursday

My dear Polly,

I hope you are not very tired this morning after last night's gaieties. I must confess that I am rather so. It was awfully jolly to see you especially as you looked so well. I hope you are really better. I wish we had had more time to talk though. I have plenty of things to say, that is if we had time for a jolly long talk, but I hope we shall have when you come home dear Polly.

But I suppose you would like to hear about the treat. I think I told you there were about 84 children there. There were also the teacher and several other people - altogether over 100 I should think. We did not have quite a common Christmas tree because the doors are so small we could never have got it in. So we had a long table with a little tree at each end and an evergreen arch over the middle, the whole thing well lighted. Miss Bearcroft kindly gave children and teacher tea before the treat began. Each of the children had 4 things, something useful, a toy, sweets and an orange and most of the teachers gave their own classes prizes. Among other things we had 2 snakes, those wooden things that twist about. Tommy Honeybourne and Billy Best had them. They were highly delighted.

We had another capital bit of fun at Annie Turner's expense. She is very much afraid of spiders so I persuaded Mother to draw a picture of one which was put on a needle book with a little scroll on the other side: "Accept this". Of course we presented it with "Accept this" uppermost. In a minute she turned it over and then her face was worth seeing as she dropped it on the chair behind her.

When all the things had been presented each teacher got something and then we sung songs and rounds till 9 o'clock when we broke up after one of the pleasantest evenings I ever spent.

I saw the eldest Miss Bourne at Hadzor the other night. Did she give you any message from me? If she did not it was only my love or something of that sort. I think I must now conclude, with love.

Hoping to see you soon, I remain your affectionate friend,

MARY DOUGLAS

Write soon.

Scaldwell Rectory
Northampton

My dear Polly,

I was very glad to get your nice letter and to hear that you are at Filey. It is a place I know very well, indeed nearly as well as I do Hanbury. Is the old Bathing Woman, Mary, still alive, also Mrs Temple the person who kept No. 28 The Crescent. I know them both very well and should be very glad to hear anything of them.

Do you like the sea. Have you been on the Brig yet - or whatever you like to call that long chain of rocks which turns out into the sea. If you go there alone don't get caught there by the tide as in some places it comes up very fast and you will not find it very easy to get up the cliff. Speaking of the cliff, beware how you sit under some parts of it as large pieces often fall off. If you look about on the head I dare say you will find some jasper etc. There are many quantity there and if you had them set they would be very pretty. We have some very pretty stones we picked up there. I wish we were coming to Filey only it might be awkward if all the hotels and lodging houses are full. We should have to sleep in the road.

You see we are out too but I expect we shall be back again before you answer this. I think we have about 10 days more. I hope you will excuse bad writing as this is a beastly pen. It is so thick. It is not mine. I hope the sea will do the little boy good, poor little chap. I wonder when you will be home again. Have you been out in a boat. We are pretty well except that we have all got bad colds. There is a nice little church here - which I am afraid is more than there is at Filey. Is the new church there finished yet.

I hope you are well and happy.
With love. Hoping to have a long letter from you soon.
I am your very affectionate friend

MARY DOUGLAS

P.S. We went to Northampton the other day and saw paper made. The foreman gave me a lot of the paper. Bank notes are made of it. I saved you a piece. It is so strong you can lift half a hundredweight with it. I have seen it done and the paper was not torn at all.   M.D.

Hanbury Rectory
Bromsgrove

My dear Polly,

I am afraid this will not be a very long epistle as I am going out in a few minutes. I am sorry I have not written sooner. How are you getting on. You asked after Mr Vevers' children. I saw them a few minutes ago. They are very well. Lizzie Holloway is still there.

We had a nice day for the Confirmation and there was a good number confirmed - 78 from this parish and some from Bradley and Himbleton. We have had lovely weather lately and the trees etc are in full leaf and I don't think I ever saw such a show of blossom on the appletrees and as for the buttercups, the fields are yellow with them. Such of the children as were at school on Whit Monday went up to the Common to play in the afternoon. Mr Smith, Mr Greenhill and Mr Vevers were there and we had such a splendid game of rounders. I don't know when I had such a good one.

I hope dear Polly you are all right and keep up your spirits. I wish you could come to the Harvest Home. Jemima and all our people are very well. Do write again soon.

With love, I remain ever your affectionate friend

MARY DOUGLAS

Hanbury Rectory
Oct. 11th 1873

My dear Polly,

I am at last going to fulfil my promise of writing. I went to Bromsgrove on Sunday but did not see you there though I went out one of the first to watch for you. How do you like Capt. Bourne's? Do you think you shall stay or not. I heard you had been ill again which I am very sorry for. Do take care of yourself.

One day last week father and I went to Kidderminster. It was so jolly. We went over one of the carpet works there. Some of the machinery is quite wonderful. Father has been at Bath at the Church Congress all this week, we expect him back today.

How long do you expect to stay at Mrs Bourne's if you do not get the place for good? I ask because I think I know of a place in the South which might suit you. I mean at my uncle's. I do not know if you would like it. Should you object to be under another? They had an under nurse till a short time ago. I do not know for certain if they want one now but if they should (which I will find out) do you think you should like it? Will you write as soon as you can and let me know. There are two children quite in the nursery and another who spends most of his time there.

What wretched weather we have had this week. It has been so cold and wet. It was by way of being a Harvest Service at Bromsgrove on Sunday. They had one or two harvest hymns and prayers but that was all. The church was not decorated or anything of that sort.

Mary Jane sends her love, is sorry to hear you have been ill, hopes you like Grafton Manor etc. Jemima also desires to be remembered to you. Father came back half an hour ago. Please write soon.

With much love, I remain dear Polly,
your affectionate friend
MARY DOUGLAS

Hanbury
(Xmas 1873/74)

My dear Polly,

I am very sorry to have been so long answering your letter but I thought I would wait for Xmas. Please accept my best wishes that you may spend a Merry Xmas and Happy New Year, which you know are most sincerely yours. And I trust and pray that the New Year may be happier than the last. And now another year is almost gone from us - one less to come this side of the grave. God alone knows whether we are nearer Heaven, as we are certainly nearer death than we were last year. Watch and pray for ye know not the day neither the hour when the Son of Man cometh. That day to each one will be the day of our death and we do not know how soon that may be - but if it is all the same to you we wont have a sermon on this occasion. I am writing remarkably bad grammar tonight which I hope you will excuse.

Have you had the same cold weather we have. It certainly is seasonable but none the less unpleasant for that. The snow is nearly six inches deep to say nothing of a very hard frost every night. The church decorations progress very slowly this year. I hope they will get done. I suppose they must somehow. The new organ has got nearly all its case on now but it is not painted yet.

Has your face been better lately? My mother has had dreadful faceache the last fortnight but it is better now I am happy to say. It is something after 12 p.m. now so it is nearly time to stop writing tonight. Have you heard Fanny Weaver is gone to service as house and parlour maid. Her father got one of his ribs broken by a bullock he was killing but he is better now. Fortunately the creature got its horns one each side of him or he must have been killed. Is not a sad thing the death of M.Ainge's father. I am very sorry to have to tell you that if you dont mean to write to her till she comes back you never will as she is gone for good. Her address is:-

Church Lench,
Evesham.

I enclose a small card if you will accept it. I wish it was something better but they say half a loaf is better than no bread, so I suppose a small thing is better than none. I hope dear Polly, that you may have a very happy Xmas with all the blessings it will bring to those who really love our Lord. And though in some respects last year was a dark and gloomy one yet I trust that it too may not have been unblest to you all. And the Xmas joy will be the brighter for troubles passed through and for the forgiveness of injuries. "Lord how often shall my brother sin against me and I forgive him?" "Until 7 times." asks St. Peter and the answer came: "I say not unto thee 7 times but until seventy times seven."

Heaviness may endure for a night but joy comes in the morning. And it will come if not in this life, when the eternal morning dawns on us it will.

I remain my dear Polly, ever your very affectionate friend,
MARY DOUGLAS

1874

Polly's job at Grafton Manor is only temporary and she starts a new job as a lady's maid for Mr and Mrs Walker in Wimbledon. Alf goes to work at Swadlincote Railway Station in Derbyshire but finds the work too dangerous and returns to Grafton Manor. Alf and Polly find the long separation hard to bear.

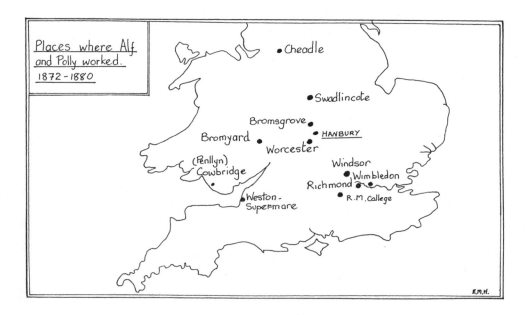

Places where Alf and Polly worked.
1872 - 1880

• Cheadle

• Swadlincote

Bromsgrove •
Bromyard •   • HANBURY
• Worcester

(Penllyn)
Cowbridge

Windsor
• Wimbledon
Richmond •
• R.M.College

• Weston-
  Super-mare

E.M.H.

Hanbury
Thursday (1874)

My dear Polly,

I do not know if you have heard of anything yet likely to suit you so I send two or three more advertizements.

Wanted for a few months by a family from abroad a children's maid who is a good needlewoman and can be well recommended. Wages £16 a year and all found. Address: A.C.Budd, 102 High Street, Croydon.

A lady at present residing at Brighton requires a respectable servant to wait on 2 children aged 7 and 4 and herself. She must be a good needlewoman.
Address: C.H.G. 42, Grenville Place, Brighton.

Wanted a young person who has acted as second nurse to take charge of two young children and give some instruction to two rather older ones. Nursery maid kept. Lady's maid helps with the two elder. Address in the first instance: A.C. care of Mr Squire, Waterloo Terrace, opposite Palace Gardens, Bayswater.

Wanted a Second Nurse where three are kept. She must have been trained in a nursery and be a thoroughly good needlewoman. She will be required to wait on the lady. Address: Mrs Strickland, Hildenley, Malton.

I hope very much to hear from you soon if you are not too busy. It is just post time so I must conclude with much love. There is no news to tell.

Your very affectionate friend,
MARY DOUGLAS

22, The Crescent, Filey

My dear Polly,

I received your letter the other day all right. We came here on Tuesday and shall I believe, stay here about a week and then go homewards stopping a night or two at different places on the way. Please excuse bad writing as I have got rheumatism in my hand. I have a few advertizements here of parlour work. Perhaps one may suit.

Wanted a Parlour Maid. Must be a Communicant of the Church of England and-have good references. Wages £16 and all found.
Apply to Mrs Norris, Abbey House, Bristol.

Wanted in a small quiet family, a House and Parlour Maid. Steady, active, obliging. Neat in dress and an early riser.
Address. Mrs Simcox, Weyhill Rectory, Andover.

Wanted immediately a Parlour Maid who thoroughly understands cleaning plate and waiting at table. Assistance given in the afternoons. No house work. Wages £16 to £18 all found.

Address. C.F. Woolwich, S.E.

This is a very jolly place. The Bowens are here. We have all been out fishing this morning. At least we went to take up a long line they set over night. We found there two ling and a conger eel which last are rather dangerous customers.

The fishermen say if you get your hand in their mouth they will bite it off and rather wriggle round your arm and twist it off. They say they make good pies. We are going to try tonight.

I had my photo done yesterday. I hope it will be successful. How are you getting on now? I saw your Mother on Sunday. She spoke so of you Polly. I think you are the joy of her life. I don't know what she would have done if you had gone with Mrs Baker. You ought to write to her as often as you can, she is so fond of hearing of you. I hope you will write to me soon and say anything you like and tell me anything. If you do I'll write you as many "nice long letters" as you call them as you like.

Much love, I remain your very affectionate friend
MARY DOUGLAS

Hanbury Rectory
Autumn 1874

My dear Polly,

You will think I am very soon fulfilling my promise of writing but the reason of my doing so is as follows. I looked in the Guardian (which came this morning) when I got home to see if there was anything which would suit you. There was one advertisement which I think might do for you. I will copy it out.

Can any lady recommend a second Nurse where three are kept, not under twenty? Must have been in the nursery.

Address. Mrs Musgrave, Hascombe Rectory, Godalming

If you think this would suit, you had better apply by the next post or get Mrs Bourne to do so as it may be snapped up. I have one or two others here which I will copy.

Superior under nurse in a gentleman's family. Age from 18 to 23, Church woman. Early riser. Good plain needlewoman, plain dress and understands her work well. Personal character. Wages from £12 to £15 all found. Good temper essential. State when disengaged.

Apply to. Mrs Whiting, 53 High St, Croydon.

Wanted 21st October for Yorkshire, a nurse for 3 children the youngest nearly two. Assistance given in the nursery. One that has been under a good nurse preferred. A churchwoman and a good needlewoman. Good references required.

Address stating wages. Mrs John Magley, Old Rectory, Mirfield, Yorkshire.

I cannot see an advertisement for a maid which would be likely to suit you. I asked mother if she knew of anything which might do but she said she did not. If there is ever anything of any sort I can do for you, do let me know dear Polly. You know I shall only be most happy. Anything you like to tell me or write about will be as safe with me as with you,

You asked me to write you one of my "nice long letters", you will think I have done it this time with a vengeance. I will spare you any more now.

With much love, I remain, dear Polly,

Your very affectionate friend

MARY DOUGLAS

Swadlincote Railway Station

Swadlincote
Sept 2nd 1874

My dear Polly,

I write just a few lines to tell you that I have arrived at my destination safe and sound. It is a very small place and is only a branch of the Midland Railway from Burton. Swadlincote is the only station on the branch. The line goes no farther. Swadlincote is full of collieries, potteries and brickyards. There is lots of big chimneys in it but there is none like our old friend Stoke chimney. I have got into some pretty good lodgings with the other porter close to the station. I have had one day at it and I think I shall like it because the Station Master is so good, he shows and tries to learn me all he can. He thinks that I shall get on well after a bit when I have got used to it. I must tell you that my job is rather hard and dirty. It is loading and unloading baggage and looking after tar sheets and checking the numbers of the trucks that goes out and comes in and doing a little writing in office. I have not been much about the place so I cannot tell you anything about it but I think it is a rather dirty place.

I am sorry to say that I cannot come to see you very often because they don't reckon to give a holiday till I have been here 12 months but I think I shall be able to get one before long and then please God we will renew old love. I have thought of you and our last meeting every hour I have been here. I don't think I shall be able to get my Phisog taken here.

I don't think I have any more to say this time. I hope to see you soon. Please write quick because I am very anxious. Please remember Old Charger to Joseph and Emily and Jim and Louisa and Bill, Sarah if not gone, and Jack and Mrs Glidden, Albutt, Jane and poor old Mrs Wilde and Ted Vale if you see him on Sunday. Tell Wilde I think I shall take his advice (keep weathering at it boy and you are bound to get on). Tell Joseph I will write to him next week.

So hoping this will find the tooth better and all kind friends in good health. (I shall expect a letter on Tuesday)

I remain yours affectionately
ALFRED HAYES (Charger)
XXXXXX
XXXX
XX
For Polly

MIDLAND RAILWAY
Swadlincote Station
September 13th 1874

My dearest Polly,

I know you will think it strange that I did not write to let you have a letter on Tuesday or Wednesday but I did write but I don't think that the letter came as I sent one to mother the same time and gave them both to the postman. So I think if one had come the other would but I shall wait till your letter comes and then I hope I shall hear more about it. I have been to Swadlincote market twice and have seen lots of girls but none like you my dearest Polly. Although my pals say I shall never do for Derbyshire if I don't talk to the girls. I say sooner than I should speak to such a lot of ragamuffins I would loose my life and they laugh at me and say: Ah, if you was to, you would have that girl out of Worcestershire after you and so I tell them that the girls in Worcestershire are worth all the girls in Derbyshire and Leicestershire too. No, my dear Polly I think about you too much and love you too well.

I shall be back in Bromsgrove on the 23rd of this month and then if you are about home or Grafton or anywhere near I wish you would meet me somewhere and then I will tell you what I mean to do with myself. I have not quite made up my mind. I want you to help me, my dear. I cannot do without your help. When I had your letter on Sunday last it brightened me up all the week till I had a letter from Mother on Friday to say that she was sorry I had not written. It made me quite bad. I thought that if one letter had not gone the other had not so I sent a letter to you and Mother by return of post. I thought that you would think that I had forgotten you but I am never happy but when I am thinking of you and I hope soon to be with you again.

Please tell me if the chap with the white waistcoat has been down to Grafton again. If he has I shall talk to him a bit when I see him. I shall also let Master Jim know a bit of my mind for bringing him down. I suppose he thought that the course was clear when old Charger and his gun were out of the way, but never mind I think that you served him just right.

Please don't forget the 23rd. Please to tell Joseph that we have been so busy that I have had no time to write to him as I promised him I would do and tell him when he comes on the Railway not to come onto any Branches but get on the Main line for when you get onto the branches they will try to keep you there always but when you get onto the main line you have a better start and can get on. The branch that I am on is a very dangerous one. There is always someone getting either killed or wounded. There has been two killed on it near Burton since I have been here and my butty has been very near killed but I have managed to keep safe so far and shall leave while I have the chance. I have sent in my notice and shall leave on 22nd.

I don't think I have any more to say just now so please remember me to Joseph, Mrs Glidden, Emily 2, Jane, Louisa and Lady Baker's maid and tell her pears are very scarce in Swadlincote. Tell Ted Vale, if you see him, that I shall very likely see him on Sunday week. My dear Polly I think that your time is nearly up at Grafton so please tell me if you have got another place and where and when you are going. So now I must wish you goodbye for a little while.

I remain to you ever loving and affectionate
ALFRED HAYES
(Charger)

Please write soon and tell me all you can.
For dearest Polly ....

Rock Hill, Bromsgrove
Sunday Oct. 11th 1874

My dear Polly,

I am rather lonely today. I do not care to go out anywhere so I am just writing a few lines to fill up my time. I wish that you were nearer so that I could come and see you. I should not care, if was as far again as Hanbury I would come but London is a little too far for one day's walk so must be contented with writing to you. I shall be glad when you will come nearer so that I can come and see you. I do not know what I shall do this winter without your company for I do not like stoping at home and I shall have nobody to come out to see me, but never mind it will not last long. 12 months will not last always and then we shall be able to have a few more quiet hours to ourselves.

I do not think I have much more to say to you but I do say success to the old Jam Pot and I hope it will be full again when we meet again at Hanbury. I have sent you 4 of my portraits and you can do what you like with them. You can send them one or two to Louisa or to anyone else. Please remember me to Louisa when you send it and tell her that Bill looks rather down hearted about her being away. I saw Joseph and two more maids at Stoke Church this morning. Joseph asked me if I had heard from you. I told him that I had not so he said "O what a Charger. She has forgotten you." but I said I do not believe you. I can trust her. And so I can, for I love you as dearly as I do my own life. God Bless you my own sweet Polly.

Jim's Emily was at Stoke all Monday night so I heard today. She went to her place on Thursday I think. I heard that she went to Grafton on Thursday for something that she left behind but I did not see her. I think I shall go over to Hanbury next Sunday. When I do I will write and tell you for I want to see Ann and the baby. I am going to church tonight but I suppose I shant have you to go with, but never mind. It wont always be like that. I have agreed with the Captain to stay on at Grafton till Lady Day but I can leave any time between now and then if I see the chance of bettering myself. I am not at the keeping but just jobbing about with the Captain and do anything that he wants me to do.

I think that is all I have to tell you this time. I will tell you the news, if there is any, next time I write and that will be about the end of the week. I hope I shall have one from you before then, so goodbye and God Bless, my darling Polly.

From your ever loving and affectionate
                    ALF

Rock Hill
Thursday Oct. 15th 1874

My dear Polly,

I got your bundle of letters on Tuesday morning. I was glad to hear that you had got amongst such nice people. I hope you are happy and comfortable. I wish I could come and see you. I hope you will come home next summer although it is a long time. It will be something for me to look forward to. I am very lonely at nights. I do not go out anywhere now. I stops at home. I went down to Grafton on Tuesday night to help Joe to wash up but if I had known I would not have went. Jane Crockett and Carrots the under house maid helped me but I did not like their company so I did not say much. Mrs Glidden came to the pantry door when the two girls were sat on the table so she says that she will write and tell you that I was courting them but you know what a one she is for making up anything so do not believe a word she or anybody else may tell you.

Wilde went down to Grafton last night between 9 and 10 and when he got to the drive gates he come upon 4 chaps and 2 girls. The chaps were all from Bromsgrove and the girls were the kitchen maid and youn Crockett, so Mrs Glidden said that I was one of the chaps and that she shall write and report me to you. I told her she was a LIAR. I was in such a temper. I would have told her some more if she had not gone away. Do not believe a word you may hear from anyone about here for they will be all false. For as long as you live I will not have anything to do with any other girl. No never. I will be FIRM and FAITHFUL believe me my dear Polly. I have not felt just right since you went. I have felt lost but I hope to see you in the Spring.

I think I shall go to live where grandfather is at Sandhurst College. That is about 25 miles from London, then if I go there I shall be able to come and see you anytime.

I think that will be a good place for me till I get a bit older. But let me go where I will it will not make any difference between me and you I hope my darling Polly.

Joe asked after you yesterday. He was glad to hear that you were getting on all right and that you had got a nice mistress. The fresh kitchen maid is a very quiet girl, rather bigger than Emily but I don't think she is such a nice girl. I do not think anything at all of any of them. I hardly ever speaks to them except Jane and Ellen. I spoke to Ellen the other day and some of them see me so they said they would tell you but I told them that you had given me leave to speak to her so that shut their mouths for them.

I am going down to Grafton tonight along with Wilde to see to his cow. I will tell you if them chaps come down again. I shall be sure to know. I went to church twice last Sunday, to Stoke in the morning and Bromsgrove at night. There I saw Jane, Mrs Glidden, Ellen and Liz Moore, Mrs Bourne's maid. I did not feel right without you. I wish you were nearer so that I could come and go to church on Sundays with you, but never mind, I shall be able to go with you every Sunday sometime and then that will make up all this time of quiet waiting, dear Polly mine.

Harriet that used to be at Grafton is come to Miss Dixon's at the Grange but I have not seen her yet but she will not make any difference to me towards my dear Polly so trust me a little while longer as I do you and then no one on earth shall come between us, God Bless you. I will let you have a letter from me every Saturday.

So now I must say goodbye. My Polly till next week goodbye.

From your ever loving and affectionate
ALF
CHARGER

Polly's duties when working for Mrs Walker in Wimbledon:

DUTIES OF UPPER HOUSEMAID

Monday	-	Drawingroom cleaned. Clothes collected for the Laundry.
Tuesday	-	Master George's bedroom and Mr Walker's dressingroom.
Wednesday	-	Mrs Walker's bedroom.
Thursday	-	Servants' bedrooms and the Ground Floor W. Closet.
Friday	-	Plate is cleaned.
Saturday	-	Pantry

The Upper Housemaid has the drawing rooms to keep clean with the grates in them.

On coming down stairs in the morning she opens the Drawing Room shutters, lays the fire - but does not light it.

Lays the breakfast in the Dining Room.

Prayers a quarter to 8 to 8 o'clock. After prayers bring in the breakfast.

After breakfast, washes up the breakfast things,

Goes up stairs to help to make the beds.

Sweep the room mentioned in the list of days.

Early dinner at ½ past one.

Servants dinner about two.

After her dinner the Upper Housemaid clears away the dinner things from the Dining Room.

Sweeps up the crumbs from the carpet.

Cleans the plate and glass used at early dinner.

Late dinner at 7 o'clock.

She waits at dinner - Cleans the plate and glass used at dinner.

Brings in tea into the Drawing Room at half past 8 o'clock

Prayers at 10 o'clock.

After prayers, bring in a tray with a jug of water and 2 or 3 tumblers.

Goes to bed.

The brushes are washed every other Tuesday.

The Upper Housemaid and Cook go out together in the morning of one Sunday and in the evening of the following Sunday.

Rock Hill, Bromsgrove.
(Thursday) October 29th 1874

My dear Polly,

I am sorry to say I could not go to Hanbury or to Stoke church last Sunday. Ever since I wrote my last letter I have been at home with rheumatic in my neck and shoulders. It is gone from my neck and shoulders now and into my face. My face is swelled nearly as big as a bushel. Please write and tell mother and Annie how it was that I could not come. I would not have missed going on any account if I had been able. For two or three days I was not able to dress myself. Please write and ask mother what day I shall go to Hanbury. I don't think I shall be able to go next Sunday for my face is that bad I can hardly bare it. I hope it will soon be better.

Our sham fight came off light. The chaps never came. It was just as I expected. There was only Ted Vale to meet them for I was not able and the others were at work. I don't think I shall trouble any more about them. Neither them nor their girls are worth picking up in the road. Mother have wrote to Grandfather but have not got an answer yet. As soon as she do I will let you know. Do not be afraid of the baker if he is consumptive for his days are numbered.

The three weeks that you have been gone seems to me 6 months for time goes very slowly now. It do not go so fast as when we were in Father Campbell's Arbour. It went too fast then. Now it don't go fast enough. I wish I could get to live somewhere near you. I have not felt right since you went.

People do say that I am altered very much and I think I am too but I hope soon to grow out of it for I know that I can trust you and I hope you do me, my Own Dear Polly.

I had a letter from Louisa this morning; she told me that she had a letter from you and that you had sent her my photograph. She said she should like to see me very much. Perhaps I shall go over to Alvechurch some Sunday morning to church and then I may see her. I wish you very many happy returns of the day, for I think that Sunday is your birthday. I cannot write any more for my head is that bad I cannot hold it upright. Don't forget to write to Mother and let her know. This letter is not quite so long as from Wimbledon to Grafton but I will send you a good long one next time when the rheumatics are got better.

Now I must say goodbye and God Bless you. I remain, to you, ever loving and affectionate

     ALF

I hope soon to see you again.

Hanbury Rectory
Bromsgrove
Saturday Night

My dear Polly,

Many happy returns of the day to you dear friend. I trust each as it comes may find you a happier and holier woman. I should say holier and happier because the holier we are the happier we are. And may the peace and love of our God ever abide with and overshadow you and ever lead you on to the rest that remaineth to God's people when their warfare is accomplished and their work done.

I would have written sooner only I waited until I could send you the answer to what you asked concerning your Mother, which I could not do sooner as I have been out. I went to see her this afternoon and am happy to be able to tell you she is much better than she has been lately. She has had a bad gathered face but is got well now. I found her, Ann and Mrs Vaughan all sitting down to tea which they kindly asked me to share and very good tea it was. They all sent you their love as soon as they heard I was going to write. Baby was very well and has taken a great fancy to me apparently.

I was very sorry to hear you had not been well lately but I hope you are better now. How are you getting on. You have not told me how you were for a long time now. I have been staying with my uncle in Dorsetshire lately. It is such a jolly place and I have any number of cousins there. So we have been a very lively party.

It is close to the river which floods considerably. Last Saturday it rose about 6 feet in 4 hours. The village was flooded to such an extent on Sunday that all the people had to go to church through the vicarage garden.

I don't think I have anything else to say at present so will conclude with all love and good wishes.

I remain your very affectionate friend
MARY DOUGLAS

Rock Hill
Bromsgrove
November 1874

(INCOMPLETE)

My dear Polly,

I got your letter this morning and I was very glad to hear from you for I am thinking of you every hour in the day. I am glad to say that I am got quite well, the rheumatic went away all at once and I am as well and as jolly as ever. I think I am better than ever I was for I feel my strength coming back very fast. I have got very thin but I shall soon pick that up again for I can eat better than ever I did.

I shall go to Hanbury on Sunday if it is anything like. It wont be a little drop of rain that will stop Old Charger. I was never at neither rain hail nor snow and I am not going to alter now. I should have liked to have been with you when you went to the Crystal Palace. If I dont go to Sandhurst College (we have not heard from grandfather yet) I shall come and see you sometime next summer but I hope I shall go to

Sandhurst. I shall be sure to go to London way when I go from home, let it be when it will.

I had a letter from Louisa on Wednesday; she told me she had had a letter from you and that you told her that I was ill and so she wrote me a letter to cheer me up a bit and it did for I was getting rather dull but I am getting on first class now thank God. I think I shall go over to Alvechurch on Sunday week to see how she is getting on. I only wish that you were no farther off than Alvechurch, you would see Old Charger very often, every Sunday if not oftener. But never mind we shall not always be so far apart. The time will come, please God when we shall meet to part no more.

That letter of Miss Douglas was a very good one. I was very glad you sent it to me for it was a very thoughtful letter. I will write and tell you all the news after Sunday.

Rock Hill, Bromsgrove
Dec. 22nd 1874

My dear Polly,

This is just a few lines to let you know how we are all getting on. I went over to Hanbury on Sunday. I am glad to say that Mother and Annie and little Nell looks capital well considering the very cold weather. Annie has been up at the Woodrow for about a month because Mrs Creswell has been ill but she was at home on Sunday. She told me that Alfred Ward had been to see her but she did not say any more but Mother told me that he asked if you were MARRIED so mother told him no but there was somebody that looked after you so I suppose that shut his mouth about you. Little Nell is getting quite good looking and grows nicely. Annie said she had not answered your letter because she was so busy at the Woodrow.

Miss Moore is going to leave Grafton but I don't know the reason. You know when Day, the under keeper, left we had another Staffordshire man named Fradley. Now he is leaving but it is on his own accord, he do not like Beard. He says he is the laziest man he ever came across. The Captain offered me the place and he was a bit surprised when I told him that I would not have it. He thought that I should jump at the offer but he was mistaken, so then I told him about my coming to Sandhurst but he wants me to have his keeper's place, but I says not for old CHARGER. It is not near enough my Polly. If it was I would not have it now. Sandhurst is the place for me and in a very short time too.

Charley the lad in the garden is going to leave very shortly. The Captain says he is too much of a man for him so he is going to get him another place as soon as he can and pack him off. We have not seen but very little of those Bromsgrove fellows since we saw about 20 of them on Saturday night but they were very civil. We gave them enough to remember the other night. I hope that your Penny Readings is not far off for such fellows to insult you but I do not think that the Wimbledon folks are ignorant fools.

It is a good lot like Christmas now for we have had snow about a foot thick for a week. It fell a week tonight and it looks like stopping. I wish you a merry Christmas and a happy new year and I sincerely hope that before the new year is far advanced we shall meet again for I do want to see you again. It seems almost years since you went. I shall stay at home this Christmas for it is no pleasure to go moping about by myself. I will stop till next Christmas and then, God sparing us, we will be jolly together for an hour or two and then we shall be alright for a week. The old Green Lane is nearly full of snow. It would suit very well now to go for a walk.

Joe said he should like to go and see your Mother some Sunday after he leaves Grafton. He wants me to go with him. I think I shall go. I have sent you a Christmas card. It is not a very good one. I was rather too late in getting it. You know what a place Bromsgrove is for getting anything. Jim and Bill and Jack wished to be remembered to you and I wish you a merry Christmas for them. Ted Vale asked after you on Sunday and wanted to know if you had heard anything about Emily No.2. He is always asking me about it. Tom Green has been very ill with Bronchitis but he is getting better now.

I think that I have told you all the news now for this time, and wishing you a merry Christmas and a happy new year and I hope you will have a truly merry Christmas and think of your old Charger making himself as contented as ever he can down in dull Worcestershire. Thank you for sending the card.

From your ever loving and affectionate
                    ALF
Write soon.

1875

Alf finds a possible solution to his loneliness - to work at the Royal Military College, Sandhurst in Berkshire where his uncle and grandfather are already employed. He would be living much nearer to Polly. His letters describe his new life as an orderly and his high hopes, but life is not that simple.

Bromsgrove
High Street

E.M.H.

Rock Hill, Bromsgrove.
Tuesday (Early January 1875)

My dear Polly,

I got your letter this morning and as you let me have my letter early this week, I will let you have yours early. I, Jim, Jack and Bill had a regular row in Bromsgrove last Saturday night with them CHAPS that we had at Grafton some time ago. I told you about it. These chaps have always called after me ever since, so they set about thirty little lads to call after me on Saturday night, so I gave one of the biggest a smack with my fist and knocked him down in the street. After then these little lads started to throw stones at us and continued to throw at us as long as we stopped in Bromsgrove (but these big ones never come near.)

I got a stick and then I went into the middle of them and gave about a dozen of them a jolly good thrashing and then most of them went off home but some of them stopped and followed us about. Then a policeman came and drove them all away and we thought we had got rid of them but when we were going down Worcester St. four of the biggest of them came from somewhere and began throwing again and one of the stones hit Jack in the ribs so Jack turned round and ran and caught one of them and gave him such a thrashing as he never expected with a cane about an inch thick, then Bill caught two more and jolly laced them then we heard no more of them except the hollering of their vengeance. I have heard since that they mean to half kill us next Saturday night but we shall be ready for a hundred of their sort. That was Saturday's performance.

On Sunday morning Jack brought Ellen to church but he did not sit with her. He sat with me and the other chaps but he took her back. He also took Miss Moore home on Sunday night. Jim went with the nurse and me and Bill went with Jane. She wished to be remembered to you and hoped you were happy in your new place. She said she often thought of you. Miss Moore is so different to you, dear Polly. Jane said, however, she has told me about a dozen times that she has got a good pair of STOCK-INGS of yours. She wants to know what she is to do WITH them. She wanted me to take them to your home when I went but I said I would ask you first, so please let me know. Joe is going to leave Grafton about the end of January. He has got another place at about £30 a year. He did not tell me where. He told me not to say anything about it because no one knows about it except him and I. We are great friends and he always asks after you. He is very glad you likes your place and likely to stop.

I do not know exactly who is going to act at the THEATRICAL but I expect it will be the Captain and Mrs Bourne and the children and perhaps some of their friends but I will let you know. I shall go to Hanbury on Sunday and have a look at Mother and Annie and Little Nell and also to do justice to the jam pot. I always have a taste when I go.

I must now say goodbye and God Bless you my own dear Polly,
From yours affectionately
ALF H Old Charger

Rock Hill, Bromsgrove
(Early January 1875)

My dear Polly,

Just a few lines to let you know how we are getting on in this part of the world. It is very cold and the snow is as deep as ever and there is no sign of it going just yet. Grafton pond bares weight and there has been a good deal of skating and sliding. It takes me all my time to look after the BROMSGROVE ROUGHS that come to see what they can catch hold of. I had a jolly row with a lot of them today and they pitched into me like mad things but they did not hurt me a great lot. They were cutting the shrubs about and playing at what we call bang. The Captain dont allow it so I went to stop it then they all began on me but I and 2 or 3 big chaps soon put them into a curious predicament. The Captain says he will summons them if they come again. They are the same party that has been on at me and Jim etc.

Jim, Jack and Bill went to Birmingham to see Emily last Saturday. They told me that she was getting on about the old style. I think that Bill has given poor old Lou the sack, for he fetched Carrots to church on Christmas day and took her back again and fetched her on Sunday night to Bromsgrove church and sat with her and he took her for a walk after church. Jack always fetches Ellen and takes her back just the same as he always did poor old Sal; in fact all three of them goes down to Grafton just the same as they did last summer. Jim I think cares for Emily a bit. I think he is the truest of the three but for poor Lou and Sal they are forgotten. They are too far off.

I think of going to Hanbury next Sunday week if the weather is anything like. I have been invited to the Theatrical performance on the 6th. I will tell you all about it next time. Did you know old Birch that used to be head keeper at Grafton before Beard? He went to America. He is dead. He died on 30th November at Kansas in N.America after a two day illness. We heard about it yesterday. Annie knew him. He used to call at Thomas Parkes when she lived there. He had only been in America 18 months. Have you heard about that dreadful Railway accident near Oxford? It was a lot of people going out to spend their Christmas holidays but it was their fate never to see Christmas day.

I remember our walk nearly to Upton last summer. I went along it tonight. It is knee deep in snow so that it hides all those rough clods. I thought of you as I was going along and thought if ever we should go along that path again together; I hope we shall have a smoother path to walk on through life for that was a very rough one and rather curious bridges over them deep ditches but we got over them alright - and I hope we shall on life's rough journey. God helping us, my own dear Polly, my time will soon be up here now and if all goes well I shall be at Sandhurst in a month and that will be a jolly time for me and you, dear Polly. I think now that I have told you all the news and if anything fresh breaks out I will let you know. I think of going over to Alvechurch to see old Lou in 2 or 3 Sundays if I can. Now I must say that they are all pretty well at Grafton and at home and I was never better in all my life than I am now and I hope you are the same.

Now I must say good-bye my dear Polly, from you ever loving
ALFRED
I HOPE YOU HAD A MERRY CHRISTMAS AND I WISH YOU A HAPPY NEW
YEAR.
I enjoyed myself nicely at home on Christmas day.

Rock Hill, Bromsgrove.
Jan 12th / 75

My dear Polly,

I did not get your letter until this morning. I do not know when it was posted but I think I might have had it before I went to Alvechurch last Sunday, but I did not see Lou. She was not at church. I did not like to go to the house because there was such a lot of the Mildmay's about and I thought perhaps it might get Lou into a bother. I saw one of her fellow servants and I expect she would tell her that I was there. I think I shall write to her and tell her what I wanted. I will ask her if Bill writes to her now; if he don't I will tell her all I know and that is a good deal. Ted Vale went with me to Alvechurch, he is as good a friend as ever I met with. He will go with me through thick and thin.

I wrote to Sally last week but I have not had an answer. I asked if she knew anything about Emily 2 . Ted Vale is often asking about her. Emily 1 is coming over here on the 18th. If I can I will tell her a good tale for I think she ought to know a little of Jim's goings on. I am going to Sandhurst either on the 2nd or 3rd of February. I do not know which yet and if I can I will go to Wimbledon on the Friday after to see my dear old Polly, for I should dearly like to see you every day. Makes the time shorter. I am afraid I shall not get the Store Keeper's place. I am not old enough, there is a good deal of responsibility. I think Grandfather will try to manage it a bit longer but my wages will be the same at the other job. The Captain gave me a sovereign for a Christmas Box and promised me another if I would stay with him until 1st February.

All the people at Grafton are pretty well. Now they have been dreadfully busy this last fortnight. There was 135 to Supper last Thursday night. The last night of the Grand Performance. I was there all night helping to wash up. Joe leaves next Monday and Miss Moore on Saturday if she (Mrs B) will let them go. I expect she will.

I got into a dreadful row on Sunday night as I was coming home from Church. I went to church with Joe and Ted Vale and as I was going up Worcester Street there was a lot of chaps threatened me but I did not take any notice of it for I have been threatened many a time before. So when I came out of church, I and Ted Vale started off home together. When we got to the Town Hall there was some chaps whistling so I said "What are you whistling at" So one of them said that they were calling their gang together. So I went on but we had not got far before a lot of them came running and whistling down the street and got in front of us; so on I and Ted went till we got down to the bridge by the Shrubbery and then there was about 50 chaps if not more, jumped out on us and one struck me several times on the top of the head and stunned me and knocked me down on the ground so Ted got between me and the crowd and just as he got me up one of the chaps struck me across the face with a thick stick and another with a belt and cut my eye very bad.

They would have done more but two of my brothers came up and then they got quiet. I then caught hold of 3 of them that I saw strike me and told them that I would summons them, then they came very penitent and went away quietly. Jim, Jack and Bill went by at the time that they were striking me and never said a word. They went by like a lot of cowards. I told them what I thought about them when I cought them.

They said that they could do nothing. They had not got any sticks. No more had we, but I and Ted Vale stood our ground. I told the Captain about it and so he sent me to the Police Court to get a Summons for them chaps today. The Captain is going to pay all expenses for me. The case will not be heard till next Tuesday. Joe, Ted Vale, Jim and one of my brothers are going as witnesses. My dear Polly, do not think any the worse of me for this, for I had nothing to do with the beginning of the row. I am none the worse for it, only my face is rather disfigured but it will soon be off. One of the chaps that I summoned was sent to Worcester gaol today for stealing iron. I think I shall stop their little games this time. Alfred Ward has left Bromsgrove but I do not know where he is gone as I did not go to Hanbury last Sunday but I shall go next Sunday and then I shall hear all about him I dare say.

I hope, dear Polly, you will be alright by the time this letter reaches you . It is very bad to be in bed and not able to get up but I hope, please God, you will soon be well. Now I must say goodbye My Dear Polly and I hope soon to see you. It seems such a long time since I saw you.

From your affectionate
     ALFRED

I will send you the Bromsgrove paper next week and then you can see about that row for yourself.
Goodbye and God bless you, My dear Polly.

Rock Hill, Bromsgrove.
19th January 1875

My dear Polly,

I am glad to hear that you are better and I hope that by this time you are quite well. I have been to Bromsgrove today to have those chaps tried. There were only two of them because the other is not come back from gaol to which he was sent last week. These two had to pay £1.9.6 or fourteen days hard labour. Neither of them paid at first but I think that both of them has had the money paid for them now. There was a good gang of us there today. There was me, Ted Vale, Jim, Bill and my two brothers but they only wanted Ted Vale as a witness.

There was a good lot of roughs threatened us as we came out of the court but we soon shut their mouths for them. I told them that I would summons them as well if they did not mind what they were at. They have been a good deal civiler this last week. I'll put a wager that they will know Alf Hayes if they should happen to see him again.

I think that I shall come up to Wimbledon on Sunday because I shall not go to Sandhurst, not till Wednesday the 3rd of February. I will polish up a bit but you know that old Charger is not a proud sort of a chap but for a that I can make myself fit to be seen. I have not troubled to smarten up much lately. I have not had much to smarten up for, but when I get near you dear Polly, I will and shall begin again. I shall be very glad when I see you and shall be very pleased to do anything in my power to please you for you are the only person in the world that I care a great deal about. I love you dearly and I am not ashamed to own it and I hope that I shall always be the same.

I did not go to Hanbury last Sunday because it was so very wet and had been wet nearly all the week. I do not know what Mother and Annie will say to me when I go for I promised to go the second Sunday after Christmas and now the fourth is turned but I must go some weekday to make it up. I had a letter from Sal last week. It was a good long one and a very nice one. I will show it to you when I come to see you. I told her about John. She said she did not care for she did not care for John much and she knew that he liked a change like the rest of the chaps about. Sal is going to send me one of her Portraits. She told me that you had sent her one of mine. I was very glad you had. I expect another letter from her in the course of a day or two. Emily was over here yesterday. She looks very well. She asked me how you was. I told her that you were rather middling so she wanted to know what was the matter. I told her that I did not know unless it was too much work.

She stayed at Grafton and a good long time. I think she was there about 5 hours. Jim was there as well but I don't think that Jim liked his situation for fear the Captain should see him. The Mrs was gone to Worcester too, with the carriage. I think that Master Bourne is gone to Sandhurst College. If so I shall have someone to talk to. Doctor Davenport is dead. I do not know whether you knew him. He died of eriscyplis in the head and face. There is no more news this time so I must say goodbye, my dear Polly. I hope to see you soon.

From your ever loving ALFRED

I will send you a paper on Saturday
Please to excuse these blots for I have upset the ink bottle.

Rock Hill, Bromsgrove
January 27th / 75

My dear Polly,

I am rather longer in answering your letter this week, but I was late home last night and that is the reason; but it is better late than never. This is my last week at Grafton and I am glad of it. I have had a good deal to do since Joe went. I have a lot of his work to do besides my own. Joe went last Thursday. The butler had a letter from him on Monday. He had arrived at his destination quite safe. Joe never left me his address. He promised me he would. I suppose he forgot.

I sent you a Bromsgrove paper on Sunday evening. Have you seen my case in it? They put me in the paper as a Saltmaker at Stoke. I shall have that corrected this week then I will send you another paper. I am going to have another of those chaps up next Tuesday. It will be the last day that I shall be here for I shall start early on Wednesday morning. I shall go to Hanbury on Sunday. I have not been since Christmas; I started to go last Sunday but it came on to rain so fast that I had to turn back. I hope that I shall see you, dear Polly, quite well and jolly as ever next Sunday week for I shall be sure to come, without something very important happens to hinder me.

The Captain and Albutt was thrown out of the cart yesterday as they were going up the street in Bromsgrove but neither of them were hurt very bad. The Captain was hurt worst of the two. He had the skin knocked off one side of his face and hurt his arm. Albutt hurt his leg against the shaft of the cart but not very bad. The horse was not a bit, for it went to Alvechurch last night to take Mrs Bourne to Mildmay's to dinner.

Albutt told me this morning that Lou was a going to give it me when she saw me for not going to see her the other Sunday when I was over there. Bill never says anything about her now. I think he has forgot all about her. He is fond of a change so Sarah says but I think he has changed for the worst this time. He don't look after Carrots as he did after Loo. He don't come down to Grafton 2 or 3 times a week and down the old Green Lane. It don't have many night visitors now. John is very thick with Ellen. He comes and fetches her to church and brings her back again. Jim don't care for any of them. He still sticks to Emily, but poor Ted Vale, none of them wont have him but he will soon be alright for Emily 2 is coming back to Grafton on Saturday as young lady's maid. There is going to be two lady's maids kept now. Miss Moore is not gone yet. She is waiting till Mrs Bourne can suit herself. I don't know when that will be, she is so hard to please.

I don't know what they will do at Grafton for an under keeper when I am gone. The Captain wanted me to stop a little longer but I told him I was wanted at Sandhurst on 3rd February. The girls at Grafton and the Stoke chaps will have to get another Charger to look after them. Mrs Glidden and Albutt have taken to calling me the foreman of the courting shop. I was very pleased with the bunch of violets. They are the first I have seen this year. I have got the others that you sent me before and I have got the rose leaves that you gave me last Summer. They are in the same pocket that I put them in at the time. I made out every word of your letter. I could make it out if it was only scribbling if it came from you, dear Polly. I have told you all the news this time; only one more letter from here. The next will be the last.

I must say goodbye now and God Bless you. Hoping to see you soon.

I remain yours affectionately ALFRED HAYES

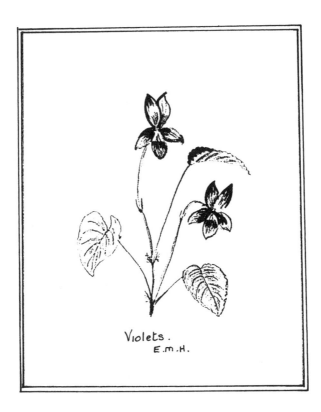

Violets.
E.m.H.

Royal Mil. College
Feb. 4th 1875

My dear Polly,

I am got quite safe to Sandhurst at last. I think that I shall like the pace very much. I do not know about what time I shall get to Wimbledon on Sunday but I shall most likely come about Middle day. I am obliged to be in at 10 o'clock at night so I can't stop very late. I went to Hanbury on Sunday last. Mother was looking capital well and so was Annie and little Nell. I will tell you all the news when I see you.

I don't expect that I shall have much time to write after this time, for there is such a lot to do but I shall stop here I think a little longer than three weeks. Some of the Grafton folks has given me a month and some of them two. The Captain told me on Monday that he should not get anyone in my place till I had been here three weeks. It cost me 11 shillings to come down here. I did not have to wait at any of the stations above a minute. I got here about half past three. My uncle met me at the station. He is a very big man something like the Superintendent at Bromsgrove - not quite so tall.

Alfred Ward is gone to Stourbridge to live. I went to Bromsgrove on Tuesday and from there to Alvechurch. I saw poor old Lou. She did not say a word about Bill. She has forgot all about him and a good thing too. Jim do not go to Grafton now on Sunday. He told me he was tired of it. I suppose he will stick to Emily now. All the better. Emily Payter is at Grafton by now. I have not seen her but Albutt was waiting for her at the station when I started. Ted Vale will be all right now and he deserves to be for he is a good chap and a true friend, different to Jack and his gang.

They likes to look after themselves rather than other folks.

Now I must say goodbye and God Bless You till Sunday and then I hope to see you about and well.

I remain, yours affectionately
ALF

A.Hayes
Care of: Mr Budd
Roy. Mil. College
Farnboro Station
Hants

34

Royal Military College
February 14th 1875

My dear Polly,

    You will think me a long time in answering your letter but I am so busy that I have not had any time till this afternoon. I have got three gentleman to valet. I have to wait at breakfast, at lunch and again at Mess at night. I do not have anything to do between Lunch and Mess. I have the afternoon to myself without I am what they call Orderly. That is to answer all bells and do anything that the gentlemen want but that don't come but once in eight days because there are eight of us and we take it in turns. I know how to do that. I have had my share of it when I was at Grafton. We wear livery. It is dark blue with a red collar and brass buttons with the letters R.M.C. on them.

    I had a letter from Ted Vale the other day. He told me that Emily Payter was come to Grafton but he had not seen her and that another lady's maid was come and Curley, that is Bill, took her home from Stoke Church last Sunday. As they were going down Grafton Lane the Captain overtook them. He was driving. He stopped and spoke to them but Ted did not know what he said, but Ted said that he heard the Captain spoke to Mrs Glidden and he said he would not have Stoke chaps or any other chaps down there. He will want Old Charger back again to give them a charge of shot and to watch them like he did last Summer, but I will write and ask Mrs Glidden all about it. She said that she would let me know all the news. I suppose that Bill has given up Carrots and took to this fresh lady's maid. He is like poor old Sally said "fond of a change". I do not think much of him. If I was to call him anything I should call him a little "FOOL".

    I am very glad that Lou has given him up for he is not good enough for a girl like Lou. At least I don't think so for I think that Lou is a good and straight forward girl and that is more than I can say for Bill. I think that Jim is a different sort. I think that he still cares for Emily, at least I hope he do for I like Emily. She is such a jolly sort of a girl. But I love you, Dear Polly, better than all and I hope that some day we shall be happy and jolly together. That will be a glorious time. Don't you think so dear Polly? I have no one to do anything for me, no mending or washing. I have to put it all out. I have not got a Grandmother alive. I live in the College. I like my place very well and I think I shall stop for a year or two and then I shall look out for something better but this is a good place for we have holidays four times a year, 3 days each time or a week at Midsummer and Christmas so that is not very bad - better than Grafton, but I shall get a day at Easter and come and see you for it seems almost a century since we parted at Hanbury on Tuesday 6th October 1874 although it is only a little over 4 months. It is only six weeks to Easter and that will soon slip away.

    When you write to your Mother please give my love to her and Annie and tell them that I have got to Sandhurst safe and sound and likes my place very well. She asked me to let her know. She also told me to tell you to let her know how the cake tasted and what sort of a one it was. There was a mince pie with it. Did you get it? I am sorry that I could not come to see you last Sunday. I have not felt right all the week through it. I was never so disappointed in all my life for I had set my mind upon it for a long time. You must keep the pot of jam a little longer. I did justice to the jam when I went to Hanbury.

Did my mother send you a Bromsgrove paper last week. She said she would. Did you see the correction that my brother put in about I being a salt maker. Now dear Polly I think I have told you all the news. I have to be Night Watch tonight but I can stand it. It wont be anything fresh to me. Now I must say goodbye and God Bless you. I will tell you all the news that I get from Grafton and Bromsgrove.

I remain
        your ever loving and affectionate
                    ALF

Please write soon.

Royal Military College
February 21st 75

My dear Polly,

I received your letter and the Valentine all right. I have not had any time to write before. I have not got any news yet from Grafton. I have not had any time to write. I had a letter from my mother this morning but she did not send me any news, but I shall most likely write to Mrs Glidden this week and then I shall be able to let you know in my next letter. I shall like to know all about the old place. The Captain has asked after me several times. I suppose he wants me to go back. There will be a rare lot of chaps down at Grafton this next summer but they wont have old Charger to keep guard. I like my place very much and I think I shall stop here as long as I did at Grafton, then it will be time for another change for the better and I hope, please God, that you will be with me to share my home, for you know that I was there at Grafton nearly seven years. I went there when I was only twelve. I might have stayed there another seven but it was too far from you, dear Polly, and not only that, there was not enough money on the score, too many hours for another thing.

I have to get up in the morning about 7 o'clock and go to bed about 10 o'clock at night. I have all the afternoon to myself and my money is about £1.2.0 a week. My wages is 18/- besides what my gentlemen give me. They have given me a sovereign in a fortnight and I don't think that is very bad. I don't have to work very hard. I can do all I have to do in about 3 hours but I have to wait at table 3 times a day, so I am obliged to stay in the College but that is nothing.

I don't have any plate to clean or glass to wash. There are men kept on purpose but still I must keep up stairs about my master's rooms for fear they should want anything and to keep their fires in. I often get wine and all sorts of stuff off them. They are very good natured. What is that young gentleman's name that you said was coming to Sandhurst from Mrs Walker's? If you tell me his name, perhaps I may know him. I have not got any news this time but if I do hear anything from Bromsgrove way I will let you know. You asked me if I meant all that those words said on the Valentine. I mean all I have said. I would not deceive you for the whole world. I love you too well, believe me, my own dear Polly.

Now I must say goodbye and God Bless you. Please remember me to Ellen and Sarah when you write to them.

I remain

    your ever loving and

           affectionate

             ALF

Royal Military College,
Sandhurst
March 7th 1875

My dear Polly,

I got your letter yesterday morning. Though it was short, it was sweet. I don't care so that you write whether it is a long or a short one. I am getting on all right and likes my place very much. I don't have any hard work to do, nor I don't have to get up early in the morning like I did when I was at Grafton. Do you remember me throwing stones up at your window under the Old Chestnut tree the morning that I went to Derby and you came and talked to me on the top of the steps. That was before six o'clock in the morning. Ah, that was a jolly time but I hope to have as jolly times again. They may not be in Grafton or in Worcestershire for we can have jolly times in Surrey or Berkshire.

I read that letter of Lou's. It is a very nice letter. She is a nice girl. Rather too good for Bill. I am glad that she has given him up for he isn't much good. I had a letter from my mother this last week but she didn't tell me much news - only that a young sweep in Bromsgrove killed his mother and then ran away. They had not caught him when Mother wrote. My brother sent me the Bromsgrove paper yesterday. I am going to send it to you today. There isn't much news about here. Only the SCARLET FEVER is very bad in this college. I have helped to carry five up to the College Hospital. They were five officers and there is one of the servants dead but it IS NOT from SCARLET FEVER but DRUNKENNESS. There is a good many drunkards here. It is all most of them think about. They are a lot of Old Soldiers and it takes a lot of drink to wet they dry throats.

My dear Polly you may rest assured that I WILL not give way to drink. I never did, nor never will. I am not a teetotaler, but I know what beer will do me good. It is only 3 weeks today till Easter Sunday, then I hope please God that we shall meet again for I do long to see you. It is nearly six months since I saw you. It seems like six years but never mind, three weeks will soon pass away. I shant fail to come. This time I hope to come twice for the officers are going away for three weeks. It is only in the vacation that I can get leave so if Lou comes over in May I shant be able to go and see her for I am obliged to be at lunch at 1 o'clock and Mess at ½ past 7 so I should only have part of the afternoon. But never mind, we shall see her again some time if it not till she has changed her name. I hope she will manage that little affair well for she deserves a good partner - better than Bill will ever make.

Now I must say goodbye and God Bless you my own dear Polly.
I remain
    yours affectionately
        OLD CHARGER

I am going to write a few lines to Lou. Write soon.

Royal Military College
Farnboro' Station, Hants
(Sunday) March 14th 1875

My dear Polly,

Just a few lines to let you know how I am getting on. I am getting on first class and now I am got settled I see that I have made a good change from game keeping to indoor service - for such is this place. I am not over worked and I have got three very nice young gentlemen to look after and as for waiting at the Mess table I can do that as well as I could a rabbit on Grafton Manor Estate. At all events I am glad that I am away from it. I only have one night's watch in a month and when I was at Grafton I had four in a week. So this is a good deal better in that way.

I am glad to tell you that the Scarlet Fever is got a good deal better. We haven't had any fresh outbreaks. All the officers that have had it are gone to the hospital and most of them are gone home on sick leave till after Easter and as for there being any danger in me coming to see you dear Polly, I don't see any in the least. I think it is only an old woman's tale about it being infectious. I don't believe for a moment that anyone can catch it in the way that people say. If it pleases God to smite people with

Scarlet Fever or anything else, they will have it and if not they wont. I don't believe in people catching different diseases by going near people that have got them because the officer that had it here first hadn't been anywhere to get it but still he had it and those that have got it since him didn't go anywhere near him. One of the gentlemen that had it and have got it now, slept in a room with two more and neither of them have got it or had it.

And there is two or three of the servants gone to the hospital to wait on them - and why don't they get it if it is infectious. I dont believe in infection in this case, not in the least, so I think that it will be quite safe in that respect to venture as far as Wimbledon on Easter Sunday, that is a fortnight today.

There is only one train from Blackwater and that is at 9 minutes to 7 in the morning and gets to Croydon about 12 minutes to 8 in the morning. There I shall have to change but what time the train starts for Wimbledon from Croydon I don't know, so I don't exactly know what time I shall get to Wimbledon. If I go to Farnborough I shall have to walk four miles and a half, so if I can manage it from Blackwater it will be all the better. You must come and meet me at the station if you can.

I haven't got any news to tell you this time but please give my love to mother and Annie when you write and tell them that I am quite well and likes my place and is getting on first class altogether. I wrote some poetry for you and sent it with Lou's letter. Did you get it? I wrote to Lou last Sunday but didn't tell her anything about her letter. I have not had an answer from her yet. Now I must say goodbye and God Bless you.

From your ever loving and affectionate
ALFRED

Please remember me to Sally and the Grafton folks when you write to them again.

Royal Military College
Farnbro' Station, Hants
(Sunday) March 21st 1875

My dear Polly,

I am writing just a few lines to let you know that I am still in the land of the living and getting on first class. I hope by this time next Sunday I shall be having a look and a bit of talk with you. I don't see any obstacle in the way yet. Our gentlemen are going away on Thursday. There is some going to stop for bad behaviour but neither of mine yet and I hope they wont. If they do they will have to wait on themselves next Sunday for I am not going to stop here because of their bad behaviour. Mine are three very nice young gents about the same age as myself.

I had a letter from Joe Gwynne and Lou this last week. Joe is getting on first rate now. He told me that he sent a letter to Mrs Glidden and Grafton and had it sent back after being at Grafton. I don't know who sent it back so he asked me to write to Ellen and ask her if she knew anything about it. If she did, write and tell me, and I would write and tell Joe. He said he shouldn't have cared if Mrs Glidden hadn't asked him to write. I have wrote to Ellen and told her all the particulars and told her to send me all the news and all the particulars back. If she sends me her letter before next Sunday I will bring it for you to see. They are a rum lot at Grafton as bad as when I and you was there. Joe is going to write to you soon. I was to remember him to you. Lou sent me a long letter, she told me that Emily was gone to live at Moseley and that Emily had thought of going out to Australia.

I told Lou to tell her that there was plenty of room in England for her yet and when England got so crowded as not to be room enough for her I would be off and let her have my place. I don't expect that will be this year nor next if ever. Jim Graves has given her up or she has given him up. I think the last is most likely. Jim has knocked off going to Grafton on a Sunday. I think John is the only regular visitor there now from Stoke. I am not sure whether Bill has knocked off or not and I don't care either. Ted Vale is the man for me. I don't care a fig for any of the others. He is a true friend and no mistake for he has proved himself more than once. I have not got much more to say, only I got the violets safe but not sound. I have got another lot or two that you sent me at Rock Hill.

Have you heard from Hanbury lately or have you heard anything of Miss Moore since she left Grafton. She told me that she was coming up London way somewhere and perhaps she should come and see you for she knew Wimbledon well. Now I must say goodbye. I will tell you all the news when I come. That will be next Sunday if I am alive and well. Goodbye and God Bless you My dear Polly.

I am your ever loving and affectionate
A. HAYES

Write soon once more before we meet.
Goodbye and God Bless. Your Charger.

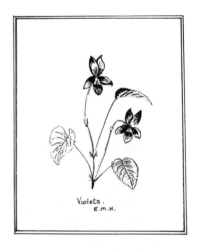

Violets.
E.M.H.

Royal Military College
Farnbro' Station, Hants
March 30th 1875

My dear Polly,

Just a few lines to let you know that I got home safe on Sunday evening. I was in college at half past six. I ought to have stopped another hour or two. I was very stiff all day yesterday so that I could not play at football or cricket but I don't care about that so as I saw you. I would give up a hundred games to see you. The next time I come I shan't go to Croydon but straight from Farnborough. It only cost me 2/3 from Wimbledon to Farnborough and it would have cost me about 3/- from Blackwater to Wimbledon via Croydon besides walking from one station to the other at Croydon. I shall know better next time.

I went to Broadmoor Asylum after dinner yesterday. There is a rum lot of folks there, most of them murderers. I did not go inside, only into the garden. It was not the right day for visitors. I would like you to see it. It is a fine piece of building, bigger than this college. When you come down here you must go and see it as well as the Wellington College and the Staff College. We have got 3 colleges as well as the Asylum just round here and yet it is the most barren country that ever I saw. If it was not for the Colleges and the Asylum there wouldn't hardly be any inhabitants. There is a good many inhabitants employed in the Colleges. More than 80 in this one.

I had a letter from home today. Mother told me that Charley, the lad that used to be in the garden at Grafton has left and gone to Birmingham to live. She didn't tell me any other news.

I am going to have my likeness taken tomorrow in my red collar, white tie and white gloves. I will send you one or two as soon as I get them. You promised to send me one of yours but you haven't yet. You know I have not got one of yours at all. I am going to have one took with my mate so that you can see what sort of a chap he is. I shall be done in plain clothes as well. I will send you some of each.

You know them stockings that you left at Grafton? Well Jane gave them to me to bring to you, so I brought them on Sunday and forgot to give them to you. I did not find that I had got them until I got out of the train at Farnborough, but you will get them some day I dare say. I forgot to ask you how Sally was getting on and where she was living. Please tell me when you write. Now I must say goodbye and God Bless you my own darling Polly.

I remain ever true, loving and affectionate
ALF

Write soon. Goodbye my dear Polly.

Royal Military College
Sandhurst
(Sunday) April 25th 1875

My dear Polly,

I am anxious to know if anything is the matter with you as you have not written this week. I wrote last Sunday. Did you get it. I hope that there is nothing the matter. I have looked every post since last Thursday for a letter but I have not seen one yet from you. I had one from Emily yesterday. She told me that she had had a letter from you and that she had written to you again. Emily is quite well which, I am afraid you are not, but I shall be very glad when your letter comes for I feel sure that there is something the matter as you have never missed one week since you have been at Wimbledon. Please write as soon as you can for I am anxious to know what is the matter.

I was on the sick list four days last week myself with a touch of the Scarletina, but it went off very light. I had it seen to in time. There is lots of men and children about here with it. I wrote to Sally last Sunday but I have not had an answer yet. I had a letter from my mother this morning. She says father is a little better and the doctors at Birmingham hope to make him strong again as the warm weather comes on but they wont tell him what is the matter with him. I can't believe that he is consumptive for it is not often that consumption sets into a person as old as he is. He was 51 on Friday 23rd April. There is not much stirring about down that part of the country. Quiet like it always was without it is two or three drunken fellows kicking up a row in a public house. That is the sort of fun that Bromsgrove people delight in.

We had a grand military funeral here on Thursday. That man that I told you of in my last letter that cut his throat. He was buried with all military honours. Most of the Captains and Officers as well as the servants of the College followed him. I did not go as I was on the sick list and could not go out. There is nothing stirring about here. All is quiet and folks seem to take it easy and I don't blame them either. There is nothing like the warm weather. I wish that you was down here so that we could go for a walk together. I don't care to go by myself. Grafton was the place for going for walks. That is a better place than if you were here for there is more to be seen. I hope that, please God, we shall have many a nice and jolly walk together before long. Not so rough as when I took you down to Upton that night after you had been to Miss Tummeys. Now I must wish you goodbye and hoping that you are quite well. Write soon.

I remain yours affectionately
ALFRED

Goodbye and God Bless you. Write soon.

Addressed to:
Miss M.Weaver, Mrs Walkers, Cottenham, S.W. Wimbledon

Royal Military College
Sandhurst
May 2nd 1875

My dear Polly,

I dare say you would wonder at my last letter but I sent it off and I dare say you had it before I had yours. I thought that there was something the matter but I hope that you are quite well and strong again. I was very middling last week with a bad cold and a stiff neck but I am glad to say that I am alright again and as well as ever. My father keeps getting better but is not able to work. The doctors at Birmingham wont tell him what is the matter with him. They are giving him cod liver oil and some strengthening medicine to take. He has to go to see them every Wednesday.

I think of going home in our next vacation - that is from 10th July to 10th September. If I go I shall go about the end of August and have the first week of September at home. Do you think that you will be able to get leave at that time? I think that about the end of August and the beginning of September is about the best time of the year. I should like you very much to come with me. I do not think I shall go if you can't come but wait till it is more convenient for you. I can only get leave twice a year. That is at Midsummer and Christmas to go any distance but we shall see more about it when the time comes. It is three months yet.

I have not heard anything of Lou yet. She promised to come and see me when she came home but she has not made her appearance yet. I am only 12 miles from Reading. It would only take her about ½ an hour to come by train.

Have you heard from home lately. How is Mother and Annie and little Nell getting on and all the folks about. I expect little Nell is getting quite big now, almost able to walk, at least she will be before we see her again. Please give my love to Mother and Annie when you write and tell them that I am getting on capital according to my sort, never was better. I was to give my mother's love to you and also to remember Ted White and all the other chaps to you and hoped that you were quite well.

Ted Vale was confirmed last Monday week. It was just 12 months on that day since I and Sall and Emily was confirmed. The time has soon passed. Have you heard anything of Sall lately. Now I think that I have said all that I have to say this time so with kind love I say GOODBYE and God Bless you.

For I ever remain,
yours affectionately
ALFRED

Write soon and tell me all the news.
Goodbye and God Bless you. M.D.P.

Royal Military College
Farnbro' Station, Hants
May 31st 1875

My dear Polly,

I am a day late this week but I was what we call ORDERLY yesterday so therefore I was very busy. I did not have time to dress myself until 7 o'clock at night. Just in time for Mess. I am glad to tell you that I am quite well and I hope that you are the same. I think that you have got a very hard place, a good deal harder than MINE for I do have most of my afternoons to myself from 2 o'clock till 7 at night but we have a busy day sometimes. Last Saturday we had 2 breakfasts, 2 lunches and two dinners. That was 6 hours hard work. This afternoon I have not got hardly anything to do.

There is not much stirring about here now. Most of the people are getting ready for Ascot races which I believe comes off on Wednesday week. I expect most of our gentlemen will go. I don't know as I shant go if I can get time. Ascot is 5 miles from here. Just a nice walk and about as barren a country as ever I saw. Nothing but common ground all the way. I thought that was a barren place when I walked from Croydon but this is worse. You know I forgot the name of the village that I came through from Croydon to Wimbledon. It was Mitcham. A village about halfway between the two places.

I shall very much like to go to Hampton Court with you and I am sure to come and see you in our next holidays if I don't go home afterwards. I would sooner come and see you than go down there for there is nobody that cares anything about me, so I don't see as it would be much pleasure for me.

My father is getting alright again so I am not quite sure whether I shall go home or not. Now have you heard from Joe Gwynne yet. I wrote to him about 2 months ago but he has never answered it. Mrs Glidden sent me the Worcestershire Chronicle this morning. I will send it to you in a day or two, there is a bit of news in it. Now I must draw to a close and with kindest love

I remain

Yours affectionately.

ALFRED

I am sorry to hear your mother is so unwell. I hope she is well again by this time. Give my love to them both when you write. Goodbye and God Bless you.

EXCERPT FOUND TUCKED INTO THE LETTER OF MAY 31ST 1875

Dear Polly the next time that you see me I shall be a tidy looking chap. I am going to shave on Sunday and cut the carrots off, and if I don't go keepering again I shall be able to look everybody in the face, so I shall be upright too.

The Wednesday after you went home from here John Palmer went to Hereford to sell a calf and pay his rent and about the afternoon sometime he found his wife drunk in the street in Hereford and some other man with her and both went off together. John is in a way about it (isn't it a blow for him.....

Royal Military College
Farnbro' Station, Hants
June 27th 1875

My dear Polly,

I did last week for the first time, neglect to write to you but I am very sorry and I hope you will forgive me for I never was so busy in my life, What with dances and balls and cricket dinners we are nearly worked to death and shall be till after next Friday the 2nd July for then we are going to have a grand ball. We were warned last night to be ready at any moment when the Quarter Master wanted us for the purpose of getting ready for this ball. We have had three days at it now getting ready. We have everything to do scrubbing the floor and polishing it with French chalk for we have no maid servants. We shall have a nice holiday soon for our gentlemen go away about 20th July. I think that is about three weeks.

Did you know Colonel Vaughan Baker, Mrs Bourne's brother. If you didn't you soon will for most all newspapers have got hold of his name. The reason is he was travelling from London to Woking in a first class Railway carriage and at Woking a young lady got into the same carriage and I believe from what I have heard he grossly insulted her and to get out of his way she opened the carriage door and got on the step when the train was going at the rate of 40 mph and she would have jumped off if he had not got hold of her. And when he got to Guildford she gave him in charge of the police and he was walked off to Guildford jail. He was tried last Thursday and committed for trial but he is bailed out for £4,000. Sir Samuel Baker is one of his Bondsmen. If you look in any newspaper you will see it. This affair has been the talk about here for more than a week.

Now for a bit of news. I had a letter from Joe Gwynne and Ted Vale last week. Joe did not tell me any news but asked me to send him some and wished me to remember him to you and said that he should like to have a line or two from you. Ted Vale told me that most likely Jim and Bill Graves would begin at Grafton as their fresh girls were going to leave. Tom Green is the thickest of the lot at Grafton now. My brother is quite cut out. Ted don't go anywhere now for he says that it is no good.

I sent you the Bromsgrove paper last Thursday. Did you get it. You will see all the news in it. I have not had the Worcester paper for a fortnight. Have you heard from Hanbury lately. How is your Mother and Annie and little Nell. I hope they are quite well. Give my best love to them when you write. Tell them that I am quite well and shall be over and see them before long. Now dear Polly, I think I have told you all this time so goodbye and God Bless you for

I ever remain yours affectionately

ALFRED CHARGER

Write soon. x x x x x x x x x x x x x

Royal Military College
Farnbro' Station
July 18th 1875

My dear Polly,

Just a few lines to let you know that I am still in the land of the living and I am glad to say quite well and I hope please God you are the same. I have given up two of my gentlemen so now I have only got my own three. We are got pretty straight again now and I suppose we shall remain so now until the Holidays which begin next Friday week and I don't care how soon that day comes for this term has been a very hard one.

I shall be very glad to come and see you for when I am writing or doing anything for you they are the happiest moments of my life and it always was so ever since I first saw you. It is now 12 months ago since I met you going to Upton Church with Sall and Lou. What a difference there is between us now. Neither of us in the same place. I and you are the nearest and quite right that it should be so. Have you heard anything of Sall lately? Is she at service or at home. I have not heard anything of her since last Christmas. Have you? Will you please remember me to her as well as Joe Gwynn and Ted Vale when you write. We are all quite well and hope that she is. I heard from Loo the other day. She is alright.

I shall most likely go home about the end of August then I shall be just right for HANBURY Harvest Home. Do you remember last year. I was at Swadlincote, just gone there. Have you heard from Hanbury lately. How is Annie? Is your mother quite well and little Nell.

Please give my best love to them and tell them that I shall come and see them if I come home in August and bring them all the news. I am glad to tell you, dear Polly, that my father still keeps getting better and all the folks at our house is quite well. My brother and Ted Vale goes to some farm house after their girls now. Jim and Bill are both widowers again. They have very bad luck. Tom Green and Jack are the only ones that goes to Grafton now. I suppose they will soon get married.

I think it is getting time, don't you, now. With my best love I conclude and say goodbye.

From yours affectionately
         CHARGER

Write soon. God Bless you.

XXXXXXX
XXXXX
XXX
X

St. Michael's Church
Upton Warren

Rock Hill, Bromsgrove
August 27th 1875

(INCOMPLETE)

My dear Polly,

I am so sorry that I have kept you so long waiting for a letter from me but I know you will forgive me when I tell you the reason. I got home quite safe from Wimbledon Station last Thursday night. About a quarter to eleven when I got to College. Then all the next day, it took me to get ready to come down here. I got to Bromsgrove Station at about twenty minutes to nine. No one did expect me except Ted Vale. He thought that I should not be home very early so he got my eldest brother to come with him to meet the 8.45 train. They did not know me at first. I had given up my ticket and was just off out of the station when Ted came and collared hold of my arm and said "Hello, where are you off to." My brother had to look at me twice before he knew me. We then went off home and just looked in. Mother did not expect me. We then went to Bromsgrove and met Tom Green and Carrots. They did not know me so I did stop to speak to them.

On Sunday morning I went to Stoke church with my brother and Ted and saw Jane and the butler from Grafton. Jane did not know me but the butler knew me in a minute. I shook hands and went part of the way home with them. None of the other Grafton servants were at church, but at night 4 or 5 of them came to Bromsgrove church. I did not go anywhere in the afternoon I was too tired. I went to Bromsgrove church at night with Jim, Ted Vale and my brother. After church I came straight home and went to Grafton. The others stayed in Bromsgrove. I was at Grafton before the girls. Tom Green brought Carrots home and two Bromsgrove chaps brought Ellen and Alice, the kitchen maid, home.

I stopped and had a little chat with Jane and Mrs Glidden. They all asked after you the first thing and all said that they should like to see you, even the butler who had never seen you nor did not know anything about you - only what the others had told him. The footman is a rum sort of a chap. Such a curious looking chap. He is cross eyed and got a good big nose piece but was very civil and agreeable. On Monday I went to see Lou at Alvechurch and took her parcel that I had from her mother's. Lou was looking very well, but I don't think she is contented. She wants to come nearer to you she said. For she says she is awful lonely where she is. So I think we shall have her London way before long. She wanted to know all the particulars about you. She was pleased to hear that you were quite well and comfortable.

I did not go anywhere much on Tuesday or Wednesday. I went to Poislands to see Beard and his wife and Bedman the underkeeper and old Wilde was there too. They was all very glad to see me. Both Mrs Beard and Wilde asked after you. I suppose Beard told Mrs Beard about me and you. Wilde was glad to hear that you was quite well. I was to remember him to you. The Captain asked me on Tuesday if I was MARRIED. I don't know who told him about it or if he said it as a joke.

(Late August 1875)

Dear Polly

I went to Hanbury yesterday. Your mother did not expect me but she looked quite well and little Nell, she is got quite a fine little girl and can nearly walk. Annie was at Mrs Creswell's nearly all day and is there a good deal of her time now, but she came home before I came away. She was glad to see me. She looked very well, better than when I saw her at Christmas. Annie told me that Alf Ward came to see her last Sunday. He has left the Police Force and I believe she said he is a stoker or something of that at some works in Birmingham. Annie don't seem to have a very good opinion of him and I don't think that your Mother thinks a great deal of him. I did not hear much news. I am going again on Saturday and then perhaps I shall hear some more. I walked from your house to Mrs Creswell's with Annie. I expect there will be a great talk about it, there always is. I don't care. I don't think Annie cares much either.

Now the reason, dear Polly, that I didn't write to you before is because I wanted to go to your home first and to get some news as well. I have not been to look after another girl so I have not found one that I care for better than I do for you. Believe me, dear Polly, I love you as dearly now as I did when I first wrote to you or before. If I ever give up you or you me I will not believe in another girl as long as ever I live, so dear Polly, set your heart at rest. Above that I can't tell you much more at this time but I will write again as soon as I get back to Sandhurst. I shall be there if I have good luck next Monday night, August 30th. So now goodbye.

Believe me, ever yours affectionately,
ALF

Royal Military College
August 31st 1875

Please excuse the black edged envelope as it is the only one that I have got.

My dear Polly,

I am glad to tell you that I am got safe back to Sandhurst again, but dear Polly, I don't think that I shall be able to come to see you again this time because I have to make up for being away. Now there has been some of the other servants doing my duty while I have been away so now I am back again they are going out while I do their duty. I have got a parcel for you and I am going to send it off now. You will get it either tonight or Wednesday morning. It is a square parcel. Most of its contents are jam and fruit but no cake. I brought it from Hanbury on Saturday. I left Mother and

Annie and little Nell quite well and wanting to see you. They would have been very pleased to see you but I told them that you would not come until next summer. I was to give their best love to you and to tell you that if Annie comes out to service at all she will come up this way. Jessie Barber and Polly Barley and Jessie Barley send their best love to you and hope to see you before long. I am got quite acquainted with a lot of the Hanbury folks now. I saw the Stoke chaps on Saturday night and Sunday morning. They all send their best respects to you, especially John and Ted Vale. It was the last that they said to me "Remember me to Mary"

I went down to Impney on Sunday afternoon and Sarah was gone to church. So I and Ted Vale went towards the church and met Sarah just at the church door.

She stood and looked at me and Ted for a minute and then came and spoke to me. I don't think she would have known me if Ted had not been with me. You know she has seen Ted since me. She was very pleased to see me and asked if you was come home. When I told her you had not she asked how you was getting on and if you was quite well and when I saw you last and such like but she did not stay long because she was going out to tea somewhere. She did not look guite so well as she did when at Grafton but she said she was quite well. She was in such a hurry that she could not stop to say any more. I wanted to ask her if she was going to leave but I had no chance. I heard at Grafton that she was but they did not know for certain.

The people at Grafton send their love to you. Ellen looks wrong somehow since she gave up John. She don't know hardly what to be at. Alice, the kitchen maid and Carrots began to run John down a little on Sunday night when I was there but Ellen soon shut them up. She said she would not have a word spoken against John in her presence so by that I think that there was some thing very peculiar that parted them. I might learn all about it some time. Jane sends her best love to you and told me to tell you that "she knew that you wished you were back at Grafton" but I contradicted her there. I don't think much of the servants there now. They are a dull lot. If it was not for Mr Gardner, the Butler, they would be as bad as mules. He keeps them alive a bit. The footman and the lady's maid are going to leave. I think it is on their own account. The footman told me that he gave notice. Now I think that I have told you all the news I can so I must conclude. If I hear any more I will tell you.

So with best love I remain yours affectionately

ALF

Write soon.

P.S. Please let your mother know if you get the parcel safe.

I have found out where my brother goes courting to. It is the Moors at Upton. Goodbye. God Bless you.

Royal Military College
Sandhurst
Farbro' Station, Hants
September 12th 1875

(INCOMPLETE)

My dear Polly

You will think that I have forgotten you altogether this time, but no, I have not forgotten you. We have been so busy at getting the place ready for the gentlemen who came back five days before their time. Next Wednesday was the day for them but they came back last Friday and we did not know anything about it until last Thursday afternoon so that threw us all behind but we are got nearly straight now. I think we shall have a nice time of it this term. At least I shall for instead of having five rooms and five gentlemen to look after I have only got three. Two of them are my old ones - the same that I had last time so I think that I am very lucky. My chum has got James Standen for one of his gentlemen. I don't know what sort of a chap he is for shelling out for we have not seen enough of him yet.

Dear Polly, I was glad to hear that you got the basket alright but you must not tell your mother that the JAM tasted of the mustard tins or else I shall get in for it when I go to Hanbury again because I told both Annie and Mother that it would not make it taste and Annie said all the time that she thought it would. The reason that the jam was put into the tins was that they would not break and another thing Mother said that if you got them alright she should not have them back again so that is the reason that you had it in the mustard tins.

Was the pears alright. They came from Mrs Creswell's. Annie went and picked them while I was at Hanbury that Saturday. I was to tell you that you need not send the basket back unless you like because yours is at home and that does as well as that one for them.

The Grafton folks are about the same as usual so Ted Vale says and he knows everything. The week that I was at home, Alice, the kitchen maid had a letter from somebody and so everybody thought it was from me as I was at home but it was not from me. But whoever it was they put Jim Graves name at the bottom of it so this kitchen maid wrote back to Jim Graves calling him every thing that was not much good and mentioned Ted Vale's name in it. So the Sunday before I came back neither Ted nor Jim saw this kitchen maid but last Sunday both Ted and Jim waited for the Grafton folks coming out of Bromsgrove church and made this girl tell them all the particulars of the letter that she had and everything belonging to it and Jim Graves told her and all the rest of them that the next letter that he had from them he would take it to Captain Bourne and hear what he would say about it, and Ted Vale told them that if they had got anything to say about him to say it to his face not behind his back in a letter and sent to other people.

I know what she said about Ted. It was something about this: That it said in the letter that she had, that she was a flirt with all the chaps in Bromsgrove and that Ellen

White was as bad, for Ted Vale has told me so and that she was going to be married and all that sort of trash so the girl thought sure enough that Jim Graves had sent the letter but I believe Alice apologised at last for being so hasty.

But the Sunday night after I got home, two Bromsgrove chaps took Ellen and Alice home and they would hardly speak to me when I saw them coming home from Stoke church the Sunday morning after. I don't know what was the reason but when I went to Grafton at night Ellen seemed as friendly as ever and so did Emma and Jane but the others I did not take much notice of. I saw the envelope of the letter that Alice had and I saw as soon as I saw it that a girl or a woman wrote it. It was not a bit like Jim's writing so I told her then that the letter came out of this house and I believe it did for it was just like Mrs Glidden's hand writing on the envelope and I think now that it was her writing.

Royal Military College
Farnbro' Station, Hants
Sept. 22nd 1875

My dear Polly,

Just a few lines to let you know that I am still in the land of the living and glad to say quite well and I hope please God that you are. We have been rather busy the last fortnight at getting the gentlemen straight and I think now that we are pretty near straight. I have not got much news to tell you. I had a letter from my brother yesterday. He told me that Hanbury Harvest Home was last Thursday and he and Ted Vale went. He did not tell me much about it but I will send you the paper as soon as I get it and then you will see most of the particulars.

Ted Vale has been rather middling lately but I think all the rest of the folks are pretty well. The reason I speak so much of Ted Vale is because he is a true friend and when we are together we are as two brothers. When all the chaps set onto me that Sunday night last winter, Ted Vale was the only one that stood by me while John, Jim and Bill and a lot more that I could mention went on and not even looked and I believe if any chap could stand the buffeting that we had that night he could stand anything. And another thing, when he writes to me he writes like a brother, so dear Polly that is the reason I think so much of Ted Vale. I have not heard any news from Grafton lately only that jolly old Wilde is gone to live in Father Campbell's house or is going. I did not hear anything about it when I was there. There was but little alteration there when I was at home only there was a path cut out through the lorals on the right hand side of the drive into Father Campbell's garden.

I think our next holidays begin on the 10th December. I don't care how soon they come for I want to go to the CRYSTAL PALACE again or some other Palace. When we went there I believe it was the happiest day that ever I remember. I should not have cared if the day had lasted till this time. I was just right then. Did you have a very heavy storm round your way last Sunday night. We had a bit of one but my brother told me that he dont remember such a heavy storm. It began about 5 o'clock and lasted until half past 9 o'clock and thundered and lightned and rained very heavy all the time. We did not have it like that. We only had a bit of a shower and a little thunder and lightning. We have had a good deal of rain since then.

I hope that when I go into Worcestershire again you will come with me. I was to tell you from your Mother that if you changed your place you was to go home but I dont want you to go until next summer then we shall be both able to go and have a good look round. I shall be looking forward to the time now until it comes. I suppose you wont have so much to do if Mrs Walker goes away for a bit. I wish I lived nearer. We should be able to have a nice time of it now but I have got only my afternoons to myself now only on a Sunday because we are at Mess or dinner every night from 8 to 9 o'clock and nights are getting dark and cold again.

It is exactly 12 months since I met you coming out of Grafton garden door against the cowshed when I came from Swadlincote and it only seems a day or two ago. Time soon passes and Lou has been at Alvechurch 12 months last Monday. Have you heard from her lately.

I was very pleased with the card you sent me and thank you very much for it. My birthday was before I went with you to the Crystal Palace on the 8th August. I have not forgotten when yours is. I will try and remember it. Now dear Polly I think I have said all I can say this time. So please give my love to Mother and Annie when you write and with best love to yourself I say goodbye and may I continue to be
                      Yours affectionately
                          CHARGER

Write soon.

Royal Military College
Farnboro Station
Octr 31st 1875

My dear Polly,

Just a line or two to let you know that I have remembered the 1st of November is your birthday and I wish you many happy returns of the day. I am going to send you a small card which I hope you will accept not for the value of the thing but just as a small token of the wishes of yours most affectionately

       ALF

Write soon.

Royal Military College
Nov. 14th 1875

My dear Polly,

I received your letter on Wednesday but I am sorry to say that I have not got the Worcester paper for there is such a lot of folks comes to me for papers to read and sometimes forgets to bring them back again. I think that I lent that Worcester paper to somebody and they forgot to bring it back again but if it do turn up I will send it. I have not got much news to tell you for I am going on about the same, slow and sure and round Bromsgrove way is very quiet. Mother told me that Wilde was tired of living at Grafton. He says that he is too near the big house, for his work is never done and Mrs Wilde says that Mrs B is so mean that she can't do anything with her. So by that I think that Wilde wont be long at Grafton, at least not to live there.

Did you get the piece of Joe's Birthday cake. What did you think of it. It travelled a good many miles, nearly 200 I should think for it is 120 from Reading to Bristol, and Tenby is a long way farther on. Joe says he is going over to Bromsgrove about February or March and says that he shall go to Grafton for a bit of skating if the ice bears when he is over there so then I suppose he will get all the news and he will be sure to let me know all that he can get hold of for we are great chums.

Our Fair went off with a great row on Tuesday night for a lot of our gents got down there and began to knock the things about throwing the caravans over so a lot of the show chaps got the Naphtha lamps and threw the Naphtha over some of the gents. Then the row began.

A lot of the chaps got their heads cracked with big sticks and stones and after a bit it got so strong that the show chaps got the guns that they shoot down these shooting tunnels with and loaded them and threatened to shoot anybody that dared to go past. They lined themselves all across the road; so some of our gents, about 20 of them, got round somehow and got at the back of them while a lot more kept the show chaps attention in front. So the lot at the back made a rush at them and before the show chaps could make out what was up they had all their guns and sticks taken from them but they fought like lions until the police came and stopped them and very soon cleared the place. Some of the gents were burned very bad, 2 or 3 have been in the hospital all the week through it. There was one or two servants got knocked about a bit but nothing to hurt.

Now dear Polly, I think that is all the news I have to tell you this time but I will send the Bromsgrove paper with this letter so you will be able to see what news there is. If you look in the deaths you will see a native of Hanbury died at Farnborough and perhaps you might know him. Now I must conclude, with best love

I am ever yours affectionately

ALFRED

Give my love to Lou and Mother and Annie when you see them.

Hanbury Rectory
Bromsgrove
Christmas Eve 1875

My dear Polly,

I am so very sorry I have not written to you before, but I have had little time for letter writing and less to say, as very little has happened here.

I am sure you will be sorry to hear that good Mrs Price has lost her husband. Poor fellow, his has been a suffering life for a long time now. I trust that he has entered into his rest.

We are all very busy preparing for Xmas, doing Church decorations and getting ready for the Sunday School Xmas treat which is a large affair as we have about 100 children. I suppose it is a very busy time for you too.

What miserable weather we have had lately, the roads have been so bad as to be almost impassable in places. It has been by turns very cold and very wet now for a long time.

I hope you have been stronger lately and that you are happy and getting on well. I have not seen your Mother for some time now but I think she is pretty well. I saw Mrs Vaughan this morning. I am sorry to say she is not so well as could be wished though well enough to come here. But I only have time to write a few lines today to wish you a very happy Xmas and New Year and every blessing

"A happy holy Xmas friend
May God grant unto thee
And happier and holier
May each one coming be
Until thy work on Earth is done
And then in Heaven shalt see
The home that Jesus came on earth
And died to gain for thee."

I remain, ever your affectionate friend,
MARY DOUGLAS

1876

This is a period of upheaval and misfortune for both Alf and Polly. During the year they have to face redundancy, serious illness, a broken engagement, two deaths and more moves. Their relationship is put under enormous strain.

R.M.C.
Sandhurst

Royal Military College
Sandhurst
(Wed) January 5th 1876

My dear Polly,

Just a few lines to let you know that I am still knocking about in the land of the living and glad to say quite well, better than on Christmas Day. We are going to have a grandish stir here this week. The first performance is the College School children's heat which comes off tomorrow afternoon (Thursday). That is going to be a tidy set out. The next is our Ball which comes off on Thursday night and I believe it will be a very good one. For nearly all the servants have got their heart in it in trying to bring it out in the first of style and we have got two or three gentlemen and ladies helping us so I think it will be a rare good one.

You asked how I should like you to come. I should like you to come very much. I should just be in my glory. There is nothing that I should like better for I shan't be there much if you don't. I shall be like a dog in a fair, lost, but I shall just go and look round just to satisfy the other servants or else they wont like it after trying so hard to get it up for they all like the most to be made of things of that sort. I shan't be much good there I know, for I can't dance but very little for I never took no delight in it and I was never brought up to much of it either. But if you were there perhaps things would be changed. Anyhow if you don't come to this one you must come to another next year here if I am here for the servants have one every year if they can get leave of the Governor. Then the Ball is not the last of the performance for the servants have a grandish supper the night after to finish up with.

So I think with all the lot we shan't die for want of amusement but how it all goes off I will tell you the next time that I write.

Now for a little news. My brother told me that there were four or five fresh girls at Grafton but Ellen is still there. They have got two fresh lady's maids and another under housemaid in Carrot's place and another kitchen maid but Jane and Mrs Glidden still sticks there. My oldest brother and Ted Vale are going to try and get in with some of them fresh ones for they have not had any luck with their girls. They have both had about 6 or 7 since I have been here and I think that Jim and Jack are going to try their hands at it so Grafton Lane will be pretty well visited again but they wont have CHARGER to look out for them again. I think that Joe Gwynne is getting tired of service for I heard that he has asked a man to get him a job at Crewe at the Carriage Works but I did not hear it from Joe himself so I don't know whether it is true or not but I dare say he will tell me the next time that he writes.

I dare say that I shall be able to come and see you again sooner than I expected for our master told us today that we should have leave again the week after next so if you can get a day I should be most happy to go out somewhere with you to the Crystal Palace or anywhere. I don't care where. How is Lizzie's arm got. Please remember me to them all. I shall be glad to see them again. Have you heard from Hanbury lately? How are all the folks at home? Give my love to them when you write again and

58

tell them that I am still kicking gently along. I am glad the ring fits alright. I shall know another time when I have to get one of rather a different pattern.

I went to that old Jew but he has not got that watch or another like it nor I did not see one in his establishment that I should like so I think that I shall go somewhere else. Now dear Polly I must draw to a close for it is nearly post time and I don't think that I have any more news, so with best love I must say goodbye and God Bless you for
I remain yours ever true
CHARGER
Write soon.

Please to excuse mistakes and bad writing for my pen is something like me rather dull.

Royal Military College
Sandhurst
January 11th 1876

My dear Polly

Just a few lines to let you know how I am getting on. I have been rather busy since the Ball for I, with some more, have been doing some gardening for our Colonel. We have been making his croquet lawn larger and putting his flower borders to rights. We have not quite done yet. I should not mind if it lasted until the gentlemen come back for it seems to agree with me better than being indoors. I seem quite my old RATE again.

Now for the Ball. I went and enjoyed myself pretty well but I went by myself as you told me. I danced but very little but went into the card room and helped some of the chaps to sing songs and in that way I enjoyed myself until 5 o'clock in the morning when we broke up. We had a very good set out. The Colonel and his wife opened it by leading off the first dance then they went away but taking it altogether it was much better than I expected. The girls and the women were most of the them dressed very well considering their station of life. I should very much have liked you to have been there for when a man goes to a Ball of that sort if he don't take a partner with him he has to beg a great deal or else you can't get a dance. So I saw that was my case so I made my exit sharp after the first dance or two but I believe most of the chaps and galls enjoyed themselves first rate and satisfied everybody. The day after the Ball we had another jolly turn out and kept it up until about 1 o'clock and the next day we had a holiday, so last week was a jolly one, began well and ended well with us.

I don't think that I have got any fresh news for you, only they have got a fresh Butler and Footman at Grafton so they are nearly all fresh down there. Ted Vale wrote to me on Sunday and he told me that he and my oldest brother went round Grafton way on Sunday afternoon and saw the two fresh maids and said good afternoon to them but they never answered so they did not get anything out of them but they are going to try again next Sunday. Tom Green goes to Dr. Woods in Bromsgrove now after the Cook there I believe, and I believe that courting the girls is all that the chaps down there think about. At least it is all that they write to me about. All the Stoke chaps wish to be remembered to you and wish you the compliments of the season. John Blunn still sticks to Botley's nurse and Ted Vale says that he hardly ever talks about Sarah without he happens to go down to Impney and sees her then he talks about her abit but it is not often that he goes there.

I am glad that you are going to ask for a day. I think that the 19th will suit me nicely. Please let me know as soon as you know if you can get it or not so that I can get leave, for our Quarter Master is as changeable as the wind and perhaps he wont let us leave just then. If you can't get the 19th perhaps you can get one day in the next week but I don't care when it is I shall be sure to get leave. I shall come and see you at any rate whether we go to the Crystal Palace or not. I wish that I was nearer to you. I would not sit in this room every night like I do. I would help you wash up or anything else so as it was in your company. How is Lizzy's arm now. I hope it is better for I know that every hand is wanted in your house and, I should think, two more pairs, so I know that you have not got much time to spare.

So if you can't write to me as usual I shan't mind for I know how you are situated and I can trust you so don't put yourself out about it for you know no news is good news. Now dear Polly I must conclude for it is post time, so with best love I say goodbye and God Bless you

From yours affectionately
CHARGER

Remember me to all the galls and I hope to be with you and them again before long.

Royal Military College
Farnbro' Station
(Mon) January 24th 1876

My dear Polly,

You will think that I am not got back to the R.M.C. as I have not written before but I have and quite safe too. I should have written yesterday only I went to a funeral of one of our College servants and did not get back until late so now I will tell you all I can. When I left you on Wednesday night I walked as sharp as ever I could to the

Station and got there just in time. If I had been a minute later I should have had to stay at Wimbledon all night but I was just lucky and got home quite safe at 11 o'clock and rather tired too. But I shouldn't mind another day or two before our gentlemen come back but I don't exactly know when it will be but anyhow I hope that I shall be able to see you once more before our work begins again.

Now for some news. Did you know Mrs Forby that was for a short time Housekeeper at Grafton and afterwards cook. I think it was before you came but she lived at Miss Dixon's of Stoke Grange last and died there this day week. She was ill a long time so Mother told me. There have been a good many deaths at Bromsgrove lately. A good many of the old inhabitants that I knew are dead and I believe that there is a great deal of sickness about there now. I will send you the paper next week. There have been some grand doings at Grafton last week, 3 or 4 parties I believe. I dare say if Ellen answers your letter she will tell you all about it for I don't know much only that there was some parties there, for I can't get hold of any news about that place now Ted Vale and his lot have shifted from that house on the top of the hill against the church and gone to Stoke Pound.

MR J BLUNN has been out for a week with his gal so I think that he is coming it fine, don't you? He had his likeness taken and is going to send me one so I shall see how he looks. I don't think that I have got any more news for you this time. I will write again about the end of the week. The sergeants here had rather a grand Ball here on Friday night and kept it up all the next day so we have had a grand time of it here lately. Now I think that I must conclude as I have told you all I know at present. If I come to see you again this term I will come on a Sunday if you don't mind. Now goodbye. Please remember me to the two Lizzies and the little one - I have forgotten her name - and with best love to yourself,

        I remain yours affectionately
        ALFRED WILLIAM HAYES

I have not forgotten Drury Lane yet.
Write soon.
Please to excuse bad writing for my pen is rather the worse for being used too soon.

Royal Military College
Farnbro' Station, Hants
February 1st 1876

My dear Polly,

I received your letter this morning and as I have nothing to do this evening I thought that I would write you a few lines just to let you know how I am getting on like. I had a bit of an accident happen last Monday night week. I had just finished writing to you and had posted the letter, then I thought I would split a bit of wood to light my fire in the morning. So while I was splitting one piece of wood the chopper slipped and cut the top nearly off my thumb. It was sharp for a minute or two but I got it bound up then, and went to the doctor's in the morning and got it straped up and they put me on the sick list for the remainder of the week, and now it is getting on nicely although it is rather sore, and I hope it will be quite well by the time our gents come back or else it will be very awkward.

Nearly all our chaps are on leave. They started last Thursday and are to be back by next Thursday. There is twelve of us left but we are to go if we like when the others come back, but there is no leave to be granted after 6th Feby so if I don't come to see you next Sunday I shan't be able to come again this term. I am not sure that I shall come this Sunday for my poor old grandfather is very ill and is not expected to live from one hour to another and I should not like to be away while he is so ill. None of us expect him to live another day. He has been ill nearly 14 weeks and has not eaten scarcely anything all the time. So dear Polly, I think that I shall give up all thought of coming again although I should like to very much.

If he does die I wont stay here much longer afterwards. It is only him that has kept me here so long. We buried one of our College servants last Sunday week and are going to bury another next Sunday. It will make 10 that have been buried from the College since I have been here but they have been nearly all old soldiers so you may guess that the R.M.C. is not a very healthy place. We have had the soldiers out this way today and they were here on Sunday. I suppose they have been looking out their places for next Autumn's Manoeuvres.

I don't think that I have any news to tell you, only that one of the fresh maids that went to Grafton a week or two ago is gone again. Got tired of that new place. It will soon begin to get pleasant down there now. It is a nice place in the summer but very dreary in the winter. I wish sometimes when I am stived* up here that I could have some of them nice times in the Green Lane and about there over again and get some PEARS and apples off Old Father Campbell's place. Them was rather jolly times and I hope to have some of the same sort again before long for I don't see being dull always but I should not mind Drury Lane sometimes for a finish up.

Mr Lowe asked my brother if he knew, the other day, how you were getting on and if I still wrote to you and if you were quite well and when you were coming down that way, but my brother told him that he could not answer all the questions. You know Mr Lowe was the man that was helping in the hayfield and he always was asking me how you were getting on before I came up here. He said that he liked you because you were a nice jolly gal. Now dear Polly, I must say goodbye. Please remember me to all at home when you write and tell them that I am getting on just tidy like now.

    With best love, I am ever yours affectionately

OLD CHARGER

Write soon.

Charley the lad in the garden at Grafton is left and gone to work at Bromsgrove Station.

Note: * "stived" A dialect word meaning enclosed, stifled or suffocated.

Royal Military College

Farnbro' Station, Hants

(Tues) February 8th 1876

My dear Polly,

    I received your letter yesterday and I am glad to hear that your work is a little easier. I expect that our work will begin sharpish next Monday. I don't know whether it will be a hard term or not yet. I shall see when it begins. My grandfather is still alive but he is dead and stiff from his feet up to his breast. I don't think that he will live the night through. I can't make out what as kept him alive for he has not taken anything except a drop of cold water since last Monday week and a very little of that for he can't swallow a morsel of anything. I had my mother up here to see him from last Friday until today. She went back this morning. (you know he is her father)

    We have got the smallpox in our village. It is at the Rectory. The parson has got it. Some of the folks are in a devil of a stew for fear they should get it. Our Quarter Master sent some of their servants to enquire about it last night but they could not find out that it was anywhere except the Parson's. If it was known up at the War Office they would not let our gentlemen come back until it was all blown over but I don't believe in it being catching. I think that if we are to have it we shall have it and all the doctors in England could not stop it. But I hope that it wont spread any farther for it is a fearful disease. I think that is all that the talk is round here.

    My thumb is getting on nicely but still rather awkward but I think it will be well enough by the time the gents come back again.

    I have not heard any news from Bromsgrove. Mother did not know any, so I suppose that it is all quiet. She said that she saw the two nurses the other day so I suppose that they were the two old ones from Grafton. Dear Polly I was glad to hear that little Nell has got that she can walk. I expect that she is getting rather mischieful now. Just beginning to use her hand a bit but she will be rare company for your Mother now. I should very much like to creep round that way tonight and have a look at them. I should make them look up, think I shouldn't. But I dare say that I shall manage to creep that way again before long. When you go there again you will be quite a stranger. You have not been there for nearly 18 months now.

What sort of a day did Lizzie have in London? Did she have a nice day. I am thinking that it is nearly time to go to Drury Lane again or else Covent Garden but I shan't have any time until Easter and then I am not quite sure how long a holiday we shall get. Now dear Polly, I think I must say goodbye as I have no more news for you. I think my agents down Bromsgrove way are getting lazy for they have not sent me much lately. Do you ever hear from Sarah now? If you write to her please remember me to her and when you write home give my love to your Mother and Annie and all the rest of the folks there. Now with best love to yourself, hoping this will find you quite well as it leaves me at present, and don't forget me to the two Lizzies and the little one. I am often wondering what games you are up to when I am down here by myself doing nothing.

From yours affectionately

CHARGER

Write soon. I have got a lot of bad pens or I am got very clumsy lately.

Royal Military College
Farnbro' Station
February 22nd 1876

My dear Polly,

I have got a bit of time this afternoon so I thought I would just write a few lines just to let you know how I am getting on. I have been very busy this last week on account of our gentlemen coming in. We had them all in on the 14th and it has taken us ever since to get the place in order: and I think that we are pretty straight again now and I think we shall have an easy time of it for a bit now. We have not got half as much work to do this term as we had last. Mine are all new ones this time but I don't think much of them at present for they are rather poor and they are not much good if they haven't got a little money. They have got as much cheek as they that are rolling in money but they can't do what they like with me. I have got used to the place now and know my way about so I don't care: but I shan't have it long for I have made up my mind to get out of it very quick.

I have not made up my mind what to take to but I think of staying about this part of the country. I have been persuaded to go into the Detective Police Force, which I think I shall: but anybody can't get there, they must get some good recommendations and I think I can get some very good ones both from here and from Captain Bourne, for the Captain told me if I ever wanted a recommendation he would give me one for anything. The Captain asked father the other day if I was coming back to him in the Spring and I believe father told him that I did not intend coming into Worcestershire again to work for a few years and I don't believe I shall. I should like to see the Captain very much I always got on very well with him.

They have had another change down there. I heard that Ellen was gone or going very shortly, and young Banner of Rock Hill was going to be a young lady's maid so I think they are not particular who they have for ladies maids now down there. I believe that old Mother Glidden is still there and Jane, but no more what we know. If I go home this next Summer I shall go and see old Mother Glidden and have a talk to her for I have a good deal to ask her. Do you still think of going home in the Summer. If you do you must manage to go with me or I with you if I stay here until then. For I should like very much to go with you home. My eldest brother thinks of coming up to see me at Easter if he can get three or four days holiday. I had a letter from Ted Vale yesterday, he did not tell me much news. He sent me John Blunn's photo. It is a very good one and I have got to send mine to John. You have not sent me yours yet. I should like it very much but any time will do.

I sent you the Surrey and Hants paper on Sunday so that you could see the account of my Grandfather's funeral. It was the largest funeral that has taken place at York Town for a great number of years for he was greatly respected by all that knew him. There was all the soldiers belonging to the establishment and all the officers that were at home followed him as well as all the servants. It will be a long while before he is forgot about here. Now dear Polly, I think that I have told you all this time so I must say goodbye. Hoping it will find you quite well as it leaves me at present.

From yours affectionately, CHARGER

Thank you very much for the violets, we have none down here. I am sorry to learn that Lizzie is going to leave for you might not get such a nice girl again. Write soon.

Violets.
E.M.H.

Royal Military College
Farnbro' Station, Hants
March 3rd 1876

My dear Polly,

I am rather late this week in answering your letter but I have not had a chance until today. But now I am glad to say that we are got about square and I think that we shall have a nice easy time of it. The gentlemen that I have got this time are not so much trouble as the ones I had last year. You know last Easter Sunday was the first time that I came to Wimbledon and if you remember right it was when I came here that I could not bring the cake and that was in February.

Dear Polly I am not going away from here just yet for I have not made up my mind yet what to get up to after I do go. I don't want to throw myself out so it is better to use dirty water until you can get clean as the saying is. You asked me to tell you the difference between the detective Police and the others. Well, the City or County Police have certain beats to go on and certain places to visit and not to go out of their county. But the Detective Police have no regular beats but go where ever they are required. I dare say that you have heard of Scotland Yard, the Headquarters of the Detectives. You may see a detective at most big railway Stations to detect rogues taking ladies dressing cases or jewel cases or fellows leaving the train to avoid paying his fare and all such like. A Detective can go on duty in plain clothes or any disguise he likes and a Policeman can't. Sometimes you can hear talk of a detective being sent to Ireland to ferret out a murder or a forgery or anything else that is a little hid and can't be brought to light for want of evidence.

So you can tell that a fellow wants all his wits about him when he joins that force. It was my uncle that persuaded me to join it if I left this and he is well known among lots of the fellows at Scotland Yard. So I think that I could get on there very well but I shall think more about it and shall see how things go at Midsummer. Dear Polly, you need not be afraid for me for you can trust Charger in any sort of company. I have been able to take care of myself a long time now. If I was to get into the worst slums of London I don't believe it would make the least difference to me now, and a detective's life is not the worst after all. But I wont say any more about it now.

Dear Polly, I think if I go home at Midsummer I shall go at about the end of August at the latest and I think it would be a good time for you because in September the days are getting short and I would like very much to go home with you if it can be arranged any how, but dont put yourself about over it. I can't go in September because our gents come back on the 10th and we always have some odd jobs to do before they come in but we shall see more about it when the time comes. Have you heard any news from Grafton lately. Did Ellen ever answer your letter. I believe she is gone from Grafton but I have heard but very little lately about any of them. Ted Vale told me that he thought Ellen was gone.

I will send you John Blunn's photo but please send it back to me as soon as you have done with it. I don't know any news, so I can't tell you any. Please give my best love to Mother and Annie and Nell when you write to them and tell them that I am just above water and struggling on tidy like, and you must not forget me to the 2 Lizzies and the little nurse.

Now I must sat goodbye with best love,
I am yours faithfully,
CHARGER

I spoke to the postman about the Valentine and he said that he forgot to stamp them on account of having such a lot of letters on that day. Do you ever hear from Sarah Bradley now. How is she? Please remember me to her when you write.

ENVELOPE
Addressed to:
Miss Weaver, Mrs Walkers, Cottenham, Wimbledon, SW.

Postmarked:
Farnboro' Station	MR	3	76
York Town	MR	3	
London SW	MR	4	76

Royal Military College
March 13th 1876

My Dear Polly,
I have kept you a long time this turn without hearing from me but I hope you will think none the worse of me. For although we have not got much work to do we can't call our time our own for Luncheon here is not over until after three of an afternoon. So we can't do much from then until six and we can't do much before Lunch and generally we have some little job or another to do such as washing up but that is not often. We have got rather an easy time of it but we can't go away or do any little job for ourselves for fear we should be called on for anything. We have got on much better this time than last but I don't know what it will be when cricket and all them sort of games comes on. I have not heard that there is to be any dancing here this time like there was last term. It will be all the better for us if there isn't.
I was rather glad to hear that Lizzie was not gone because perhaps if another had come she might have been disagreeable or some other ailment belonging to her. Fresh

faces always make some differences or another. You are all pretty old servants there now. All have been there over a twelvemonth - something different to the Grafton lot. My brother tells me that some of the last new ones there is gone again so I suppose that Mrs Bourne has been coming out in her true colours. I thought perhaps that it was the early PEARS that they had been after but it is rather too early for them yet. I should not mind two or three pocketfuls now just to moisten my mouth but they are a little too far off or else some of them would have to come. If old Long have not picked them all when I go home in August I'll open his eye for some of them.

He has not got young Charlie to tell him everything now. I believe he is gone to the carriage works at Bromsgrove Station. Poor old Wilde's wife is very ill again and they don't expect her to live and I believe his daughter is going to be married soon so I suppose there will be great doings down at Old Father Campbell's house after a bit. I have been thinking all day today what rare games we used to have in that one place. It could tell some tales if it could speak. Have you heard anything of the place lately. I never hear how the folks at Grafton House are getting on. I can't never get to hear how old Mother Glidden is getting on. I mean to write to her some day when I have a little time to throw away but I don't for a moment suppose that she will answer it.

Have you heard where Ellen is gone to from there. I will have a good look round the place when I have a chance. I'll pick up all the fresh news there is to get. I think my Uncle is going down to see my mother at Easter and he says that he shant come back until he has had a talk to Captain Bourne. I don't know what as induced him to want to have a talk with him but fancy I suppose. I am glad to say that my thumb is getting nearly well but is rather tender at present. It is not grown together properly. It is rather dumpy. It will never be the proper shape again. Dear Polly, have you heard from your home lately. How are all of them about there. I hope they are quite well. Give my love to them when you write. It seems a long time since I saw any of them and it must seem longer to you. I know it was a very wet day when I was there last and your mother wanted me to have an umbrella for fear the rain should spoil my coat but the rain never hurt me nor my coat. It was not the first time I had been out in the rain.

Now dear Polly, I think I must conclude for I have no more news to tell you. Only what you know - that Easter is coming and then we shall have a bit of holiday. That is the thing that I am looking forward to. I hope the weather will change a little before then. It has been two raw winter days here yesterday and today. It is a little finer just now.

Now goodbye with best love, I am yours affectionately

ALF

Write soon.

(Crested notepaper)
Royal Military College
April 2nd / 76

My dear Polly,

I am longer than ever this time in answering your letter but all last week we had not a bit of time for anything. Last Thursday week we had a grand Funeral here. It was Colonel Chesney's so there were a lot of officers from Aldershot camp followed him and after the Funeral they came to the RMC to have lunch. When they got here there were no joints on the table or the table laid or any servants there to wait on them for we were all at the Funeral and we did not hurry back. So when our Governor saw how things were he swore and danced about like a mad fellow.

There were six of us told to be ready for the lunch. We were all to be full dressed and be in the dining room at 3 o'clock. I was lucky enough to be among the six and so instead of getting dressed and getting the lunch ready for them we all started off to see the Funeral and of course we got back too late to wait at the lunch after all. The Officers had to go back without any. But our old Governor made us lay the lunch table and get dressed and wait in the dining room every day since last Thursday week until yesterday and we had to wait an hour each day just for punishment, so we six have not had a bit of time to ourselves for more than a week. For the regular lunch is not off the table until nearly half past three and then we have got to lay for the other afterwards so it was six o'clock before we were done and we were for Mess again at half past seven so you see what chance I have had.

Dear Polly, what nice weather it is. We shall very soon have summer here. It is a fortnight today until Easter Sunday. I am not quite sure whether I shall be able to come and see you on Easter Sunday or not yet, but I shall be sure to, some time during the fortnight that our gentlemen are away. I am not sure whether my brother will come or not yet at Easter for his master is rather a funny old file and perhaps he wont give him leave. Dear Polly, I shant expect you to have a day with me at Easter for I don't feel inclined for any pleasure yet. I will stay until the summer and see what that will bring forth. I should not mind going to Hanbury harvest home next year if I am at home when it comes off. Or any of the picnics about there.

I suppose that Jim Graves and Bill and John will be taking their girls out for a walk by this time for it is such a nice fine day. I believe that all the servants have left Grafton that were there when we were. I am not quite sure whether Jane is gone but all the others are. Have Mrs Walker still got the house full. I should ask her if I were you to get somebody to help just to see what she would say and if then you can't get anybody else, send for me. I can do anything I know you want me to do. For I believe without any bragging I should make a good HOUSEMAID or nurse or anything in that line of business.

Now I must say goodbye with best love,
I remain yours affectionately
ALF HAYES

Write soon.

R.M.College
(Sunday) April 9th 1876

My dear Polly,

It is not often that I write twice to your once, but you see now I am getting very considerate, but the reason I am writing is that I think I shall be able to come and see you this day week (Easter Sunday) for our gentlemen go away on Wednesday the 12th and are going to stay until the 1st May, so I shall ask leave for next Sunday. I will let you know if I get it by next Saturday. It is a very nice afternoon now although it was a little wet this morning, and a nice time to go for a walk, I think. We shall have some nice weather now I think. I hope that next Sunday will be a fine day for I shall very much like to have a look at you and I want to say something to you too.

How have you been off for work lately. We have not had much to do lately. Now we didn't want much and I don't expect that we shall do much while the gentlemen are away. If we don't get a day or two's leave for I think we are entitled to it, for while the gentlemen are here we are on our feet a good many hours from 6 in the morning until 11 at night. But we are not at work all them hours but still we have to be here. I suppose that you will soon be losing the little nurse. It is getting sharp into April now. I believe that my brother is coming up to see me next week but we are not sure yet. I should like him to come the Saturday before Easter and all of us go (you I mean) to Hampton Court on Easter Monday. There is going to be some grand doings there I believe on that day but I don't think that I should be able to get leave or you either. So we will let it drop for we can't always have things our own way and turn out very likely for the best.

Did any of your people go to the Boat Race yesterday. Nearly all of our gents went excepting a few of the poor ones. I think Cambridge were the winners this year. Have you heard from home lately. How are all of them there . Is your Mother quite well and Annie and little Nell. Please give my love to them all when you write. I should think that 'Nelly' is getting quite a nice little girl by this time. She must be getting on for two years old now. I should like to see them all again before long.

Now, dear Polly I think that I have said all I can this time for I don't think that I have got any news for you - only that Joe Gwynne has left his place in Wales and is at Home for the present. Do you ever hear from Sarah Bradley now. Is she still at Corbett's. Please remember me to her if you ever write to her.

Now goodbye, with best love
I am ever yours affectionately
ALF

I will send you a line or two if I get leave and if I don't on Saturday.

Write soon.

R.M.College
Farnboro' Station
April 18th 1876

My dearest Polly,

I am just writing these few lines to let you know that I have got back to the R.M.C. safe and sound again. I was obliged to stay in all day yesterday on account of being watch at night so I could not go where I intended going and I am orderly today so I can't go this evening but I must go one evening this week. We shant have anything to do so I shall have a good chance. I have done nothing either yesterday or today and I am obliged to be inside in case I should be wanted. Our Quarter Master told us today if we BEHAVED ourselves we should have some more holiday before they come back but he did not say when or for how long. I think that he is getting very generous lately, but I think he is doing it to obtain some end or another. There must be something in the wind, I think.

Dear Polly, did you get home quite safe on Sunday night. I hope you did. I have thought since that I might have went home again with you and have come down here by the first train in the morning. I should have been here quite soon enough if I had. I am hardly believing that I have been to see you, I was with you so short a time. But short visits keep up memory. I suppose that you are not so well off as we are for time. I believe this is the easiest time that I ever had. I wish your place was like it sometimes, then there would be something to encourage you but perhaps Mrs Walker would think you would be getting into LAZY habits, think she wouldn't but she wont give you a chance.

Is Lizzy gone for her holiday. If she went on Monday her holiday is half gone. When she was telling fortunes out of the cup she ought to have told another day or two on to her holiday. I did not think of it or I would just for fun. You must do it when you have your holidays, then perhaps you will have a day or two longer. I think I must do it too or get Lizzy to do it for me.

Today we had six of our servants sent away for being DRUNK or tight which ever you like to call it, so they have not done themselves much good with their Easter holidays. I was not among that gang. I was out of luck then you see but I think it was bad luck for them. There was one or two of the funeral party there though. My Uncle is gone off into Yorkshire so I am by myself for a bit. He is gone for a week, but I expect my brother will be here in a day or two. Then I shall be alright again. I dare say that he will have some news to tell me. If he do I shall be able to let you into the light of some of them when I write next time.

Now dear Polly, I think that I have told you all I know at present but I thought that I would just scribble a few lines to let you know that I am got here alright again, hoping you did the same and hoping that the Lizzy left at home and the little one are quite well.

With best love,
    I am yours affectionately,
                ALF

Write soon. I am just going to write to Ted Vale.

Royal Military College
Farnboro' Station
April 28th 1876

I think of writing to Lou on Sunday if I have time.

My dear Polly,

    I have been rather a long time writing this time but I had my brother here from last Saturday until Wednesday so we went all about the place and did not have much time for anything else. He was looking very well and was very glad to see me. He asked how you were getting on and I told him as well as ever you could. All our old acquaintances wished to be remembered to you. And Ted Vale sent rather a funny account of Sally Bradley. He says that she left or rather ran away with the Butler at Corbett's about a month ago sometime about the end of March but he has not heard anything more of her so that accounts for her not answering your letter, she was too much wrapped up in the affairs of the Butler friend. He says that he can't tell how true the tale is but he knows that Sarah went on the evening and on the following morning the Butler was missed and has not heard anything more of them since. So I think if Sal gets up to those games she wont be much good for herself. If I could find out her address I would write to her but perhaps she would be above answering it for she has not answered two that I have wrote before.

    Dear Polly, I went down to see them grand relations of mine on Monday and stayed there about 4 hours. She showed us (I and my brother) all over the garden and all about the place and had Tea with them and had a good long talk with them.

    We stayed there until $\frac{1}{2}$ past 9 o'clock at night and when we were coming away Mrs Kelsey, one of the ladies, asked us to come down again on Wednesday before my brother went home so we went and had dinner with them and they did just feed us up on wine and stuff until I was glad to get away. I did not refuse anything or perhaps they would not have offered me anything again. I know how to work them sort of folks. I can tell you that both of us got into their books. I have got to go any time that I have got an hour to spare but that wont be until the summer comes for our gentlemen are come back. They came in on Wednesday the 26th. They would have stopped until 1st May, only at the end of May the gentlemen go to London to play a cricket match with Woolwich and the match generally lasts two or three days so our old Governor makes them come back 3 days sooner to make out for it.

I dont know whether any of us will be able to get leave when the cricket match comes off. If I can I'll come and see you but I am not sure that we shall be able to get it. My brother had his likeness taken while he was here but he has not got them yet. The man is going to send them to me and I am to keep one and send the rest on to him, so when I get it I will send it to you so that you can see what sort of chap he is. I know that he has got a girl for she wrote to him while he was here from Wolverhampton. Have you had a photo taken yet. I hope you have. You know you must not forget Old Charger when you get them.

Have you heard that Joe Gwynne has gone to Crewe to work. My brother and the rest of the chaps saw him the Saturday before Easter. He told them that he would write to me and let me know all the particulars about his place.

Now I don't think that I have any more news for you this time. Has Lizzy come back from her holiday yet. Please remember me to her and the rest. Have you heard from home lately. How they all are at home. Please give my love to them when you write and tell them that I am looking forward to the time when I shall see them again if I have good luck.

Now I must say goodbye and with best love,
                    I remain yours ever affectionately
                                    ALF
Write soon.

I have forgot to tell you that Jane at Grafton asked after me the other Saturday. I told my brother to tell her to write. I don't know whether she will..

Hanbury Rectory
19th May 1876

My dear Polly,

I was beginning to meditate sending you a small piece of the flower commonly called "Forget-me-not" when your letter arrived the other morning. I hope you have been well all this long time. How jolly it will be when you come home wont it. We shall be very glad to get you back amongst us. It seems a long time since we met. Does it not. I saw your Mother last night. She asked me to tell you that she has been very unwell lately with a bad gathered face, but she is now much better. The gathering broke some days ago. Your aunt Vaughan is also pretty well. They both send their love.

Have you heard what a bad accident poor little Bessie Cottrill had a short time since. She fell out of a wagon and broke her leg. I suppose you know the Cottrill's have left Hanbury some time back. Poor Mr Baylis at the Howning's died last Tuesday. He had been ill about 3 weeks. The funeral is fixed for tomorrow. Hanbury is looking so pretty in its bright young green but they have cut down a great many trees lately, so it is hardly so green as usual. If it is, if you would like some flowers I will send you a few some day if you will let me know. I heard from M. Ainge yesterday. She is very well. Her address is: Wigmore Hall, Kingsland, Herefordshire, if you want to write to her.

I remain dear Polly,
Your affectionate friend
MARY DOUGLAS

Royal Military College
Farnboro Station
July 2nd 1876

Let me know if you can what month you go home. You need not be afraid to TRUST ME. Alf.

Dear Polly,

I was very pleased to have a few lines from you for I had begun to think that you were above writing to, but I was glad to see that you was not. I am very sorry to hear that your work is so hard for I thought you had got an easy time of it. Now I suppose the nurse has been gone some time. If you don't mind yourself a little you will be knocked up. If you would take my advice you would study the 11th Commandment ("Man mind thyself") I would not work myself to death for anybody again. I have done it before now but never again. I never heard of you cutting your hand before. How did you do it and how long ago. I hope that you have got it well again before now. For one hand is nor much to do a lot of work with. You wants two.

I am afraid that it is worry more than the heat that makes you get thin but don't worry about anything. Take things cool and the work that can't be done, leave undone and then if the people don't like it give them it straight. Tip, don't stand any of their nonsense or else you will soon make an old woman of yourself. I used to try to please everybody but I soon found that I did not please anybody so now I am on another system. I pleases myself and I can find that is the best way and gets just as well thought of so if I was you I would do the same.

You asked me what I meant by changing the course of my life. What I have just told you is part of the way in which I have changed. But another way is when I and you were "SWEETHEARTS" I was trying to make some end for us in the future. Everything that I did, I put something by for the future never thinking of the present. I may say, starting a home for a married man but now all that is gone out. A thing of the past. I never think of the future now. I never ask myself now - what will be the best thing to gain an honest livelihood in time to come. I simply keep jogging along quiet and contented. But as for Religion. I hold with you there but I am the same that I always was in that way.

I am sorry that your Mother don't write to you for a letter from Home would help to cheer you up a bit. I know one from Home do me. Perhaps your Mother is put out over I and you parting, but never mind, it will soon blow over and be as right as ninepence in time.

Master Bertie Bourne came here to see me last Wednesday. He said that he was coming by on his way to Aldershot so he thought that he would call and see me. He had not come straight from home. He has been out with the Militia for about a month and is staying at Aldershot for examination. He did not tell me any news, only that the Captain and Mrs B were quite well and all the rest of them too. I think it was very kind of him to come and see me. It is not many that would do it. I have heard that Sarah Bradley did not go far with her butler lover for she is at her own home in Shropshire. Now perhaps she thinks that she has picked up a crooked stick which I think is most likely. If I knew her address I would give her a bit of advice and see if I could not make her see her folly.

I had a letter from Emily Eaton the other day. She is quite well and still in Birmingham but not in the same place. She has been at this, where she is, about 6 weeks. Now I think that I have told you all I can. Bromsgrove Fair was last Saturday week but I have not heard any news about it. Now I must say goodbye for it is nearly church time. Hoping that you will pardon the way in which I have wrote this and that I shall hear from you again before long.

With best love,
    I remain your faithful Friend
            ALF HAYES (CHARGER)

Note:
(Polly wrote to Alf on May 14th 1876, four weeks after he visited her in Wimbledon to say that she thought it proper to forget him. See Alf's letter of May 14th 1877)

Emily Eaton

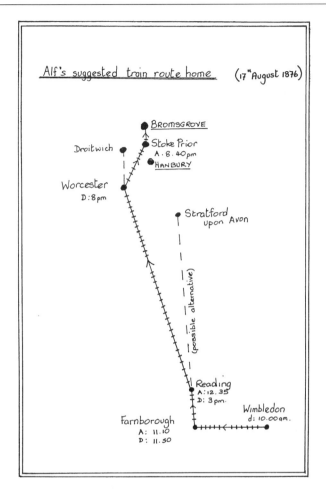

Alf's suggested train route home (17ᵗʰ August 1876)

BROMSGROVE
Stoke Prior
A. 8. 40 pm
Droitwich
HANBURY
Worcester
D : 8 pm
Stratford
upon Avon
(possible alternative)
Reading
A: 12. 35
D: 3 pm.
Wimbledon
d: 10.00 am.
Farnborough
A: 11.10
D: 11.50

Royal Military College
August 17th 1876

Dear Polly,

I did not expect to see a letter from you so soon. I intended to have written to you this week about going home. I think that I shall be able to go with you on Wednesday if all is well. I will drop you another line by Tuesday night. But where shall I meet you? Will you come as far as Farnboro' and I will meet you there and then go on to Reading, but it will be rather late when we get to Stoke. It will be 8.40 at night; and to get there by that time you will have to start from Wimbledon by 10 o'clock and that train gets to Farnboro' about 11.10 and the train starts from Farnboro' for Reading at 11.50 and gets to Reading at 12.35.

Now if you think that you can come the way that I have said and if the time will suit you please let me know. You must only take a ticket from Wimbledon to Farnboro' at first because it is on another line to Reading. We shall have to stay a very long time either at Reading or Oxford. There is a train starts from Reading about

1 o'clock but it doesn't go to Worcester but branches off for Stratford; then the next train starts about 3 o'clock and gets to Worcester at 6 o'clock, then we can either go to Droitwich or wait at Worcester until 8 o'clock then go straight on. This is the way that I went home last summer.

I think that I have explained the route as well as I can; and if you think that you can come by it I shall be most happy to travel with you. If there is anything that you can't understand in it, let me know and I will right it if I can.

Now hoping to see you soon, I am yours sincerely

ALF HAYES

Please excuse bad writing for I have got a bad hand.

P.S. It will be a great deal out of the way for me to come to London and start from there, but it will be quite straight for you to come Farnboro' and Reading way.

Royal Military College
Farnboro Station
(Mon) Sept. 25th 1876

My dear Polly,

I received your letter by the first post this morning. I was very glad to see one. I expected it. I thought you would have got to Weston-SuperMare earlier in the week. That was the reason that I wrote to your Mother, for I asked her to send it on to you, but I suppose that you got it at home without any sending. If I were you I would make the best of my time while you are there. What I mean is, enjoy yourself and pass the time as pleasantly as you can. I expect that you have plenty of company and at the seaside there is always something fresh to see. I only wish that I could come and pass some of the time away with you. I have never seen the sea yet but I have both read and heard what it is like. I may have a chance of seeing it some day, but any how I hope that you will enjoy yourself while you are there and come back home a great deal better for your holiday. I am glad to hear that Mr Walker behaved so well to you. Though it was more than you expected it was no more than he ought to have done but it shows that he is a gentleman.

We are rather busy down here just now for we are going to have a ball down here on Wednesday night, the 27th, and some athletic sports next week so we shall have something to cheer us up a bit for there is not much while the gents are here except plenty of work. And I have a little business to attend to nearly every night, for my chum - the one that had his likeness taken with me - has picked up with a girl just lately and I have to put him right to go and see her but he is rather flat.

For three or four nights she has disappointed him and he says he wont go any more but I persuades him to go and off he goes and sometimes he blows me up for telling him to go. There is something to do with him I can tell you. Dear Polly, tell me what sort of place Weston-Super-Mare is and how you like it when you write. I believe it is a nice place. One or two of our gentlemen come from there. Is anybody from Hanbury with you or are you by yourself. Let me know all the particulars when you write.

Did you see in the Bromsgrove paper last Saturday week how my brother Herbert got a telling for doing another man a good turn. It was a man who was put into the County Court and Herb told him what to do to get out of it. So instead of the man keeping it to himself, he told the judge. So Herb had to go and the judge told him to mind his own business and not give advice in future. I will put the bit of paper in this letter for you to see.

I have not heard from any of the chaps from Stoke since I have been back but I expect a letter from Ted Vale in a day or two. I suppose that you know that all the Grafton people are away - servants and all - and Mrs Baker is staying in the house. It seems to me just such another turn out as it was when Mrs Bourne got the better of the fever that she had about 6 years ago. They all went away then. Now dear Polly I must say goodbye for the present. I will write again very soon. So with fondest love I hope this will find you much better and looking likely for improving. So goodbye and God Bless you

      I am yours most affectionately
           ALF

Write soon.
Please excuse slovenliness

BROMSGROVE COUNTY COURT
before R.Harington Esq

The Statute of Limitations

John Wells, Bromsgrove butcher sued Oliver Baden, nailer for £10 3s 9d, balance of an account due for meat sold and delivered. Mr Baden, Birmingham appeared for the plaintiff and Mr Buller (Buller and Bickley) Birmingham, for the defendant. At the commencement of the case it was stated that the defendant pleaded the Statute of Limitations, but this plea had not been entered up and His Honour at first refused to allow it. Mr Buller accordingly said he must ask for an adjournment inasmuch as his client had been given to understand by a junior clerk at the County Court office that it would be sufficient for him to bring his books and make the plea on the hearing of the case. The defendant was sworn and he said that he went to the County Court office for the purpose of giving notice that he should dispute the debt. In a conversation with one of the junior clerks, the latter told him if the debt had not been contracted or acknowledged within six years it did not matter about a "special paper". It would be sufficient for him to bring his books and state his plea on the day of the hearing. His Honour said that being so he should require the attendence of the clerk. Accordingly Herbert Hayes attended and said he remembered the defendant attending at the office and stating that he should defend the action. He told the debt was six years old and that Mr Wells had entered it only the day before to save the statute. He told the defendant to come to the court and defend the case if he didn't owe the money and that he could not plead the Statute of Limitations. His Honour: I think you had better confine yourself to attending to your own business and not to giving advice. That being the case he should allow the plea. The verdict was for the defendant on the score of statutable limitation.

From: Bromsgrove, Droitwich and Redditch Messenger 16th Sep. 1876

Hanbury Rectory
27th Sept. 1876

My dear Polly,

I received your letter alright yesterday morning and was very glad to hear of your safe arrival. I hope you will be really the better for your stay at Weston. Do be careful and not catch cold or do too much or tire yourself. I know you find it difficult to keep quiet but I hope you will try. Your mother is very anxious about you and it would be a great comfort to her to think you were taking care of yourself - I saw her yesterday and she sent her love.

I am sorry to say Mrs Pugh's little boy met with a bad accident. He was climbing up a large bough of an elm tree, which fell off some time ago but was still leaning against the tree and hanging by the bark, when it fell on him and crushed him. His thigh is broken and he is otherwise hurt but how much I cannot say just at present. Joseph Fisher has also met with a bad accident. He was draining at some distance from here, and the earth fell in and buried him up to the neck. His collar bone is broken and he is hurt besides. I believe he was taken at once to the Infirmary (Worcester). I hope they will both get over their injuries but I am afraid they are both very delicate.

How do you like Weston? I hope you mean to let me know how you get on and how you are. I hope the Weston Dr's give a better account of you than they did at Droitwich. Does Lady Georgina ever go to see you? We had had a great deal of wet and some very heavy tempest since you went. I hope you are having nice weather and enjoying yourself.

Is there good bathing at Weston? I am sorry you are not able to enjoy it but I should think the water would be very cold now. I don't think I have much more to tell you just now so I will conclude with much love and hoping soon to hear a better report of you. Father desires to be kindly remembered to you and hopes you will be better before long and come home much the better for your seaside visit.

I remain ever your affectionate friend
MARY DOUGLAS

HANBURY

Distressing Accident

An accident of a very distressing nature happened here on Monday to a little lad named Pugh, about seven years of age, the son of labouring parents. In a meadow continuous to the National Schools, and near to a public footpath, stands a large elm tree, one of the lower and spreading branches of which had been used by the school children to swing on. This branch had of late years been rotten and unsafe for the purpose, but the youngsters, not withstanding they had been cautioned not to do so, had persisted in using it for the purpose of their pastime. The lad in question was so engaged on Monday, when the branch suddenly parted from the tree and fell, crushing him in a shocking manner across the loins and lower part of the body. Assistance was at hand as soon as possible and the poor child was released from his perilous position and removed to the General Infirmary at Worcester, where according to our latest advices he lies in an exceedingly critical state.

From: Bromsgrove, Droitwich and Redditch Messenger. 27th September 1876

Hanbury
Oct.7th 1876

My dear Polly,

Thanks for your letter which came the other day. I hope as you may bathe that Weston is having the desired effect of making you stronger. How are you feeling. Do you think you are really better? I saw your Mother the other day and showed her your letter which she was very glad to see. I was to tell you I had seen her and that she was pretty well.

Hanbury presented a very gay appearance last Friday when the Michaelmas Mop was held. I was there about the middle of the day. 200 or 300 people were gathered round the Arms and several shows etc. were in Barley's field. Little Pugh is getting on well. We have had nice warm weather here this week. I hope you have had it as warm but not as wet, for it has not been fine here for 24 hours together. I am glad to say Fanny Garratt is much better.

I suppose you heard your cousin Richard Barley has been home. I did not see him as I should have liked to have done as, although I was there, he was not at home. You come home next Friday do you not?

As I do not think I have anything else to tell you, I will conclude
    with love from your affectionate friend
                   MARY DOUGLAS

P.S. I saw Mary Ainge yesterday, do you know she is to be married before long?

                  Royal Military College
                     Farnboro Station
                   October 8th 1876

(Note: With printed crest. Alf comments "Another nice monogram.")

My dear Polly,

So that you shan't be disappointed of a letter from me on Tuesday morning I am writing now. I was very glad to hear that you are getting better and I hope that you will continue to do so. You will get stronger after a bit. You pretty near wore your strength out while you were at Wimbledon. I am rather glad that you are away from there. If you had went back you would have knocked yourself up completely and it would have taken you a long time to have regained your health and strength again. But now I hope please God that you will soon be alright again.

When do you go away from Weston. It must be getting near three weeks since you went. Let me know when you go. Lady G— Vernon is a proper sort of a lady. I wish that I could drop across one like her but I haven't such luck. Dear Polly, our Ball came off on Tuesday night last and a very good one it was. There was about 200 Ladies and Gentlemen there besides our own so I think it was a very good turn out. It was on until 5 o'clock in the morning. There was no bed for us poor chaps all that night. You know it is not much sport for us. We shall have another to-do on Friday and Saturday for our Athletic Sports come off on them days and that will be sport for the Gents but extra work for us. It always is, but we must not grumble. It won't make it any the better.

That is a very nice letter of Miss Walker's - a nice sisterly one. I see she speaks about Master Bourne's death so you see that they soon get hold of it. Well, he was a nice young gentleman. One that I liked very much and I was truly sorry when I heard of his death. I believe that the Captain is a good deal cut up over it. My Mother says that he looks ten years older. They are all come back to Grafton again. There will be a great alteration I know in the Captain. A great difference to what there used to be. I shall never forget the day the Captain first allowed Master Bertie to use a gun. Me and the Captain were stood under one of the trees in the Orchard talking when Master

Bourne let the gun off and I suppose he was afraid of it for he discharged it straight at us and some of the shots struck the Captain. My word he did walk into him. He ordered him into his room and told him that he should not have a gun any more, but the threat did not last long. He was out again the next day, but to see the face that Master Bertie pulled. That is what I remember so well.

I am glad to say that my little chum has picked up with another sweet heart. He is a rum un after the girls. Now today is his first start with the fresh one. I don't know how he will get on with her. He was rather glad that the other broke it off for it was too far for him to go to see her. When you say it was most as bad a case as when I lost MY GIRL, it was not for he had been courting about 2 months and I had been courting about 2 years. You see there is a great deal of difference, don't you think so. And another thing, when he lost his girl his love for her was burnt out but mine was not. It did not make a bit of difference to me in that way. I thought just as much of you then and loved you as dearly as when I knew you first so Dear Polly don't contrast the two again for I can't bear to think of the time.

I think it ought to be forgot or it may cause some unhappiness in some future time. And as for not saying much the night we parted, I could not. My heart was too full and time was very short. I was thinking what would happen before we met again. You know when you or anyone else is parting from one they love, to go a long way off, an almost silent voice whispers "I wonder when and where we shall meet again." That is just how it was with me that night. Now dear Polly, I must conclude for it is near post time and with fondest love I must say goodbye and God Bless you

From yours most affectionately

ALF (CHARGER)

Write soon.

I have put Miss Walker's letter in with this. Please remember me to your Mother and Annie when you write.

You must go and see my mother again if you can when you get home again.

BROMSGROVE
THE DEATH OF MR.R.V.BOURNE

It is with unfeigned sorrow that we have to record the death of Mr Robert Valentine Bourne, eldest son of Major and Mrs Bourne, of Grafton Manor. The deceased, who was generally beloved for his very amiable disposition, was in the nineteenth year of his age and had just been gazetted as a sub-lieutenant in the Worcester Militia. He was with his regiment at the camp on Salisbury Plain, and it was there, in all probability, that he contracted the illness which has proved fatal to him. At any rate immediately on his return home he was seized with typhoid fever. The case was under the care of Mr.H.Prosser, and Dr. Balthazar Foster, of Birmingham, was in almost constant consultative attendance but it was one admitting of scarcely any hope from the first, and the deceased succumbed to the malady on Sunday morning last. His death will be mourned by a wide circle of friends who were unremitting in their inquiries during the whole time of the deceased's illness which extended over a period of nearly three weeks and we need scarcely add that a large amount of sympathy is felt throughout the neighbourhood with the deceased's parents. The funeral which was of a private character, took place at the Cemetery, Bromsgrove, at noon on Wednesday. The service was performed by the Vicar (the Rev. Canon Murray) and by the Rev.A.St.John Mildmay, Rector of Alvechurch. The mourners were Mr Bourne and his son Mr Gilbert Bourne, the Revs G.H.Bourne and F.Hopkinson, uncles of the deceased; Lieut-Colonel Arbuthnot and Mr F.P.Murray. The funeral cortege was followed by the Hon. and Rev.H.Douglas and others. Many beautiful wreaths and crosses of flowers were placed upon the coffin in the grave by the hands of loving friends.

Bromsgrove, Droitwich & Redditch Weekly Messenger. Saturday, Sept. 9th 1876

"My little chum"

Royal Military College
Farnboro Station
Oct. 16th 1876

My dear Polly,

I was obliged to disappoint you of your letter on Tuesday (You will get this on Wednesday) for last week was our Athletic Sports. They were on most of the week and did not finish up until late on Saturday night so of course we, as usual, had all the things to clear away. It did not matter, Sunday or not, we had to do it. That is the worst of a Military place, when a thing wants doing it is done let it be what day or time it may, so we were at work all Sunday morning. Then we had all our usual work to do afterwards so it was church time at night when we got done then Mess after that so you can guess I did not have much time to spare today for we have got an extra lunch on today so you must excuse mistakes. We are going to have some Theatricles here next week and then I suppose we shall have a little more work, but I suppose we shall get it over in time. It will all bring Christmas nearer and then I say "Jack up!"

Dear Polly I was very sorry to hear that you were got worse. You must take care of yourself a little longer or else it may bring on some lasting disease which I hope and trust it won't. I hope by this time that you are got pretty near yourself again. Let me know when you leave Weston. My Mother asked when you were going to see her again the last time she wrote. I have not wrote to her or any of them at home for three weeks now. I have not had time but I must try and write sometime this week.

Dear Polly you asked when I should see you again. I am afraid it will be some time for I don't think that I shall go home again before I am got settled in some place for good if all my people at home keep well, but if anything should happen to either of them I should go directly. Now I think that I must say goodbye for this lunch is going on the table. I hope I shall be able to write again at the end of the week. I am writing this so that you should not be disappointed after Wednesday. Now goodbye Dear Polly, with fondest love I say goodbye hoping it will still find you improving.

> I am yours ever affectionately
> ALF

Write and let me know when you go away.

> Hanbury
> 18th Oct. 1876

My dear Polly,

Thank you for your letter which came to hand yesterday morning. I am very sorry you are so little better. I had hoped to have heard you were much better. Are you coming back on Friday? How do you mean to get from the Station home?

You must mind and not take cold on the journey. William Phillips died this morning. He has been much worse for some time past. I daresay you have heard Mrs Creswell has got a baby. Whether it is a boy or a girl I am not at liberty to state as I don't know. I don't think there is much more to be said at present, so I will conclude with love from

> Your affectionate friend
> MARY DOUGLAS

On the back in a different and very shaky hand is:-
Leave Bristol (?) past 7
Leave Bristol half past one
Leave Weston

Royal Military College
Farnboro' Station
(Sat) October 28th 1876

My dear Polly,

I am rather a long time in answering your letter this time but you must forgive me as we are in a very unsettled state just at present. It is believed that there is to be a great alteration in this college at Christmas. The Quarter Master and all the people that have had the management of the College for the last 20 years have got to leave at Christmas. So they have got to settle all back accounts and leave every thing straight for others to take over. That is the reason that we are in such a muddle and I don't think that we shall be ever straight again for we have all got to turn out at Christmas and I am sure that things wont be all straight by then so Dear Polly you must not be disappointed if I don't just answer your letters just at the time. I believe that there is only going to be 25 servants kept here after Christmas instead of 60. Of course the oldest servants will stand the best chance of stopping but I would not stay if I had the chance.

I have made up my mind to get into the Detective Police Force and I will get in either by hook or by crook. I will try my best and I am sure that I have never failed in anything that I have given my mind to. If I don't get into the Detectives direct I will go into the Metropolitan and rise, but I think that I shall manage it without. I have indeed made up my mind to go to London after I leave here. I have got my eye on three more jobs but they won't come in until I have failed in the Detective Force. My uncle and all will be leaving at the same time as we others so I shan't have anything to keep me here.

I should very much like to see you then I could explain things to you better than I can on this paper, but I am afraid Dear Polly that it will be some time before I see you again without you come up London way to live. I should very much like for you to be living somewhere near me. It would be much better for both of us but if your mother don't want you to go far away don't you. For I would not like you to upset her for she is indeed a good mother to you. And we shall be sure to meet again sometime perhaps to part no more until death. Dear Polly, I am glad to hear that you are got back home again but I am sorry to hear that you are still so middling. I hope that by the time this reaches you, you will feel better. I wish you were as strong as me. Nothing don't seem to hurt me.

You must go and see my mother as soon as you can. She is very anxious to see you again. I know she and all the rest will make you welcome if it is only for my sake. I believe that they are very fond of me especially the little ones. You can go any time that you like (except washing days which won't be very comfortable). My mother is always asking when you are coming to see her. I dare say she will have a lot to tell you about Alf when you do go. We are going to have another Ball here on the 7th so I suppose that we shall have a little more extra to do then. And then there is the fair that is held here on the 8th/9th. The one that our gents always gets into a row at. Then I don't think that there is anything else stirring just about here so I will say goodbye for the present. I will try and write so that you can get the letter on Wednesday the 1st. Now please give my best love to Mother, Annie and all enquiring friends especially Ted Vale if you see him.

With fondest love I remain yours for ever.

ALF

Write soon. You will get this on Sunday.

Royal Military College
Farnboro Station
(Sat) Nov. 18th 1876

My Dear Polly,

I was very glad to hear that you had come to Richmond to live and it rather surprised me; but I am very glad that you are come for we are nearer together than when you were at Wimbledon. I know Mrs Caustin well and likewise old Maslin that used to be with her. I suppose she isn't with her now. Do you know where she is?. I knew Mr Caustin very well; but he as been dead some few years now. I have been out shooting with him and Captain Bourne many times. He was a very nice man and I believe Mrs Caustin is a very nice lady. Old Long's son (the Sailor) used to be Page Boy there about 6 years ago. So I have known something about them for a long time, and I would advise you Dear Polly, to stay with her if you think that you can manage to do what she wants you to do. I think it is a good deal better than Mrs Walker's and Richmond is a nice place and I think it will suit you.

Dear Polly you never told me how you managed to get to Mrs Caustin's. Did Mrs Bourne recommend you? For I thought that you were going somewhere in London but I think you have got a better place. I shall stick up about this part of the country if you think that you can manage to stop there. I was not aware until My Mother wrote that you did not like me going into the Police Force. She told me that she thought that you did not like it so I won't go into it. I would sooner stay here than do anything that I thought you would not like. One of the gentlemen that I am looking after now is trying to get me a Gamekeeper's place. He is not quite sure whether he will get it or not yet but he says that he will let me know by 1st of December.

If he don't succeed in getting that he is going to try for something else. I don't think that I shall be obliged to leave here yet. I have been picked out to stop on if I like and I will do it sooner than go into the Police if you don't like it, but I hope to get the gamekeeper's place. I shall never be satisfied until I am amongst it again. My Mother wants me to go into Worcestershire again but I don't see it. I don't always want to be messing about home. Dear Polly when your letter came this morning my

89

chum Jimmy was going to open it, for his girl (the one that I told you about last week) is gone to live there and he thought that she had been writing to me instead of him but he noticed the writing and saw it was yours so he brought it up to me. I believe that he has got Richmond on the Brain as he is always talking about it.

Dear Polly I don't know hardly what to tell you about staying at Richmond as you have not been there hardly long enough to know what the place is but if you think that you can do the work without doing yourself any harm, stay by all means and perhaps as the Spring comes on you will get stronger for this time of year is very trying to strong people let alone weak ones. I don't suppose that you have got any complaint on you such as DECLINE or CONSUMPTION to prevent you from gaining your strength. I sincerely hope not. Do not put yourself about. Take things as they come and as coolly as possible and when I come to see you, if she don't allow such as me to come to her house, I can see you somewhere else just as well. I don't care about going inside the house, any place will do for me. Do you remember the summer house in front of Campbell's house? Many a happy moment have I spent there with you. Now dear Polly I will say goodbye for the present and I have told you all the news I know this time. I will write again most likely about Friday.

Now goodbye and God Bless you, with fondest love

I remain yours for ever

ALF

Royal Military College
Farnboro Station
December 3rd 1876

My dear Polly

I received your letter on Friday night. I was very glad to get it for I had been look-ing for it all the week. Now I must ask you a few questions. When did you get to Windsor? Did you get my last letter before you left Richmond? Have you been out much yet and what sort of a place do you think Windsor is? Please tell me what sort of a place the hospital is and how the rules are, for when I come I shall want to stay with you more than 2 hours. That ain't half long enough. It isn't hardly worth com-ing for. But I shall come. They ort to allow more than two hours. You must try and get out for a bit if you can without getting yourself into a bother. I shall most likely come before Christmas but I am not quite sure yet. I am going to leave the College on 31st December if not before. I shall see when the gentlemen are gone. They go on 15th or 16th of this month.

I don't think that I am going far away from this place. The Gamekeeper's place that I told you about, I can't get for the man is not going to leave just at present, but the gentleman is looking for a place for me. I have been persuaded to take a Warder's place at Broadmoor Lunatic Asylum and Reading jail. They are in want of Warders at both places but Broadmoor is the best. It is rather rough the first six months but after that you are a gentleman. Nothing to do only walk about and about £60 a year and everything found, that is after you have been there a short time. It is £45 to start with and everything found so I don't think as that is very dusty. I am going to try at Broadmoor most likely tomorrow and then I shall see more about it.

I will tell you all the particulars when I see you. I think I might do a good deal worse. All that I want is to keep myself steady and then I am bound to get on. I have asked Captain Bourne to recommend me and I know he will give me a good character, and I shall get 2 years good character from here so I think I ought to be able to get on.

Dear Polly when I come to see you I shall take the train from Wokingham to Windsor and walk from Windsor station. My chum wont come with me then, he was only humbuging when he said that he would come but he wants to see you very bad. If I get to Broadmoor he must come and see you there. He is rather downhearted about me leaving. He says he wont stay here if I go right away. I don't know what makes him think so much of me. You would think he was my brother. I took my prayer book to chapel last Sunday and sung fine. We have not got a choir but sing ourselves and we makes a fine noise I can tell you. My brother Fred has joined the Bromsgrove church choir so I suppose that he is getting on quite grand. They all expects me home at Christmas but I think they will be disappointed for I shan't go home without I am obliged.

The chaps here are talking about having another Ball but I don't think that they will get it, at least not till after Christmas then most of us young chaps will be gone so that it wont be a very lively one. We are going to have another grand Ball here amongst the gents on the 6th. It will be the last one here for years I expect for the Cadets that are coming in next Spring are not allowed to have Balls or any parties of any sort. This place wont be up to much when they are here. It will be like a big school.

Now dear Polly I think that I must say goodbye for I have told you all the news that is worth knowing, but I must not forget to tell you that it is my little sister's birthday tomorrow - the 4th, but I am sure I can't tell you how old she is. Now hoping that this will find you still improving - with fondest love. Goodbye.

I am yours ever affectionately

ALF

Write soon

ENVELOPE
Addressed to:
Miss M. Weaver, St Andrew's Hospital. Clewer, Nr. Windsor. p.p.

Postmarked:
Farnboro' Station DEC 3 76
Windsor

St. Andrew's
Convalescent Hospital
Clewer

Printed: HANBURY RECTORY
BROMSGROVE
5th Decr. 1876

My dear Polly,

    I was indeed sorry to hear the bad news in your letter this morning. It must have been a terrible blow to you and must, I feel sure, be a terrible consciousness to live under. The thought of death hanging over one is awful to all, but particularly I think to the young. Truly, dear Polly, the Advent call has come to you - "Prepare to meet thy God. Since we know not the day neither the hour when the Son of Man cometh." I don't well know how to tell you how deeply I feel with and for you, dear Polly. Words look very cold and heartless on paper and I'm not good at expressing my thoughts but I think you know me well enough to know that I am not so really and don't measure my heart by my words. But you must try not to be more down hearted than you can help.

    I wish I could do anything for you. You will be much in my thoughts and prayers. But I hope you may still have a long and happy life. What Doctor was it you saw? Did he not give you any hope of recovery? Your life ought to be a very holy one that you may be ready whenever the Master may in His own good time call you. Think of His wonderous Love, and let us pray that in all things we may be enabled to use His prayer - "not my will but Thine be done." And let us try to remember that it is our Loving Father who orders all our life for us, be it health or sickness, joy or sorrow and that He knows what is best for each of us. I am just going to see your Mother as I promised to do when I heard from you. I shall not tell her all you have told me though,

92

but only prepare her mind for it then you can tell her all when you write - but however she is told it will be a sad grief to her I fear.

I am afraid this letter wont do much towards cheering you up. There is not much news to tell you, in fact the only bit I can think of is that Miss Greenhill is going to be married in about 3 weeks. I hope you will write some times when you can and let me know how you are. You know I shall be always pleased to write to you, or do anything I can for you. That God may bless, help and comfort you, dear Polly, is the earnest prayer of

> your ever affectionate friend
> MARY DOUGLAS

> Royal Military College
> Farnboro Station
> Dec. 6th 1876

My dear Polly,

You will say "Well done Alf" this time in being such a good boy to write again so soon, but I received your letter this evening and I have not got much work to do. I thought I could not do a better thing than write you a few lines. This is our Ball night and most all the chaps are gone, my chum amongst the rest so I have got it all to myself. I am very glad indeed to hear that Lizzie came to see you. She is a brick and I shan't forget her for it. I will go and see them if I go anywhere. I think that Lizzie was a very thoughtful girl to come and see you. I know it did you as much good as a pail full of doctor's stuff would do you. How did she look? Was she quite well? Tell. And how did she say all the rest of the folks up there were? Please remember me to them when you write and tell them that I will try to go and see them about Christmas time if I can't before.

Dear Polly, I will come as soon as I can after our Gents are gone away but I think that I will come on a week day, as Sunday is rather a bad day to travel and I shall want to be at the Hospital before the clock strikes two for I don't want to waste a second if I am only to be allowed 2 hours - which is not hardly long enough for a fellow like me that as to come a short distance, but I suppose I shall have to put up with it just for once and I don't suppose they will be hard on me to turn me out just as the clock strikes four. Anyhow we shall see about that when I get there.

Dear Polly, I expect that I shall go to Broadmoor, but not until after Christmas. You know I shan't go there if I can get a Gamekeeper's place before then for I would sooner be a Gamekeeper than a Warder because the Gamekeeping would suit me best. My uncle wants me to go to Broadmoor because it is near here and he don't want me to go away from this part of the country as long as he is here for I am his only relative about here that he cares anything about. He as told me often that if it has not been for me England would not have held him after my Grandfather died, so I think that I shall try and stay about here.

Dear Polly, I am sorry to hear that the doctor says that your HEART is affected, but I think that he might be wrong for I don't think that your heart being affected would make you keep so weak. I think that you have worn your self out with worrying yourself and trying to do work that was too hard for you and I hope, please God, as the Spring comes round you will be quite your self again. I only wish that I was a little more settled. I would not want you to go to service again but I would take you, and your service should be with me - which time I hope wont be long. I will try my best to get settled and begin to make some head for the future in which I hope God is helping me to succeed.

Now dear Polly I think that I have told you nearly all that I have to say. Mother, Herb and Fred send their best love to you and all sorts of good wishes. And Mother says that when I come to see you we must go to Windsor Castle for it was there that she and father spent their WEDDING DAY. Father is very middling again now. I expect that he will have a job to get through the winter.

Ted Vale wishes to be remembered to you and wants to know how you are getting on and lots of other people ask after you. Now dear Polly, goodbye for the present. Hope this will find you still improving. With fondest love

       I remain still yours most affectionately

                  ALF

Write soon.

I will let you know as soon as I can which day I can come.

I shall want to let them girls at Wimbledon know what day I can go to see them too.

          Printed: HANBURY RECTORY
                BROMSGROVE
                8th Dec. 1876

My dear child,

I am indeed sorry to hear that you are so unwell again. It seems you are not quite up to the exertion needed for service. But indeed I am not surprised for you know you were far from strong when you left home and tho' you have every care and consideration shown you, you can hardly expect but that you will knock up unless you gather more strength to begin with. I hear they think your heart is a little affected. This always makes people feel very ill sometimes under exertion, as if they could not carry on at all and they are often not nearly so ill as they feel and think they are. I hope this is your case. This affliction of the heart generally counts for weakness and the best things for it are rest or very light work, good nourishment, patience and peace of mind.

You must not be cast down or distress yourself. Remember at all times even when you feel worst and things seem very hard and trying, that you are in God's special keeping and that you may and should commit yourself without anxiety to his holy keeping. Look on God as your real friend and Father, and he will let you keep hope for ever yours. Commit everything unto the Lord, David says. God will provide for you my child. You must try and show your love for him by trusting in him and not fretting. Think what he would have you do and try to do. Be very regular in your prayers, prepare carefully and tell God all your troubles and ask for help to do what he would have you do. I shall remember you in prayer.

I am sure your mistress is kind to you and you had better ask her to advise you what to do. If you came home again we must try to help you to get stronger before going out again. May God bless you my dear child.

> I am yours sincerely in Christ Jesus
> HENRY DOUGLAS

> Royal Military College
> Farnboro Station
> Dec 17th 1876

My dear Polly

I have been rather longer this time in answering your welcome letter but you must please excuse me as this week has been a very busy one for us, for we have been cleaning up the place a bit and putting things to right. It is always the case just before the gentlemen go away for the Duke of Cambridge is expected here to see the gents. So of course it would not do to let him come and find the place in a dirty state, so that is what we have been up to this last week and then there was the gents traps to pack up. We were two days at that. But now it is all done and we are pretty near free, for the gentlemen went away on the 16th and now I suppose that we that are going to leave, can do so as soon as we like.

I don't just know when I shall go for I can't make up my mind whether to go home or not. You know I should like to spend Christmas at home then I should not like to be messing about at home after that, and it is not worth while going all that way just for a couple of days, so I don't hardly know what to do at present. And another thing, I stand a chance of getting a Game keeper's place near Oxford close to the place that I told you of before only I think a better one but I shan't know anything more about it until I hear from a gentleman again. He was one of my masters here and he is going to let me know whether I have got it or not as soon as he has seen the Head Keeper at this place. So you see I am rather unsettled at present.

Dear Polly, I think that I shall be able to come and see you on either Wednesday or Thursday. I have not asked leave yet but it will be one of them days but I will let you know which it will be. I want, if I can get leave, to see you on Wednesday and go to see the folks at Wimbledon on Thursday for I don't want to stay in the College any longer than I can help.

Have you seen the account in the paper about the Murder of two policemen near Hungerford by poachers. It is a very brutal affair. It appears that they were jumped out upon and one of them deliberately shot before another of them could do anything to help themselves and the other that was not shot run away, it is supposed, for help. He was pursued and caught about 200 yards from the place where the other one was shot. When they had caught him they battered his brains out. It is only 3 weeks ago that the same sort of thing was done in Somersetshire and they have not caught the men that done it yet. If things go on at this rate there will be a job to get men to be policemen. I am glad that I gave up the idea of being one now.

Now dear Polly, I think that I have told you all this time for I hope to see you before this day week and then I shall be able to tell you everything better than I can write it. Mother and all the rest send their love to you and hope that you are still on the mend. You can write and tell the folks at Wimbledon and I will try to go to see them on Thursday. Now goodbye. Hoping this will find you much better. With fondest love

I remain yours affectionately

ALF

Please to excuse the shortness of the letter. It is not so long as yours.

ENVELOPE
Addressed to:
Miss M Weaver, St Andrew's Hospital, Clewer, Nr Windsor.

Postmarked:

Farnboro Station	DE	18	76
Windsor	DE	18	76
York Town	DE	18	76

Royal Military College
Farnboro College
December 20th 1876

My dear Polly,

I know that you were disappointed in not seeing me today but I went to Reading yesterday after a place and did not get back, the reason I will explain to you when I see you. I expect that I shall go to see another place tomorrow but I am not sure yet - until the post comes in tonight so therefore I cannot come to see you tomorrow. I don't think that I shall be able to see you before the 26th for you can see by what I have told you how I am situated at present. You know I would not disappoint you without a reason; I never did. The place that I expect to go to see about tomorrow is at Colonel Loyd Lindsay's. A nice place the other side of Reading. I dare say if you have read the paper lately you saw about one of his keepers being shot by a poacher. Well, he is not expected to recover so he wants another man in his place and one of the gentlemen that I have been looking after here lately, is trying to get it for me, but I don't know whether I shall get it until he writes again. This Colonel Lindsay's place is not the one I told you about in my last letter, that one was close to Oxford and this one is in Berkshire and a much better place I think.

Dear Polly, have you read the account of the Berkshire Police murder near Hungerford. I will send a paper so that you can see it. Now dear Polly, I must say goodbye as I have got another letter to write to the gentleman that is taking so much trouble about me. I am extremely sorry that I disappointed you today but I hope to see you on the 26th if not before.

So with fondest love I am still yours affectionately
ALF

P.S. I shan't be able to go to Wimbledon this week I am afraid. If I can't go before I see you, I will write again. You may expect another letter from me at the end of the week.
Goodbye and God Bless you.

Royal Military College
Farnboro Station
Dec. 28th 1876

My dear Polly,

I now write as I promised you. I got home quite safe about half past seven that night. I went back by the G.W.Railway instead of the S.W. for I found by enquiring that I could go straight to Reading by the G.W.R. and arrive there in time to take the train to Blackwater which I did and got to my journey's end safe and sound "cups" and all. Dear Polly, it only seems like a dream - I coming to see you - for the time was so short, but never mind, it wont be always so. The next time we meet I dare say that we shall be able to have two days or more instead of two hours, at least let us hope so.

I went to Wimbledon yesterday and found them all well but not expecting to see me that day. I went and knocked at the door and a fresh girl came to answer it, so I asked for Lizzie, but I don't think the girl understood what I said for she left the door open and was going to tell Lizzie I suppose. It was just dinnertime and they were having theirs but before the girl could get a step from the door, Lizzie cought sight of me and bawls out "Why, it's our Alf" and she came running to see me and I spent my time very jolly with them talking about old games. I told them that I thought that you were better and they seemed very glad to hear it. They were very pleased with their cups and Little Lizzie used hers for dinner and again at Teatime and they each made a bargain to wash their own for fear of breaking them and after Tea, Lizzie wrapped hers up in paper and put it away. Both Lizzies told me they wished you were back again. The one that they have got there now is not such a jolly girl as you were when you were there.

I did not like the look of her either. I believe that she has got a very sly temper by what I saw of her. She did not say much. She was very quiet. She asked a few riddles at Teatime and I think that is about all that she did do. I dare say when Lizzie comes to see you she will tell you some of the riddles that I told them for they seemed to please her a good lot and she said that mine were the best. Taking it all together we spent a very jolly evening. There was only one thing wanting and that was YOU. We all wished you were there and we all hoped to meet together next Christmas if we were spared. I stayed there until about 8 o'clock and then took my departure amidst all sorts of good wishes and arrived home about half past ten.

I don't think that I have any more to tell you about them. If I have forgot anything I dare say Lizzie will tell you when she comes to see you next week. She is going to bring you some Mince Pies and stuff. There were afraid you would not be allowed to eat them but I told them to take them and you would manage the rest. Now dear Polly I must say goodbye as I have not got any more news to tell you. I am not sure that I am going home on Saturday. I will let you know if I do. So wishing you a happy New Year and many of them (for my sake), with fondest love

I remain yours ever affectionately

ALF

Goodbye and God Bless you. Please to excuse bad writing and mistakes for my pen is rather middling.

1877

Alf has returned to Bromsgrove and starts work as a gamekeeper at Grafton Manor again. A number of local events prove most newsworthy. Frail Polly struggles to cope with her new job in Windsor but worried friends advise her to come home.

Grafton Manor. Bromsgrove

Rock Hill
Bromsgrove
Jan 8th 1877

My dear Polly,

I received your letter on Saturday and very glad I was to see it. I had been looking out for one, for two or three days. I was very glad to hear of your going to your place on Tuesday but don't you get trying to do things that you are not able to do. Take things as quiet as ever you can and not worry yourself and you will see that you can get on ever so much better. I hope to be somewhere up nearer you before long but I don't exactly know when I am going for I have not had a letter yet but I expect one tomorrow morning. For you see letters that are wrote on Sunday never get here until Tuesday and this gentleman always writes business letters on Sundays, so I think I shall get one tomorrow morning. I will let you know as soon as I know.

Now for some news. I have been knocking about first at one place then another. I have had Ted Vale for my companion most of the time but we have not been any distance from home yet and I don't think that we shall go far. I have thought of going over to see Lou but I don't know whether I shall yet for I have not heard anything off her for sometime and I wrote to her but she never answered my letter so I don't think her hardly worth going to see and Ted Vale will be engaged after Thursday, for his young woman is coming back then. She as been spending her Christmas at home, so after Thursday I shall be by myself. I went to the Randan's with the Captain on Saturday. He did not hardly know me. I don't know what have altered me so much as people don't seem to know me. I am going out again with the Captain on Wednesday if I am not gone to the other place.

Dear Polly, I saw Sarah Bradley last night coming from church, her and Jane and another fresh one was there and me and Ted was together. So after church me and Ted walked up the street a little way until we met. Ted stopped and spoke to them and I went on for I did not see them until I looked back and saw Ted talking to them, so of course then, I went up and spoke. Sarah looked and stared for a bit, then I said "Why Sarah, don't you know me" and I don't really think that she would have known me if I had not spoke. She seemed very glad to see me and asked very kindly after you, in fact all her talk was about you. She said that she should like to see you very much. I told her how you were and how you had been going on these last two years and every particular.

I believe, by what she told me last night that she is going to Mrs Caustin's with Mrs Bourne. She is her maid but only for a short time, but I dare say that she will write and tell you every thing. Dear Polly, if you have time, answer her letter for she seemed rather put about as you did not answer her letter before, and I think if she is going up near you to live it will be company for you, so try and keep in with her. She and Jane send their very best love to you and hopes to hear of you being strong again soon, and Ted Vale sends all sorts of good wishes. And Mother, Herb and Fred send their love to you. Now I must say goodbye, for it is getting dark, so with fondest love I say goodbye hoping this will find you a great deal better and still improving for it is the earnest wish

     of yours most affectionately

          ALF (Charger)

I will send you the Bromsgrove paper so that you can see about Jemimah Bicknell
Goodbye. Write soon.

CONCEALMENT OF BIRTH AT HANBURY

On Friday, the 19th instant, at the County Magistrates' Clerk's Office, before E.Bearcroft, Esq. (in the chair), and the Rev. W.Lea, Jemima Bicknell was brought up in custody of Supt. Tyler, charged with endeavouring to conceal the birth of her female child. Prisoner was cook at Hanbury Rectory, and some suspicion seems to have been entertained that she was in the family way, but she attributed her appearance to other causes. On the evening of the 29th December she complained of being unwell, but laid her illness to her having eaten an orange, and it was arranged that if she felt worse during the night she should knock the floor for Olive Whatton, the lady's maid, but she did not do so. Next morning in answer to the latter as to the state of her health, she said she had been sick during the night, but was at her work as usual. During the morning a char-woman employed at the Rectory went to the prisoner's bedroom, and from certain indications there, the prisoner was accused of having given birth to a child, which she admitted, and was put to bed.

Mr.J.R.Mahoney, assistant to Messrs. Roden and Fayrer came about two o'clock in the afternoon, when she had admitted having been confined between twelve and one o'clock of the previous night, but in answer to a question from him said the child had not cried or stirred. The child was found in a box in the prisoner's bedroom, wrapped in some apparel, where she stated she had placed it. Mr. Mahoney said he had made a post-mortem examination of the body of the infant, and was of opinion that it died during the process of birth. Prisoner admitted to P.C.Bannister that she had made no preparation for the birth of the child. Prisoner made no defence, and was committed to take her trial at the assizes.

From: Bromsgrove, Droitwich and Redditch Weekly Messenger. 27th January 1877.

Rock Hill
Bromsgrove
January 16th 1877

My dear Polly,

You will see by my address that I am still at home, but I have not had much leisure time for I was at Grafton along with the Captain a shooting and rabbiting last week and he wants me to go again this week, but I don't quite see it, for I want to look about me a bit now I am here for perhaps I shan't have such another chance. I don't know when I am going to my place for I have not heard from the gentleman yet although I expect a letter every day. I fancy when I get the letter I shall have to pack off there and then, so I have got myself in readiness, but if he don't write very soon I shall either write to him or else give it up altogether for something else. He may have written and the letter was misdirected or something but anyhow I have not had it. Perhaps when I write again he shall have done something about it. He told me at Reading Station that he would let me know before the 20th and the time is up on Saturday.

Dear Polly, I don't think there is much news of any sort stirring about here just now but I will try and tell you what there is. I had a trip yesterday, first to Alvechurch to see Lou. She did not expect me. When I got there I saw Mrs Mildmay at the back door so she asked me if I wanted to see Mr Mildmay. I told her 'No, I wanted to see Miss Garrett," then she says "Oh, she as been gone from here twelve months." So of course I couldn't believe her, but thought I would stop and see if Lou would turn up, so she did at last and came and spoke to me. I did not hardly know her but I did not remark it to her, but she is altered.

I don't think she is above half as stout as she used to be nor she hadn't got half the colour that she used to have. She asked all about you and where you were. She said she had given up all hope of seeing either of us again as she had not heard anything of either of us for a long time. She says that she should like to see you very much and she shall do it if you are about that part when she goes home again. She sends her best love and respects and hopes to hear of you being in good health soon.

Secondly I left Alvechurch about 12 o'clock and went to Birmingham and I found out Emily Eaton and called on her on my way back. She is living just this side of Brum. Well, I met with a surprise here for I rang the bell and Emily came and opened the door, so directly I saw her I said "You are just the person I want to see." So she says "Me. I think you have made a mistake, Sir" Then the truth seemed to flash across her mind for she cries out "Why it's Charger." Then of course she asked me in and I stayed there about 2 hours. She seemed very glad to see me and her first words nearly were "How is Mary (Polly)." So I told her all the particulars. She said that she should come and live down Reading way if you and Lou got down there for she says that she as no friends up where she is and nobody that cares anything about her. The other girl that lives with her told me that she was always talking about the games that we used to have at Grafton. So I suppose she as not had such happy times since. I think that she is sorry that Jim Graves gave her up, by what she said. She wanted to know all about him. Emily sends her kind love to you and hopes to see you again some day. Dear Polly, you must not think any the worse of me for going to see these two girls for I went to see them simply as a friend and I have told you most of what passed between us so I hope you wont be jealous.

PROBABLE CONTINUATION SHEET:

Dear Polly I saw Sarah Bradley and Jane at Stoke church on Sunday morning. Sarah told me she had written to you and told you all the news. So I suppose she told you of the alterations at Grafton. It is not like the same place. The old servants such as Long and Jane and the Butler seem to have the rule of the house and outside too. The young servants are obliged to look twice before they speak. I would not live there again for a good deal. Sarah says she is tired of it already and if she don't soon go to Richmond or wherever it is, she shall leave altogether. She told me on Sunday that she had a good reason to believe that she is not going to travel with Mrs Bourne but Mrs B had not said anything to her about it yet. She and Jane send their best love to you.

I don't think that I have much more to say this time. I think of going over to Hanbury to see Annie and Mother again this week. I shall call at the Firs as I go past. Dear Polly, I sent you the paper on Sunday and I cut a piece out with Miss Bicknell's affair on. She is to be tried next Friday at Droitwich. I will send the whole account if I can get it. Now dear Polly. I must say goodbye for the present and I hope this will find you in your new place quiet and comfortable.

So with fondest love, I remain yours most affectionately

ALF

Write soon.

Hanbury
17th Jan 1877

My dear Polly,

You will think me a long time answering your letter, but I hope you will forgive me as I went out for a week the day I received it and since have been uncertain where to address to you as Ann told me you were kept prisoner by the floods. Are they gone down yet.

I am rather sorry you have taken a situation already as you had the chance to rest longer. It seems to me inspite of the present outlay it would have been the best economy. Your mother wanted me to say, in which I quite agree, that if you find you can manage your new work without hurting yourself, well and good, but if not she earnestly wishes you not to attempt anything else and to come home at once. Persisting in work when you are as unfit as you are at present cannot be right for yourself or fair to those for whom you are working. I hope you are feeling stronger and that you will get on well. Are you any better?

You will think the Xmas present I promised you a long while coming but I hope you will accept it now on the principle of better late than never. I will tell you about the school treat when we have it but I can't say for certain when that will be, but before very long now I hope. I don't think I have anything else to tell you this time, so will conclude

with love from your affectionate friend
MARY DOUGLAS

IN PENCIL IN A DIFFERENT HAND:
   If I went we should have to leave it till Saturday.

   Take a basin cloth to the nursery for Miss - to wipe up water from Baths.

   If I see him I can't speak to him.

   If you like we can go now or stop till daylight but I think we had better go tonight for you to see about your flowers
S. Mat   XXVI   30 - 46
S. Mark   XIV   26 - 42
S. Luke   XXII   40 - 46
S. John   XVIII   1.2

Note: Mary Douglas makes no reference to the trial of Jemima Bicknell although the events took place at the Rectory which is her home.

Rock Hill
Bromsgrove
Jan'y 31st 1877

My darling Polly,

You must excuse me this time in being so long writing this week for although I am still at Rock Hill I have got plenty of work to do just now. I have been at Grafton almost every day since this day week, but today the Captain is gone to Lord Ward's a shooting so I thought that I would slip in and write to you. I am sort of temporary gamekeeper. I expect that I shant go after this week for I don't like the goings on. Father's master has been after me to help in the garden down there. I have been two or three days when I am not wanted at Grafton so I have got most of my time filled up except Sunday.

Dear Polly, I was very glad to see by your last letter that you had got to your new place. I hope you will like it. You must tell me all the particulars when you write again for perhaps by that time you will have seen what it is like and how it is likely to suit you. And as for going to Confession, I don't think you ought to go if you don't believe in it, but if they seem offended, go, for I don't think they can do you any harm and I don't understand it so I can't tell you what I would do if I was in your place. But if you look at the First Epistle to St. John, the first chapter and the last two or 3 verses you will see what he says. I think it says that if we confess our sins he (meaning God) is faithful and just to forgive us our sins. I don't think that confessing to a priest can't do anybody any good, so I think if I were you I would see how I could get on without going. And again Daniel says in the O.T. in the 9th Chapter and 9th verse of Daniel.

He says "To the Lord our God belong mercies and forgivenesses." So my idea of confession is that it is no good confessing to a man of any sort. Dear Polly, I can't be a very good hand at preaching so you must not laugh at what I have told you. I have only given you my idea. Now for a little news. The Grafton folks go away today. The carriage has gone by twice since I have been writing so I expect that Albutt has been to take them to the station. I saw Mrs Bourne on Monday for the first time to speak to her since I have been here. I was going from the Hall door to the Gun rack and she stopped me in the passage. She asked me how I was and a few other questions but I could not stop or perhaps she would have said more. I have not seen any of the Grafton servants to speak to them since last Sunday week. I believe they are all gone for a holiday today.

Dear Polly, I sent you the Bromsgrove paper on Saturday so that you could see Jemimah Bicknell's trial. She's committed to the Assizes so she will be in prison more than a month before the trial comes off, which is in March. If she don't get sent to hard labour it will be a lesson for her. Not only to her but one or two more that are rather fast about here. She will find it jolly cold in jail this time of year for the winter is just commenced here. It snowed here yesterday and the day before but there is none left, but it is very cold. Now dear Polly, I think that I have told you all this time. I hope that I shall have better news to tell you next time and when you write to the folks at Wimbledon please remember me to them and tell them how I am getting on just about the same.

Now goodbye, with fondest love

I am yours most affectionately

ALF

WEDNESDAY

Concealment of Birth at Hanbury

Jemima Bicknell (23) a domestic servant, pleaded guilty to trying to conceal the birth of her female child at Hanbury Rectory, 30th December 1876. The Hon. and Rev. H. Douglas whose rectory she was a domestic servant gave her a good character, and his Lordship only sentenced her fourteen days hard labour.

From:Bromsgrove, Droitwich and Redditch Weekly Messenger. 3rd March 1877

INCOMPLETE

Rock Hill
Bromsgrove
(Tues) Feby 27th 1877

My darling Polly,

I was very glad to see a letter from you this morning, and I am writing now to tell you a little news. I sent you a paper on Monday. You will see in it most of the town news and some country news too so you will have a good idea of how the things in general are going on. But I must tell you some fresher news. You know Old Smith at the Bowling Green, the man that the Captain used to have such rows with about the

1877

Game. Well, lately he has been rather hard up for cash and was to give notice to leave his farm as of last Saturday, the 24th, so as for him to get out of it by the 25th March. So on Saturday last he went out of the house about half past seven in the morning and as he did not turn up again that day, some of his men and old Botley went to search for him but could not find him until about six o'clock on Sunday morning.

Then they found him stood straight up in a ditch full of water, quite dead. He must have walked into it and stood there until he sank in over his head. He must have been some time dying. It is the most deliberate affair that I or anyone else ever heard of. It is the top of the talk about here. The inquest is to be held today. The whole account of it will be in the paper on Saturday. The Worcester Assizes begin today, so about tomorrow Jemimah Bicknell will know what she as to do. It will all be in the Bromsgrove paper next Saturday. I will send it to you then you will be able to see.

It is only a rumour that Joe Stanton still sticks to her, but it might be true for all that. I know she did not go the right way to work to keep his love. If she had told him all about it when he asked her only two days before it happened, she might have been at the Douglas's now, for Joe's mother says that she would have had her at her house if she had known about it before. And I believe if Joe was to go and give evidence against her it would be a great deal worse for her. She don't deserve his love for not trusting him. I think she ought to have trusted him before anyone else but she will know all about it tomorrow and I hope she will get off for Joe's sake as well as her own for I believe Joe is a steady going on chap.

Dear Polly, I have said enough about that so I must tell you a little of home affairs. My brother Fred as got the sack from his young lady; but it is too bad for he did not deserve it. He is a steady easy going chap and quite capable of taking care of himself and guarding the honour of any respectable young woman but people will talk and make mischief so they have parted, Fred and Miss Johnson. But it will come to something yet for Fred is going to find everything out. He had found a lot out already and is on the track of the folks that started it and I expect they will have to look around themselves too. Our friend Master Beard is the starter of it but I think he has got a taiter* this time. Fred is going to see him on Sunday. I think the girl thinks a good deal of him for she wont send anything back that Fred as given her and she told him last Sunday night that she should never think of any other young man as long as Fred remained in Bromsgrove. I know Fred thinks a good deal of her or else he would not be at so much trouble in finding out all the mischief that as parted them.

Dear Polly, I am still at home and I don't think I shall go to that place near Reading. I have not heard from the man once. I don't expect my letter was sweet enough for him. I don't think that I shall go far away again. I like jobbing about for I have my nights and Sundays to myself and not very long hours in the day - from 7 until 5, so that is not bad and it will do until I can see something to suit me. I was at the keeping all last week because the nailers are on strike and they are all over the place, so I was asked to look out for them. Joe Gwynne is at home bad, he is not able to go on with his work. I have not seen him but he as been to our house but I was out so I did not see him.

Note: *'taiter' means hot potato, a tricky problem.

MYSTERIOUS DEATH BY DROWNING

On Tuesday an inquest was held at the Dog and Pheasant, Worcester Street, Bromsgrove, before Ralph Docker Esq, and a respectable jury of whom Mr. W.Jefferies was the foreman, touching the death of Mr William Smith, of the Bowling Green Farm, Grafton Manor, about a mile and a half from Bromsgrove. Mr J.R.Horton attended to watch the proceedings in the interests of the relatives of the deceased.

Shadrach Gilder, Rock Hill, cowman, said the body the jury had viewed was that of his late master, in whose employment he had been for two years. He last saw him alive on Friday, 23rd February, at about half-past seven o'clock in the evening. Next (Saturday) morning, about ten o'clock he heard that he was missing from home, and he and others went in search of him about the farm at midnight of that day, and continued the search for him on Sunday morning, when he and the deceased's son, Mr. Alfred Smith, discovered him at about seven o'clock in a pool on the farm known as Lancashire Pool. This pool was near a hedge dividing fields, two fields from the house, from whence it could be partially seen.

To Mr. Horton: The pool could not be seen from the windows of the house.

A juryman said it could be seen from the farm buildings.

Examination continues: The pool was "pretty well" for depth and he should think that at the spot where the deceased was found the water was twelve feet deep. It was about the middle of the pool - about three or four yards from the bank. The body was floating upright in a slightly stooping position, having the hair of the head close to the surface, causing a wave or ripple which led to his discovery. The deceased's hat was by the side of the pool, but not within six or seven yards of his body.

The deceased's clothes were not disarranged in the least but were as they appeared in his usual condition when walking about the farm.

In reply to the Coroner, a juryman said the pool where the body was found would be about 300 yards from the Worcester turnpike-road, and anyone in the vicinity of it could be seen from the road for a considerable distance half a mile at least.

Emily Millichip, a domestic servant at the Bowling Green, said she last saw her master alive on Saturday morning about half-past nine o'clock. Deceased was then by the back door. He didn't come down to his breakfast at the usual hour that morning, which was eight o'clock. She did not see him again from that time till his body was brought in about eight o'clock on Sunday morning. Deceased was at home on Friday evening; she saw him about ten o'clock, very soon after which she went to bed. The deceased was then in the sitting-room with Mrs. Smith and Mr

Robert Smith. a grown-up son. She could not tell what time the deceased went to bed but it appeared to be very soon afterwards that she heard him come up stairs.

To Mr. Horton: It was unusual for the deceased not to get up to his breakfast. Her mistress took the deceased up a cup of tea. So far as she (witness) saw of the deceased when he was at the door on Saturday morning there was nothing unusual in his manner.

Mr R.Prosser, surgeon, Bromsgrove, deposed to having known deceased intimately. In conseqence of what he heard respecting him about four o'clock on Saturday he went to his house, where he found search being made for him. Inquiries were instituted and witness came on to Bromsgrove and informed some of the deceased's friends. He had a note from Mr. Botteley at about ten o'clock at night stating that the deceased had not then been found, and asking whether he considered it advisable to inform the police.

Witness subsequently went and assisted in the search till two o'clock in the morning.

To the foreman: He waited on Superintendent Tyler, who did not however, appear to take any part in the search.

The Coroner said that circumstances might be explained; it did not affect the main points of the case.

Examination continued: Witness was not present when the body was found but saw it soon after. The deceased was then dressed in his usual every day clothes, which were in perfect order. No garment was missing, but the hat, he understood, was brought off a tree. There were no marks of violence on the body with the exception of a few slight scratches on the face, probably produced by his having fallen through briars on the bank. The scratches were of recent infliction and in fact were bleeding when he saw the body. The hands were bleached, and the general appearance of the body was that of having been in the water for some hours. There was no disorganisation - there could not be any; and no indication of the cause of death - whether death took place before or subsequently to its being placed in the water. He had seen the deceased up to within a week or two before his death, and he then appeared as he usually did - a kindly, agreeable, and well-disposed man.

MYSTERIOUS DEATH BY DROWNING

The Coroner said this was all the evidence it was necessary for him to call. The circumstances of the case lay in a very small compass. There was no evidence to lead them to a conclusion as to how the body (of Mr Smith) got in the water. The case seemed perfectly free from suspicion or suggestion of any kind, and it was quite as possible - in fact very likely - that the deceased, in passing by the pond, might have accidently fallen into the water. There was no reason - no suggestion as far as they could learn, that the deceased had taken away his own life.

And it might have been that he fell in the pool from a sudden seizure or something of the kind. However all they knew was that the deceased was found there, and unless the jury thought it necessary that a post mortem examination should be held, to discover the cause of death, he proposed to leave the case where it stood. Of course the cause of death could be proved if they thought it material. If however, on the other hand, they thought the case free from suspicion they would find their verdict upon the evidence already adduced.

The room having been cleared, the jury were left in consultation and at the end of about twenty minutes, on the public being admitted, the foreman said their unanimous verdict was "That the deceased was found drowned, without marks of violence; but by what means he got into the water there was no evidence to prove." He was also requested by a majority of the jurymen to state that in their opinion the deceased "might have slipped in, when in the act of viewing the pool."

The Coroner: That is no part of your verdict.

From: Bromsgrove, Droitwich and Redditch Weekly Messenger. 3rd March 1877

Rock Hill
Bromsgrove
(Thurs) March 8th 1877

My darling Polly,

You see I am still at the old place, but I am getting on pretty well, and I thought by your last letter that you were pretty near comfortable. I can pretty near tell when I read

110

your letters if you are better or worse without you telling me, but if you tell me I am more certain. Do you go to a doctor now and what do you think of yourself now. I want to hear you say, "I am quite well." and then I shall be alright (for a week) for I often think about your health. You are so far away. I never have a chance to see for myself; and as for myself, if I was not just the thing you would soon hear about it. So please say in your next letter how you are and all about it.

I sent you a paper on Monday so that you would see all the news. Jemimah Bicknell only got 14 days as your mother told, and a good job for her, it might have been worse. Mr Douglas spoke for her. Dear Polly you would see most of the particulars about old Smith, but the evidence was so wrapped up at the inquest that people who really did not know the facts could not learn anything about it. There was a few lies told too. Just to hide that he did commit suicide for just before he did it, he insured his life for £1,000 and if the jury had brought in a verdict of suicide, his friends would not have got the money, so there was something in it. He had only been missed 2½ hours before the workmen began to drag the pools for him, and the one that he was found in was the first one to be dragged, but they did not succeed the first time and that was about 12 o'clock on Saturday morning. He was found about 7 o'clock Sunday morning.

So I think - and so do a good many more - that if his friends did not suspect something wrong they would not have the pools dragged for him so soon after they had seen him. I have seen the place where he done it and the men that pulled him out. One of the men that helped to get him out was Mr Butler Botley's gardener, and the other one was Bird, Mrs Jones' man, and the man Gilder that gave evidence at the inquest. And all of them say that he must have jumped in and hid his hat after he was in the water for they could not get at it without going through the pool after it, so you can guess that something was wrong. Dear Polly the reason that I am telling you so much about this is because it is the top of the talk here and you and I know the people concerned so well.

I saw Jane from Grafton on Sunday, she asked after you and I was to give her love to you. I asked if Sarah was at Richmond, she said she was so she will be coming to see you some of these fine days if she has not been. All the Grafton folk are away ecxcept the Capt. and he is away all day. They are having a lot of repairs done. I suppose it will be the last time the Capt. will have done there for he has bought an estate somewhere near Hereford and I have heard that he is going to live there. He is going to give up the shooting so Beard told me, so I am sure that he wont be long after he has done that. I went with my brother Fred to see Beard last Sunday morning about what he had said about Fred and his lass. He denied everything so I suppose he is a liar or else the girl's friends are. Fred is going to see the girl again on 25th March, then I suppose we shall hear the rights of it. Fred is rather put about over it, but I tell him, time will work wonders.

Now dear Polly I must say goodbye for it is near post time and I have told you all that is worth knowing. Mother, Fred, Herb and all at home sends their best love to you and they have asked "When is she coming again?" Now Polly, Goodbye and God

Bless You,
    With fondest love
               I am yours ever affectionately
                        ALF
 Write soon.

Rock Hill

              Bromsgrove
           March 25th 1877

My dear Polly,

I am writing to you on a Sunday for a wonder. There is not so many people coming in and out as there is generally. All the folks are gone out except me and Father and Mother, so I have got a quiet $\frac{1}{2}$ hour to write to you. I have but very little news to tell. I saw Joe Gwynne last Saturday week. He looked very middling but he is not altered a bit since he was at Grafton with us except got thinner. He as been at home 8 weeks with bad health. He talks about going back to work about Easter Wednesday. The work that he is doing is to heavy for him. He seemed very glad to see me. He said that I am not altered much only I have not got quite such a good colour; so I don't know what so many people think I am altered for, or what there was in me that they did not know me at first. Joe sends his best respects and well wishes.

Dear Polly, I have found out if John Blunn is married or not. He isn't. He was asked in church for the last time today. I have heard that they have been living together for some time and old Aldham went down to John's father and told him that if John would be married, he would marry them for the ordinary fee instead of the double fee (which is always charged during Lent) but how true this tale is I don't know. I hardly ever see him to speak to him. I have seen him and her going down towards their house at Charford at 10 o'clock on Saturday nights with parcels but I don't suppose there is any harm in that. I don't think that John is such a soft spot. Nobody knows anything about him. Butcher and Curl says that he never speaks to them like he used to do and Ted Vale can't get anything out of him.

Dear Polly, I am at home still. I will tell you the reason I am staying. We are afraid that father will be laid up again before long. He seems to get worse and he as such a red colour just as he had two years ago, and if he should be laid up, Mr Horton wants me to do his work, but if father can get through this and next month he may go through the summer. We are afraid that he wont get through another bad illness like he had two years ago. I am at work with him every day. Father said just now that he thought that his course was nearly run. He can feel himself getting weaker every day. He looks stout and well but I am afraid that his inside is going. Now dear Polly, you can see why I am staying at home. It is not my wish that I am staying. I shall get away if I may.

I don't think I have much more to tell you. If I were you, I should go and see Sal, it will be an outing for you and it won't do you any harm. Please remember me to her if you go. I shall most likely see her again if I am at home when she gets back to Grafton. Shall you have any holiday this Easter. If you do you will be able to go to Reading. You will find it a nice little town. Go from the G.W.Railway. It is only about a 9d ride but of course you know best about your own affairs. I know you would be welcome at Louisa's home. Please remember me to Louisa when you write. Now Polly, I think I must say goodbye for the present. I will send the paper with this letter so you will be able to see what news there is. So hoping this will find you quite well.

With fondest love,
   I am yours affectionately,
      ALF
Please excuse writing for my hand is rather shaky.

     Hanbury
     26th March
     Easter 1877

My dear Polly,

Many thanks for your letter and photo. It is a very good one and I think you certainly look better in it. It is a long time since I heard from you before. I was under the impression it was your turn to write or I should have done so. How nice it has been to have a little fine weather. You must have had enough wet weather to satisfy you for some time to come. To judge by the pictures in the papers, Windsor must have looked very forlorn. Are you anywhere near the Castle? You ought to have a good chance of seeing the Queen.

I think your Mother seems pretty well. I saw her one day last week. I suppose you have a good many extra services now. We have evening service at the Big Church on Wednesdays, at St Mark's on Thursdays and at Broughton on Fridays. I am very glad you think you can manage your work and very much hope you will be able to do so. But don't overdo yourself because you know that would not pay. I am afraid I must not stay to write any more as I must go to my Father, so I will conclude wishing you, dear Polly, a very happy Easter and all its blessings.

I remain your affectionate friend,
          MARY DOUGLAS

Bill on the back:

1   14   11½
1   4   9
2   19   8½
2   17

Rock Hill
Bromsgrove
(Tues) April 3rd 1877

My dear Polly,

It is a wet day today so I can't do much, for wet days are rather against gardening, so I have a quiet half hour to write to you. There is not much stirring about here, only there was a man scalded to death at Stoke Works on Saturday. His home was at Hill Top, close to where old Long lives. The man was tight and fell backwards into the pan of boiling Brine. It was done at about ½ past ten on Saturday night and he died at 12 o'clock on Sunday morning. He is to be buried on Wednesday.

There is going to be a Military Funeral at Bromsgrove this afternoon. A man that used to work at Bromsgrove Station Wagon Works. His name is Tustin. He was struck by a fellow workman with a pair of iron tongs about 12 months ago, and that blow and consumption together, as killed him. He was in the Rifle Corps so they are going to bury him with Military Honours today at 4 o'clock. You will be able to see the whole account of it in next Saturday's paper which I will send you as soon as I get it.

Dear Polly, you asked me to get you some flowers but I am sorry to say I can't just now for it is the worst time of year for them just at present, For the snowdrops and crocuses are just done and the other Spring flowers are hardly out and father is badly off for flowers in the greenhouse this Spring for he as had a new cystern (for hot water) put in and the chaps that done it as been most of the winter at it. So he has not had time to get his flowers to grow. I will remember you when there is any about.

I know you would have liked some for your performance. I am sorry I can't get any. I don't know when I shall go to Hanbury again for it is a busy time just now. I dare say I shall see a chance some time. I must try and go on a Sunday next time. I have not seen Anne for nearly 12 months now. I must go as far as the Firs to see her if I can't go any further. My brother Fred is knocking about without a young woman at present. He would not have any thing to say to her on the 25th as he promised, so I suppose it is all up. You said do I remember last Easter Sunday. I do, and I have good reason to remember it. It was the last time I saw you before the (on the 16th April). I remember the day and the date well, but never mind, it was all for the best. I think Herbert and his young woman have dissolved partnership. She is gone to Evesham and I have not seen any letter for some time now and he never says anything about her like he used to.

I, with a lot more chaps, walked to Kidderminster on Good Friday. We had a rare nice day and we walked until we were tired. We came back round by Droitwich. I was that tired that I have not been all right since. I was rather stiff. The man that lives at the Swan at Upton, was tried last Tuesday. He was fined £2 but none of the people that was there were interfered with so Ted Vale is alright this time. Dear Polly, I believe that John Blunn is to be married next Saturday. I have heard so but I don't know if it is the truth. I don't think anybody knows anything about it except themselves. Now dear Polly, I think I must say goodbye. You must excuse bad writing for I have got hold of Herb's pen and it don't suit me. Now goodbye.

With best love, I am yours faithfully,

ALF

Write soon. Don't be surprised if you hear of me being a gamekeeper.

Rock Hill,
Bromsgrove,
15th April 1877

My dear Polly,

You must forgive me this time for not answering your letter sooner for I have been very busy all this week. You know I told you last week that you were not to be surprised if you heard of me being a Game keeper. I have been a Game keeping more than a week. Captain Bourne's under keeper has left him so he came and asked me if I would mind coming back to him for he did not know of anybody that would suit as well as I should. So I have taken the place, but it is quite different to what it used to be. I am more my own master than I used to be. If I stay on with the Captain, most likely I shall go down to his new place that he has bought, for he is going to keep a lot of game down there. Most likely Beard is going there after the season is over then if the Captain keeps the shooting on at Grafton Manor I shall stand a good chance of getting Beard's place. If the Captain gives up Grafton I shall have to go with Beard down to the other place. We don't hardly know what is going to be done yet.

Dear Polly, you asked why I don't say more about myself in my letters. Well, I can't say much. I am the same old Charger you knew a long while ago, not altered a little bit, only grown uglier. I often think of the good times that we had in that Green Lane when I go past there of a night, for Grafton is in my beat now just the same as it used to be. I often wish that you were here or somewhere about. I am getting like I used to be before you pulled me out of the mire. I keep going on from week's end to week's end and never see any fresh faces but always the same people and the same things.

Both Beard and his wife ask about you very often and old Lowe that works in the garden, he asked about you yesterday and all the old hands ask about you.

Dear Polly, you asked me what I meant by It means blow up and the 16th April means Easter Sunday. You know Easter Sunday was on 16th April last year and it was the last time I saw you before you thought it proper to send me the "travelling ticket". It is exactly 12 months today since I walked with you from Mrs Walker's to Wimbledon Station and that was the time I thought you ought to have told me, if you meant it, that you wished to discontinue the acquaintance. For you know in the next letter you told me and it was only a little over a week afterwards, but I know most of the facts concerning the whole affair. I have learnt it from one and another, but some day I hope you will tell me from your own lips. Dear Polly, don't be cross for what I have said. It was you mentioning the subject in your other letter that made me think about it. The subject always makes me think all manner of things and I never like bringing it up and I hope it was all for the best.

I was glad to hear of you having a trip but you ought to have seen Sal. She would have been so pleased especially if you had taken her by surprise. What did Lizzy, the cook at Mrs Walker's say to you? Is she quite well. I suppose she will be getting married before long. Please remember me to her and to little Lizzy when you write. It will be a nice holiday for you to go to Wimbledon for a week in the summer. I wish I could get a week's holiday and go too, but no fear, no more holidays for me I expect. How much holiday shall you have in the summer. I suppose all the young ladies will go away for their holiday, the same as the gentlemen at the R.M.C. used to do.

Dear Polly, you must please give my love to your mother and Annie when you write and tell them what I am doing for I don't know when I shall be able to go and see them again. My father is still about the same, no worse nor any better. The weather has been rather cold these last few days. He will be alright I think as the days get warmer. Now I must say goodbye.

    With fondest love,

        I am yours affectionately,

            ALF

Hanbury
7th May 1877

My dear Polly,

I am very sorry indeed that you are worse again. I still stick, as you supposed I should, to my old tale that you had better come home again. Of course what you say about earning a living is all quite true but I don't see that you do it very well by working for a few weeks and then getting knocked up as you do. I fear you will, if you keep on so, be knocked up completely and be unable to do anything for yourself.

Now what I would propose to you is this - to come home as soon as you can after leaving the hospital. You know something about dressmaking do you not? Another dressmaker is wanted now here and Sarah Barber wants someone to help her as Jessie is going to be married on Thursday to John Stanton. So you could either work with Sarah or on your own account and if you liked to fill up spare time with fancy work, you could do so and I believe could get a sale for it in Bromsgrove. Your Mother thinks you might work say till Michaelmas with Sarah and learn all she can teach and then set up on your own account. I know you might earn more at Service but I fear your being completely done up and unable to do anything for yourself.

Your Mother, I think, would be much happier if you were with her. At all events do give the plan full consideration and I would say, if I may, ask God to guide you in this matter. I think you would be right to come home as by so doing you would have a better chance of health. You see, a little extra hurry or so forth hurts you and to that you would be less liable here than elsewhere.

I send you a few flowers. I would have written on Saturday but did not know if you had a Sunday delivery and I did not think the flowers would like being shut up so long. I don't think I must write any more now or it will be past post time before I have got the flowers. So goodbye for the present.

I remain your affectionate friend,
MARY DOUGLAS

Rock Hill,
Bromsgrove,
May 14th 1877

My dear Polly,

I was very pleased to see a letter from you on Saturday and I am writing as soon as I could find time. I thought by your letter that you were very down hearted. I can generally tell when I read you letters what sort of spirits you were in when you wrote them. I don't hardly wonder at your being down hearted, being a long way from home and friends and having such ill health. I agree with Miss Douglas. I think that it would be better for you to come nearer home, if not live at home, for you are now a long way from home and living amongst strangers, and nobody that cares anything about you. While at home, you would be well cared for and plenty of friends (that would be glad to do anything for you) that can't do anything now you are so far away.

You can do what you like about staying at St. Stephen's until the term is out for I don't suppose it will make much difference, but after that I advise you to come this way, it will be better for you and it will be doing what I wish. It is not like if you were a strong girl for then I believe, away from home is the best place, but in your case I say you are best nearer home and I think if you think the matter over a few days you will agree with me.

Dear Polly, you said in your last letter that you thought I had forgotten you, but I think you know better don't you? I can't help thinking about you. If I wished to forget I could not but I never have. I think now as I thought two years ago. You know what we were then. I hope we are the same now. I am.

It is 12 months today I received your letter telling me that you had thought proper to forget me. I can't help speaking about it, but believe me dear Polly, it did not make a morsel of difference to me then nor now. So let the matter rest and let the past be passed and look for a brighter future. If you come home we shall see more of each other and see things in a different light to what we see them now. So I think if you do as Miss Douglas advises it will be better for you and for me too. Tell me what you think about it when you write. Dear Polly I have said all I can this time and you have got my opinion about you coming home.

So I will tell you all the news I can. Mrs Bourne is come home and the children. I saw Sal Bradley yesterday. She is going to stay at Grafton. She told me that she had got a letter from you and I thought she looked rather curious at me too, though as if you had told her something about me but perhaps it was only fancy and she told me that you were in the Hospital. It looked like she thought that you did not let me know all them sort of things, but I am always fancying some foolishness. We are very good friends and I like her very well so I don't think there is anything wrong. Dear Polly it is no trouble for Herbert to send the paper. It is a pleasure and it will help to pass an hour away and news from home is always welcome so the paper will accompany this. I must say goodbye for it is post time. Hoping this will find you much better. You have all best wishes from Mother and all the rest at home. So I says goodbye.

With fondest love,
> I am yours ever
> ALF

Write soon.

Rock Hill,
Bromsgrove,
May 22nd 1877

My dear Polly,

I do not see any way of our meeting as things are arranged. It is better for you to get off at Droitwich, as Miss Douglas is going to meet you, for I know you will be tired after riding such a long way. So I don't think I shall be able to see you on Wednesday, but if you think that you could walk as far as our house on Sunday afternoon you could have some tea and then I could walk back with you. I am so tied on Sundays that I have not got much leisure time, but it will be better after a bit as soon as the nailers go to work again.

If you can't come on Sunday could you come by the Carrier on Tuesday. I should be at home by teatime and could walk back with you, but I should like you to come on Sunday. When I see you I shall be better able to tell you how I am situated. Now hoping you will get home safe and sound and find all the people at home quite well. Wishing to see you on Sunday.

I am yours affectionately,
ALF

Please write and tell me which day you can come.

Rock Hill,
Bromsgrove.
June 25th 1877

My dear Polly,

I am so sorry that I have been so long in answering your letter but I have not hardly been at home these last few days for the farmers have begun mowing and it takes all our time in looking after the mowers. I was out all day yesterday (Sunday) or I would have written then. The nailers are gone to work again so after the mowing we shant be so busy for a week or two. Dear Polly, I was sorry to hear that your charge was so restless but I think if you keep sticking to her as you have done you will master her. Don't let her think that you are afraid of her. I hope by this time she is a little more comfortable to deal with.

I saw Miss Cole and Mr Griffin walking up Rock Hill the other night. I should not have known her if it had not been for her sweetheart. She was dressed in black. Dear

Polly, there is no news of any account to tell you. Bromsgrove Fair is to be held today so that will take most of the people's attention. I don't expect that I shall go. I shant have any time without it is at night and then I expect I shall be tired. I shall go one night in the week if the Theatre comes. I should have liked for you to have been here to have gone with me. I don't seem to enjoy myself at such places now if some body is not with me, but I dare say that we shall be able to go somewhere together before the summer is out.

That man that threatened me is going to be tried tomorrow. It will be a fine set out I know. Lots of people are glad that this man is cought.

He is a very old poacher and has dared anybody to catch or touch him. He found his mistake out when he came on my beat. It will be a long trial for there is a lot to come out. The Captain will be one witness. We are going to have him up for Trespass. There is nothing fresh going on at Grafton. All the folks are about the same. The footman asked after you the other day. Of course I tell them that you are quite well and going on first rate. The girls in the kitchen are always asking how you are. They seem to take a great interest in you but I think it is for want of something else to say. Albert is gone to Captain Bough's. He went last Thursday. We have had one letter from him but he did not tell us what work he had to do or anything of the particulars. We shall hear more about him when he writes again.

Father is rather middling. He has got fresh cold, and a cold takes more effect on him than it would on anybody else. He is going to work this morning but he could hardly walk. Fred still sticks at Grafton. He goes there every night. I expect he will be taking some of them to the Fair. I shall hear something about it when I go there this morning. You know I am writing this before Breakfast - about 7 o'clock. I was afraid if I did not write now I shouldn't have a chance again today. Now I must say goodbye for the present. Hoping this will find you quite well and your charge still improving for I want you back in this part of the country again. I seem to lose you all ways. So with fondest love

        I am yours ever affectionately

              ALF

Write soon.

Rock Hill,
Bromsgrove
August 26th 1877

My dear Polly,

I am just writing to tell you a few of the events that have occurred since you were here. I have seen the Captain and settled with him about going into the house, he pressed me rather hard and made all manner of excuses to try and make me go into the house, but I stood firm and I had to tell him at last that I would sooner leave him altogether than go indoors. I told him plain that I did not like indoor service and another thing, I did not like the servants in the house. I told him that all the upper servants in the house wanted the servants under them to do all the work and therefore they had to work very hard. I did not tell him this until he told me that I should have an easy place. The Captain looked rather old (fashioned) at me but I stood my ground, so at last he told me that he would let the matter rest until after the shooting season. William is going to stay at Grafton until they can get somebody. I will tell you all the particulars when I see you.

Dear Polly, since you have been to our house people says that we are married. The Capt. asked me about it the other day and he asked Beard who my sweetheart was, so of course Beard told him. Beard told me that the Captain looked quite pleased about it and said that he knew you and that you was a very respectable young person. That is something, ain't it? The Theatre is still in Bromsgrove. It is going to stay all the week. I should like you to come over here next Sunday, the 2nd September - if you can and it is a fine day - to go and get some nuts. If it is a fine week all this next week all the nuts will be ripe.

You could come over either before or after dinner. Which would suit you best? Only just let us know. You know you are quite welcome. Old woman Jeff wants to know when you are coming again. I don't think I have got any more to tell you because I hope to see you next Sunday. I have heard from Harry Lowman and he sent me his photo in his soldier's dress. I will give it to you if you will come next Sunday.

Now goodbye, with fondest love
        I remain yours affectionately
           ALF

Rock Hill,
Bromsgrove
Sep. 7th 1877

My dear Polly,

I shall like you to come to our house on Sunday if you can. I am rather tied just now for Beard is gone out until Monday so I shant have much time to myself. If you could come before dinner you could rest abit and then come out somewhere in the afternoon. I shall have to be out all Sunday afternoon and you could come with me. Please write by return to say if you will come. Mrs Caustin is at Grafton now. I must say goodbye for it is getting late. Hoping to see you on Sunday.

I remain yours affectionately
ALF

Rock Hill,
Bromsgrove
Oct 11th 1877

My dear Polly,

I shall come to your house on Sunday. I shall be there about 3 o'clock. You can come and meet me if you like. I don't know yet if I shall have to go out watching on Sunday night, but whether I do or not I shall come for I have a chance of going to church which I should not have if I staid at home. I rather liked going to that little chapel, we will go again if you like next Sunday.

Joe Gwynne is gone to Mrs Caustin's today. He came to our house yesterday but none of us was at home but I think Herbert saw them in the town. There is nothing afresh happened at Grafton. I see Sarah pretty near every day now. I think it is all about the same down there. I shall see you on Sunday so I shall say goodbye for the present.

With fondest love,
I am yours affectionately
ALF

Rock Hill,
Bromsgrove
Oct. 16th 1877

My dear Polly,

As I have got safe home again, I will tell you a few incidents that have happened about here since I saw you on Sunday. I had it very windy all the way home. I thought sometimes the trees were coming down on the top of me, the wind made them crack so and as I was coming past Stoke Heath (across the Park) the wind nearly took me off my feet. I never was in such a wind in my life, but I got home alright. About 1 o'clock on Monday morning a great branch from the tree at the back of our house blew onto the top of our house and knocked the top off the chimney and knocked a lot of tiles off too. It pretty nearly frightened us out of our senses. I thought the house was tumbling down but no more damage was done.

There is a great many trees torn up about here and ricks blown down. Grafton Lane was full of trees and branches and men had to go with axes to clear the way before anybody could get down. There is a great deal of damage done all round here. I don't know how you folks stood it round Hanbury but it is many years since there was such a wind before. I expect we shall hear of a deal of damage done at sea especially if the wind was as strong as it was on land. But let us hope it was not.

Dear Polly, I heard today that Mr Lowe was a good deal better and they think he will get alright again, it might have been worse. Mother is a good deal better, she will soon be alright again. I have not been to see Polly Barley yet but I think I shall go either tomorrow or Thursday night.

Those people that we were talking about on Sunday that starved that woman at Penge, has got a reprieve so they wont be hung. Louie was very proud of her cuffs, they were very soon put away so that nobody should not touch them. I saw Sarah yesterday. She was going to the station to meet her father she said. She was in a hurry so she did not stop to say much. Now dear Polly, I must say good bye and mind to take care of yourself while you are out. Hoping you will be comfortable and have no more Fits.

I conclude with fondest love.
I am yours affectionately
ALF

THE GALE ON SUNDAY NIGHT

Collieries

A meteorological correspondent of The Globe of Monday night drew the attention of colliery managers to the rapid atmospherical changes during the past few days and pointed out that the downward motion of the barometer coupled with mercurial changes of pressure equal to 320 pounds on the square foot within a few hours, indicated conditions likely to lead to falls of roof and explosions.

Birmingham

The gale of Sunday night surpassed in violence anything which has been experienced for many years. It seems to have swept the entire country but though its effects have been felt very much in the destruction of property it would seem so far as at present can be ascertained to have been singularly free from injury to human life. Birmingham from its elevated position experienced the full force of it, especially in the more exposed suburbs on the southern side.

Bromsgrove

The gale commenced about eight o'clock when the wind increased in velocity blowing huge clouds of dust along the streets to the great discomfort of all who were out of doors. The greatest violence was experienced between one and three o'clock on Monday morning. The heaviest gusts reached as high a point as ninety miles an hour.

The first destructive effects of the gale began to tell upon insecure tiles and chimney pots and to hurl them into the street. Few persons were permitted to enjoy their slumbers for the howling of the wind, the rattling of windows and in many cases the shaking of buildings.

Telegraphic communication with Bromsgrove - Birmingham and Worcester directions - was entirely cut off during Monday morning. It was restored in the afternoon. Owing to obstructions, the mail-cart to Alcester was unable to proceed till a late hour. The part where the greatest destruction has been dealt in our immediate neighbourhood, is the avenue of poplars at the lower end of Old Station Road. Scarcely one of nearly thirty of these has escaped the full fury of the wind. Some four or five of them, together with a large elm have been blown down bodily raising with their roots, large quantities of earth and bringing up bodily a section of drain pipes. The upturned roots and fallen trunks entirely filling up the road for fifty or sixty yards. A great many of the employees at the railway works experienced great difficulty in surmounting the obstacles.

The Bristol train

The mail train which leaves Birmingham for Bristol at 2.45 a.m. had a narrow escape in coming down the decline into Bromsgrove Station on Monday morning. The driver of the engine became aware that it had come across some obstruction, which it was apparently carrying before it. As soon as possible he brought his train to a stand-still, which was about a hundred yards before reaching the station, when it was found that the engine had been carrying with it the upper portion of a signal post which had been blown across the metals. The escape of the train from more serious disaster may be looked upon as most providential.

Bromsgrove

In the town itself the streets were strewn with stray tiles and brick bats. The most serious incident of this kind seems to have been at Mr.Sanders in St. John Street where a chimney which stood singly was blown down but rested bodily against an adjoining stack.

The chimney of a cottage at Stoney Hill occupied by a man named Taylor was blown down between one and two o'clock in the morning, and though a great portion of it crashed through the roof into the bedroom beneath occupied by some of the family, no injury to life or limb occurred.

Finstall, Rednal and the Lickey Hills

At Finstall several large trees were blown down, an elm completely blocked the Alcester Road near the Cross Inn. At Rednal a large poplar was broken short and obstructed the road for several hours. The same may be stated of the firs on and about the Lickey Hills. Numbers of these are overturned in the plantations and lie in rows, "like the mower's work at close of day."

Worcester

From Worcester we learn that scarcely a house in the city escaped. At the prison the buildings were considerably damaged and one of the roofs was blown off but luckily without injuring anyone. At Diglis some new premises being erected at Messrs. Webb's Chemical Works were blown into the canal and swamped a barge.

London

The damage to and destruction of property in London by the gale was more extensive than was at first reported. On Monday numbers of vessels due in London on the previous day arrived in the river some of them with the loss of anchor, chains and damage to sails and rigging.

Buckinghamshire

At Haddenham in Bucks a windmill and a large quantity of corn were consumed by fire through friction caused by the brake of the mill giving way during the storm.

Somerset

At Crewkerne during the gale a large chimney stack 112 feet high was hurled to the ground and fell directly across a cottage occupied by a family named Prince killing four of the occupants instantly.

From: Bromsgrove, Droitwich and Redditch Weekly Messenger. 20th October 1877

Rock Hill
Bromsgrove
November 28th 1877

My dear Polly,

I was very glad to see a letter from you on Monday and to hear that you are getting on so well. I went to Hanbury on Sunday and found everybody quite well. I did not get there until 6 o'clock and Jessie Barber was there so Jessie and your mother went off to chapel while me and Nellie took care of the house but we were not long by ourselves for *Nance came in soon after. When me and Nellie were by ourselves I asked where Auntie Polly was, she hesitated for a minute then she says, "Why to Manster" so then I said "Why that is a long way off isn't it." So she says "Yes to Cheagle" So you are got into a funny part of the country.

Your Mother told me that Lady Vernon had written to you on Friday so I expect that she would tell you all about the people at Hanbury. Poor Polly Barley is no better. I have not been to see her yet but your Mother told me that Polly has said she should like a wood pigeon so I shot her one today and shall take it over tomorrow night. Old Nance had a bit of a squabble with the Matron up at The Firs last week. Nance flared up at her and told her what she thought about her so the Matron told her she would tell Lady Vernon on Monday, so I don't know how it is settled but you will hear all about it on Friday for Nance or Mother will write to you then. Your Mother is rather anxious about you yet. She told me that when Mr Baylis came back from taking you to the station and told her that you had got to go by another route and would not get to your destination until 9 o'clock, she was quite upset and was not right again until you wrote to say that you were alright.

She likes me to go and see her and Nellie is quite concerned for she made Mother get out your white teapot and some lump sugar before I came, then when I did not come she says to her Grandmother "I could cry, couldn't you Grandma." She was soon on my knee when I did get there.

Now dear Polly, I must say a little about myself. I am still going on about the same and am quite well. I thought of going to Birmingham about next Monday so when I write again I shall be able to tell you when I shall get my photos. I am glad that you have made such good friends with the housemaids. I will send you three or four of my photos when I get them so you can do what you like with them but tell that gardener that he will have a gamekeeper's fist in his face if he gets annoying you. Tell him I am looking out for him. Dear Polly, I like that letter very much that Miss Mary sent to you. She is a little brick and she writes what she means. I must now conclude for I want this letter to go tonight and it is getting late. Mrs Brown is still improving and all our people are pretty well so having told you all the news I must say goodbye. Sarah and Jane send their love but I have not told them where you are yet.

So with fondest love,
I am ever yours affectionately
ALF
Write soon. Goodbye and God Bless you.

Note: * From now on Polly's sister Ann is referred to by Alf as Nance.

1878

Alf and Polly are farther apart than ever. Alf is working as a gamekeeper in Herefordshire and hopes to have a home for Polly soon. Polly, still needing to support herself, takes a job in Cheadle near Manchester. They both feel impatient with the delays. Alf remains optimistic but Polly is increasingly ill and unhappy.

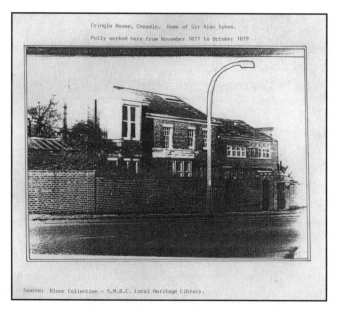

Cringle House, Cheadle, Home of Sir Alan Sykes.
Polly worked here from November 1877 to October 1879

Source: Bloor Collection - S.M.B.C. Local Heritage Library

Rock Hill
Bromsgrove
9th January 1878

My dear Polly,

I was so neared knocked up yesterday that I was not able to write for we had a hard days shooting on Monday and the Ball on Monday night and another days shooting on Tuesday. So I was near done up and I have got such a bad cold that I can't hardly stand up.

Now Polly the first thing I must tell you is about going with the Captain. I have settled to go with him, but it is not just as I wanted it but I have made a fresh agreement with him so that Beard can't humbug me about as he has done here. This is what the Captain said to me!

"Alfred I am very glad that you have made up your mind to go with me to Cowarne. I can't do just yet as you would wish but I will try to do so in the course of time. I want you to go with Beard and get a stock of Game on the estate and then when I have got a little more ready money I will divide the estate into two different beats and you shall have one part and Beard the other. Until then things must go on about the same as they have done here."

So Polly, I think, though things don't look quite bright just now it will be brighter in time. The Captain is going to build two keeper's houses on the estate but not till the Spring and when I have been down there a bit I shall see more about the place and make some different arrangements if I see that things don't go on just as they ought to. I think I can see my way clear to get on nicely if things goes on anything like straight. I am going to this Cowarne about the second week of February so I shant be about here long now. I might have some alterations in my agreement now before I go if I can see that I can better myself in any way. If I do I will tell you.

Now the next thing is the Ball. It came off on the 7th as I told you and a very merry night we all spent. It began about 8 o'clock. Mrs Bourne did not come for it was a wet night. The Captain and the young ladies came and stayed through 2 or 3 dances. I think we had 16 dances altogether. There was about 50 other servants from most of the gentlemen's houses around. I had 5 dances and was knocked up for I found dancing very hard work for you know I am not used to it and another thing I am not a very excellent dancer. Rather awkward. I can't tell you who was the belle of the Ball for everybody was very neatly and tidily dressed and all could dance much about the same as one another. But I heard in the house that a Miss Amiss (Joe Carwell's sweet heart) was considered the most costly dressed, but I did not think so. I thought Sarah Bradley was dressed as nice as any of them. She wore a white dress and blue ribbons about it. I think her dress was not white muslin much stronger stuff than that. Anyhow she looked the best dressed to my eye.

She is going to write to you one of these days so I expect she will tell you all about it. We kept the Ball rolling until half past 6 on Tuesday morning so you can guess that we made the most of it. I should have enjoyed myself a great deal better if I had had you there for I was one by myself for there was nobody there that I took any interest in but I can't grumble for I enjoyed myself very much and it was easy to get a partner to dance with. Everyone was ready when they were asked.

Dear Polly I did not go to Hanbury on Sunday for I was out at work all day. I shall go next Sunday. I have only 6 photos taken. I will send you 1 more next week. I must now say goodbye for it is post time and Herb is waiting to take it.

So with fondest love,
I am yours faithfully
ALF

Rock Hill
Bromsgrove
23rd January 1878

My dear Polly,

Here I am sound and well again so I am going to tell you a few of the incidents that have happened at this respected domicile since I wrote last. First of all I have got rid of my cold so I am in a perfect state of health (as Ted Vale says). The next is that I have got to go down to Much Cowarne as soon as I like after tomorrow, but I don't suppose that I shall go for a week or 9 days for I am not quite ready. For after I leave here I shall have to lead a Batchelor's life again, but I hope it wont be for long. The next thing Polly, is Fred's photo has arrived so I am going to send the one that he gave me to you. I think it is much better taken than mine were and when I have mine taken again, Worcester will be the place that I shall go to.

Please remember me to little Lizzy when you write again and tell her that the Photo that she as got is a bad one if she thinks that I look ill, for the day I had it taken I was as well as ever I was in my life. It was the bad light that made it turn out so bad. I have got one here that looks twenty times as light as that one. Dear Polly I shant go to Cowarne before you write again. I will send you a line or two the day that I go so that you will know. Mrs Bourne is not going away yet. I believe that they are going to stay another week at Grafton yet. I have not seen Sarah to speak to her since you wrote so I have not been able to deliver your message. I was glad to hear of your going to the Pantomime. Which performance did you see? The afternoon or night? I shall learn some of the little ditties that are on the bit of paper that you sent me - they are rather good.

Dear Polly you must forgive me for thinking bad of you the other week for my thick head is always fancying some nonsense or another. I had got a cold and a lot of work to do and I suppose that made me bad tempered but now I am all serene again. I hope that your cold is got better and your cough too. You must take great care of yourself for this weather is very trying. Often weak people fall off this time of year. I always feel uneasy when you say that you have got anything the matter with you for I think you are knocking yourself up again. You know that people can kill themselves with kindness as well as with hard work. I don't want you to kill yourself with either just yet. Ted Vale and Jane Graves asked where you were on Saturday. They wished to be remembered to you. Ted Vale has been in Shropshire for more than a week spending his Christmas holiday with his sweetheart at her home. This is the second time that he as been. He is getting quite grand.

Did I tell you that our Cottage Hospital is opened about 3 weeks and is nearly full of patients. Mrs Phillips that Mr Hooper used to lodge at Hanbury is one of the patients. I don't know what is the matter with her. I have not been to see Polly Barley since you have been away. I don't hardly like to go unless I could meet with some of them and go in with them. I should like to see them again before I go away. Your Mother thinks that I have never seen them and she tells me what sort of a woman your Aunt is and how she talks and what little Jessie is like and all sorts. She little thinks that I know them all. I have never told her that I have been.

Dear Polly you have been away nearly 3 months now - it is eleven weeks. Time flies very fast. I am beginning to look forward to the time when we shall meet again. Now I must say goodbye for I have told you all the news.

I shall have something to tell you next time I write. I shall go next Sunday I expect. For the last time for a while. Now goodbye and God Bless you.

With fondest love
            I am yours ever affectionately
                        ALF

I will send you the paper next week.

OPENING OF BROMSGROVE COTTAGE HOSPITAL
1st January 1878

1st June 1876

A meeting of the representatives of various Friendly Societies was held. Chairman Mr Coxall, a new resident, said there was a need to provide a cottage hospital. A Hospital Sunday was arranged to collect money.

29th June 1876

The Friendly Societies were in favour and willing to contribute annually. A committee of town's people was set up and approached the Bailiff, Mr Prosser, to ask for a Town Meeting. A requisition was signed.

18th July 1876

A Town Meeting was held at the Town Hall and a committee appointed. There were "almost insurmountable difficulties." After several months of searching, no suitable site had been found for building, or suitable premises that were immediately attainable for conversion. The committee persevered.

19th January 1877

A row of cottages on Mount Pleasant was leased for fourteen years at £32 per annum on the understanding that the premises could be reconverted at the end of the term if required. They were converted free of charge by architect Mr Cotton.

The Cottage Hospital

The building contained 3 lofty wards of 3 beds each, an operating ward, kitchen, suitable appartments for matron etc,. The wards were well lit, ventilated and the walls were decorated with pictures. A corridor ran the whole length of the front. A carriageway at the back catered for accidents and opened into an operating ward which led to an accident ward.

Grand Opening on New Year's Day 1878

There was a procession from the Institute at 12 o'clock to the hospital. Among those present were Mrs Corbett (wife of Mr.J.Corbett, MP and president of the hospital), Dr Batten (Medical officer in charge), Mrs Bourne and the Misses Bourne (Grafton Manor). A blessing was given by Rev. G. Murray and a report on the progress of the hospital was given by Mr. Nichols in which he said that £500 had been needed, of which £414 6s 3d had been collected.

Dr.Swete (Worcester) congratulated everyone and said it was only 20 years since the first Cottage Hospital had been established. It would be an inestimable blessing to the poor, for it would be open to all. No one would be refused on religious grounds. He asked people to consider the agony of having to travel 12 - 14 miles to Worcester or Birmingham, but pointed out that now patients could be attended at once. The hospital was not just for accidents but for illness so that family members could continue their usual occupations.

The hospital was then opened for inspection and hundreds visited the building. The first patient was accepted the following day.

From: Bromsgrove, Droitwich and Redditch Weekly Messenger.

The Little Elms
Much Cowarne
Nr. Bromyard
20th February 1878

My dear Polly,

At last I have got a few minutes, so I will try and tell you what has happened to me these last few days. I have got to my lodgings and I am very comfortable. My land-lady is a widow and there is no children only one son and he is grown up. They are very nice people and I don't regret the change that I have made; for Cowarne in a few years and a little expense will be made a nice place. It is a place that have been great-ly neglected. The farmers are much better sorted than they are about Bromsgrove. They all wear smock frocks and goes to work just the same as any other of the men. And all the people around are very good natured, the best I ever saw, and another thing it is a capital place for cider and hops.

The people about say it is a very pretty place in the summer when the fruit and hops are about. I shall be able to tell you more about it when I have been here a little longer. There is not much game here yet; but it is a capital place for game and in the course of a few years I believe we shall have as good a lot as anybody. There is a few pheas-ant now and a few partridges but not half like they were at Grafton. Yes Polly, I think that you and I could get on here very well when things are put a bit straight for every-body that are at Cowarne are doing very well. The two old keepers came here very poor men, now the head keeper is going to have one of the farms on the estate and the other one has saved about £500 and neither of them have not had very big wages.

The head man had 16/- and the under man had 13/- per week so that was not anything very grand and these things give me a little hope of getting on. The worst of the place is it is such a long way from any town. It is 7 miles from Bromyard and 8 from Hereford. A carrier goes to Hereford twice a week so we can get anything we want by him. There is a shop or two about so we are not very bad off.

Dear Polly, you asked if there was a church near. There is one on the estate and two or three a short distance away. The church on the estate belongs to the Captain. It is going to be rebuilt this year and going to have 3 more bells put to it, there will be 6 then. The Captain is going to build the tower to it in memory of poor Master Bertie. The place will be all alive with workmen this summer so we shant be by ourselves.

Now Polly I must thank you for the Valentine that you sent me. It is the best worded one that ever I had sent me. It was the only one that I had. I hope that you had an armful. Dear Polly, have you heard from Nance lately? Has she sent you Alfred Ward's address? I shall be able to write to him in the course of a few days. We are got nearly settled. Give my love to your Mother when you write and let me know how Polly Barley is if you hear. I don't think that she will last long. The month of March is a very trying month for people like her, poor girl. I feel sorry for her for she is so young and in such good spirits too. It is turned 3 months since you went away. It will soon be 12. I keep counting the months but they go by very slow but if I keeps counting I shall win. Now Polly I think that I have told you most all that I have got to tell.

I shall write to your Mother perhaps this week. I shall see what turns up. I have taken to my old day to write and I will try and keep to it. Now My Polly goodbye for the present, hoping this will find you all serene as it leaves me.

Yours ever affectionately,
ALF

Write on Sunday

Little Elms
Much Cowarne

St. Pauls, Worcester
19th March 1878

Dear Polly,

I was at Hanbury yesterday for a few hours and went to see your Mother who I am glad to say seemed pretty well. She told me you were expecting a letter from me, which was news, as I was fully under the impression that I had written last. I know I intended to write and then thought, I suppose, that I had done so. I beg your pardon for my very stupid mistake. How are you getting on now? I hope you are stronger. Do you like Cheadle? I like Worcester very much. There is plenty of work as ours is a large and very poor parish. We have about 4,000 people - all poor, unless it be the publicans who I am sorry to say drive much too good a trade for the welfare of the people.

I am afraid I have very little news to tell which could by any possibility be interesting to anyone who is unacquainted with St. Pauls. One goes on at much the same thing day after day until one can't think of any news at least one does not know any. I began this some hours ago and have since been out all the afternoon to one sick or poor person after another so I have no more to tell than if I had finished this when I began it. We had a concert in the schoolroom about a fortnight ago for the poor. It was very successful the room being crammed as full as ever it could hold and I'm sorry to say a good many people could not get in at all. We have much better congregations now than at first. We have daily morning and evening prayer. No one comes at present in the mornings but there are generally a nice few in the evening. I will conclude with love and hoping to hear from you as soon as you can make it convenient to write. I remain your affectionate friend

M.DOUGLAS

Note: Mary Douglas has left Hanbury Rectory and moved with her parents to work in the parish of St. Paul's, Worcester.

Much Cowarne
Nr Bromyard
31st March 1878

My dear Polly,

I was very sorry when I read your letter to see that you are not well. I hope that you wont be knocked up again. If you feel that you can't do your work don't stay to worry yourself but come home, for I know that you would sooner work yourself to death than put anybody to any inconvenience, but you must not do it. You will ruin yourself for life if you do. I am glad that you told me what the doctor told you about your teeth. I have thought a good many times that your teeth had something to do with your health and if I were you I should take the doctor's advice and then see what you are like afterwards. But if you have any sound teeth don't have them taken out, only the decayed ones, for dear Polly, you know that nothing artificial is like the real thing and I don't think that you will find false teeth like your own.

There is a good many people about nowadays that have false teeth and no doubt it is a good invention. Captain Bourne wears a set but I don't think that I should like them for myself. But if it is anything to improve your health I shall be glad to hear of it being done, but I will leave it to you. Of course you know what is best for your own comfort, but I do sincerely hope that you won't be ill again for I don't know what I should do if you were to. We are so far from each other or else we could advise one another and work things out for the best. As it is we must help ourselves and make the best of it but I hope it will only be for a short time and then we will fight our battles together.

Dear Polly, I expected to hear that you were not alright. For the last 3 or 4 days before I had your letter a sort of dullness came over me and I could not shake it off. It has happened once or twice before but this time my landlady noticed it and asked me what was the matter so I told her I did not know but I expected some bad news and sure enough I had some. Dear Polly do you think that we are farther off one another in heart as we are in distance? No, I say not. We are farther in distance but closer in our feelings towards each other. I have thought a good deal about you lately and I think the more I think about you the better I love you. So Polly you must think like me and look forward to the time when we shall meet again and I hope, not to part for a long time. That is what I am doing and that is what keeps me in such good spirits. I think that I am better now in health than ever I was. Beard says that I look better now than ever I did since he as known me, so I don't think the work will knock me up. I won't let it and you must be the same.

It as been very wintery here ever since last Saturday week. It as snowed every day until today but now I think it will go. I hope it will for the time of year is coming on that we might expect some finer weather.

Dear Polly, do you think that our letters get fewer and farther between? It is true we don't write so regular but we always write in the same spirit as of old, but I can't write here as I could at home for you know that anybody can't do as they like when in lodgings. I think a letter unexpected does more good than one that is expected. It do me. I am writing this on Sunday but you wont have it until Tuesday for there is no post out from here on Sunday. I am glad to hear that little Lizzy is getting on so well. Please remember me to her when you write.

You must send me a bit of wedding cake if you get any from Wimbledon. I should like to see them gals again. When we get settled we will invite them won't we? Now Polly I think I must shut up or else I shant have anything to say in my next letter. Did you get the paper I sent you? That young man that murdered his sweetheart is to be hung tomorrow.

Now goodbye with fondest love.
Believe me to be yours most affectionately
ALF

Recipe for toothache.

Take a piece of clean cotton and dip it in a strong solution of Ammonia and put it to the tooth that is affected, it may cause you to laugh but that wont hurt you. The pain will be gone.

Much Cowarne
Nr. Bromyard
April 15th 1878

My dearest Polly,

I am always late now but better late than never. I should have written yesterday but the house was full of folks so that I hadn't got a chance. Now that I am writing I will tell you all that I can think of and I hope that it will find you in better health now. First of all I must tell you that I am alright and getting on pretty tidy. I think that I shall soon want you to help me. I do think that you are already mine only I am letting you out for a holiday and that I shall soon want you home again.

My landlady quizzes me sometimes and wants to know something but I don't tell her. She suspects me. I have never told her about you but she guesses that I am engaged, for last Sunday week she went out to Tea, to an old man's and his daughters. So she asked me before she went which I was going to send my love to so I told her that I had not got any love for either of them but she could give my respects to all of them. So then she said "Now Alfred I am sure that you have got somebody." I did not tell her then that I had, so she isn't sure yet. I should like you to come down here and see how things are going on. I know you would like it. Mrs Beard often asks when are you going to spend a week with her. She would be glad to see you and so would Beard. He often talks about you and always seriously. I get on very well with him now. He is not like the same man as he used to be. So if you think of having a holiday this summer you will know where to come to. I should so like to see you.

Yesterday afternoon was so nice I wished many a time that you were within walking distance. I wouldn't have been by myself long but the time flies fast. We shall soon meet again. You have been at Cheadle more than 6 months now. The months pass one by one waiting for nothing. Dear Polly, I wrote to Nance about 10 days ago, a good long letter, and told her to let her mother have it so that I shant have to write to her for a little while for I have not got much time to spare, only on a Sunday. Then generally our house is full of one and another. I always makes time to write to you for I always get uneasy if I lets it go over a week. I often writes in a hurry. That is the reason that it is such a scribble sometimes.

I am sorry that someone opened A.Ward's letter for it would expose him to some order. I wrote a good stiff letter to him but not such a one that I should have done if I had my own way. Now Polly, I think that I have told you all that I can think about just now. I must tell you more next time if I can find out that I have forgot anything. So I must say goodbye with fondest love
I am yours most affectionately
ALF

Goodbye and God Bless you. Tell me what the Dr. says about your teeth next time you write.

Addressed to:
Miss Weaver, Cringle House, Cheadle, Manchester.
Postmarked:
Bromyard   AP   16   78
Manchester   17   AP   78

Much Cowarne
Nr. Bromyard
April 29th 1878

My dearest Polly,

I am so sorry to have kept you so long without a letter. I intended to have wrote the next day after I received yours but I am so busy now that I have to wait my chance. We have got a lot of strange people at work on the estate so it takes Beard and I all our time to look after them. They are felling timber and peeling the bark of it so I hope as soon as that is done we shall get rid of them for they worry us a good bit at this time of year now the pheasants are nesting and laying about but for all that I am getting on alright.

Dear Polly, I am so sorry that you are not so well. I wished for once in my life that I was a rich man then I could try and do something for the benefit of your health. I can't feel contented while I know you are so unwell. I can't tell what to do to benefit you in any way but I do think that the Manchester air don't agree with you. You ought to be in a country place far from any smoky dirty town. It almost seems a pity that you went to Manchester. I did not like the idea of it at first but that I think was my own selfishness for I never thought but what you would be alright there or else you should have stayed at home a little longer and I would have worked for you. But I hope as the warm weather comes you will get around again for this time of year is very trying to all weak people. I have good faith that you will get around all right again soon for I believe it is only weakness that you are suffering from.

I shall be glad when I can have you down here. I am sure this country air would suit you too. I am heartier since I came down here than I have been for some time. Dear Polly, do not trouble yourself about what my people at home would say if they knew that you were not well for they know that it would not make any difference to me. I am the same Alf you knew at Grafton 4 years ago. The same that stuck to you at Wimbledon and have done so ever since and if it please God that I should, I will marry you in spite of all that people say, for Polly, I can love no other girl as I have loved you. So make yourself at rest about that.

Dear Polly I think that the dentist that you went to is a very dear one. I never heard of such a price as £18 (22½ weeks pay) for a set of teeth. You could get a very nice set for about £7/10/- at Bromsgrove and I thought that was dear. I think you had better stop a bit and perhaps you will see something more reasonable. For I think £18 a very unreasonable price. It is 15/- per tooth while you can get one single tooth put in for 5/- at any dentist in this part of the country. I think Manchester is rather a dear place if dentistry as the ruling of it. Polly, I sent you the Bromsgrove paper last week to see Jessie Cole's wedding in it. I was rather surprised for I did not think it was so near. I wonder if she wore that dress that you sent her back. If she did I should think that she looked rather lovely. Now Polly I must say goodbye once more. I have not got any news to tell you this time. All is about the same. Please give my love to your mother when you write and all enquiring friends, hoping, dear Polly, that this will find you in better health. With fondest love,

I am ever, yours affectionately,

ALF

Much Cowarne
Nr. Bromyard
Sunday June 9th 1878

My dear Polly,

You will think that I have forgotten you altogether this time, as I have been so long in answering your letter. I have not had time for anything lately. I hope it wont last long. I can't get 5 minutes to myself now. We have got nearly 200 young pheasants now and they take a great deal of looking after. With that and other work we have got our hands full at present, but we must not grumble but look forward to easier times for I can stand it very well as regards health so I don't care. I think it will be better after this year.

Mr Bourne and the three young ladies are at Cowarne now but the weather is so dreadful wet that they can't enjoy themselves as they would like to. The young ladies seem quite delighted with the place, they think it a lovely place and say they would like to live here but Mrs B don't like it so much; but I think she will like it when it is put straight and their house built. It will make a great difference. Miss Beatrice is grown quite a woman. She wears a long dress and looks quite *nobby. I was quite surprised when I saw her, she is as big as her mother and a great deal like her. They will all soon be grown up. How the time flies. It don't seen long since they were quite little things.

Dear Polly, how are you getting on now and what sort of a lot of fresh fellow servants have you got and how are you getting on together? I am beginning to look forward to the time when we shall meet again. You have been at Cheadle nearly 7 months now. It will soon be 12.

I often wish that you were close here so that I could see you oftener. I don't think that there was ever a two parted as we have been. We have never been together very much but always a long distance apart. I hope that this is the last long distance that will be between us, but let us hope for the best, think for the worst and take whatever comes. That's the way isn't it, and always leads to the best at last.

Dear Polly, have you heard from home lately. How are everybody and how are they getting on? Give my love to them. My Mother and Louey and Frank have been very middling lately. I think they are getting better now. They send their love to you.

The fever is very bad about Bromsgrove and a good many have died lately. Have you heard from Sarah since she went home. I have heard rather a bad account of her this last week. I heard that she had got into a mess (The F___W_y) but I don't know how true it is. I heard it from Mr Stubbs the butcher at Grafton. Please don't say anything about it until we are sure. Time will show. I hope she has not been such a fool.

Dear Polly, I will send you a Hereford paper this week then you will see the account of the Dinmore Murder. It is rather a mysterious affair and causes a great deal of excitement about here as it is close to us. I don't think that I have much more to say this time, so I must say goodbye. Albutt and Stubbs asked after you yesterday.

They are staying at Cowarne with the missus. Now Polly I must say goodbye. Hoping this will find you quite well.

With fondest love, I am your ever faithful
Write soon.   ALF

Note: * 'Nobby' means superior or smart.

Much Cowarne
Bromyard
June 24th 1878

My dearest Polly,

I am doing rather an unusual thing in writing twice to your once, but I have got an hour to spare today, so I think I can't do a better thing than write to you. I have not got much news to tell you for I have not heard from home lately. When I wrote my last letter the Captain and Mrs Bourne were here. It was very wet all the time they were here and the day they went away it was fine and as been fine ever since. Albutt and the butler and one of the girls were here but they don't like Cowarne, it is too dirty for them. I told them that they were seeing Cowarne in its worst state but they would not have it. If they were here today I know they would tell a different story, it is beautiful here today. Most of the farmers have begun mowing and the weather looks promising at present for a good hay harvest. I hope it will hold dry for many reasons.

Dear Polly, I wish you could be down here for a week or so just to see the place. I know it would suit your task especially in fine weather. The Captain, I think, is going to build two keeper's houses and going to make the present keeper's houses into farms. That is his idea at present but he may alter his mind again. As soon as I can see things a little straighter I shall be able to tell you where we shall live and then I shall ask you to come and see the place, then I hope you wont refuse. If you do you will perhaps see me at Cheadle after you. You might see me as it is, some fine day. I have had an invitation from a young man living at Manchester. He was at Cowarne all Whit Week and he made me accept his invitation but I am not sure that I shall. If I do it will be on purpose to see you. It wont be just yet anyhow. Dear Polly, it is Bromsgrove Fair day today and I believe it will be a very good pleasure fair this year. I believe that there is two Theatres. There are lots of shows of different sorts. It is grander than it has been for some years, so I have heard. I should like to have had a look round it with you. I should like to have a bit of an outing now. I have not been anywhere or to anything since I have been here. Is there any Picnics at Manchester this year and how do you get on amongst it. Shall you come to Hanbury Harvest Home this year? Albutt, when he was here, bet me 5/- that you would and that I should be there too. He went home and told my brother that you and I were coming to the Harvest Home but I know I shant go if you don't. I should like to be there with you.

Now Polly, I have not got any more news this time, but I hope you are all serene and in good health as I am happy to say I am. Mrs Beard often says "I wonder if Mary will come down here this year." I tell her I don't know. I hope some day to say yes. Dear Polly, have you heard from home lately? How are they all. I have not had time to write to your mother lately. Please give my love to her and hope she and all are quite well. I expect little Nelly will be big Nelly before we see her again. Let me know all the news when you write.

Now Polly, goodbye and God Bless you.
With fondest love, I am ever yours
ALF

Much Cowarne
Bromyard
July 24th 1878

Dear Polly,

You seem to be rather doubtful about us ever seeing one another again and that we shall always be parted as we are now. I will tell you how I think it is. It has always been our lot to be parted, and always long distances and we have not enjoyed so many long walks and pleasant chats as others may have done and we see others doing different to what we are doing but, Polly, our future may be as bright as those that see each other every day. I often think that it is a long time since I saw you and that I ought to be nearer to you but I can tell you that we are doing what hundreds can't do and that is we can trust one another. So Polly let us look for brighter things and put our trust in God and all will come right in the end.

I keep looking forward at the future and I am trying to gain one point and I think after a bit I shall gain it. That one point is, Polly, a comfortable home and a happy life in the future. Sometimes it seems a long time to wait but then I think if we can get a comfortable home at first it will be better than shifting about. So I think we are taking the wisest course. So Polly, cheer up and keep looking forward and you will see that we are on the right track. I should like to see you oftener. I should not mind if it

142

was every day but I know it can't be, but yet it is not impossible. So Polly think with me, when the proper time comes we shall meet again and it may be very soon or perhaps a 12 month. So cheer up and keep up your spirits until then.

Dear Polly we ought to be at Bromsgrove this week. It is the Agricultural Show there and I believe it will be a very good one for most all the gentry round takes an interest in it. It will last 3 days. It is the first time that anything of the sort has happened in Bromsgrove so it will be a treat to a good many. I am sorry to learn that Nance is so middling. I was not aware that she was obliged to give up her work nor I did not think that her thumb was so bad. If I was in her place I would take it easy for a month or two and take no notice what people said about going back to the Firs. I think she ought to stay away. I will write to her and give her my advice and as for Nelly being made into a boy, you tell her that Boys are made of pepper and snuff and all such dirty stuff while little girls are made of sugar and spice and all that is nice. It is much better to be a little girl. The suit must stop for her little brother when she has one.

I had heard that Herb kept company with some young woman in Bromsgrove but I did not know who it was and I don't think that I knows the girl now. The weather has been very hot this last week. It very nearly melted me out of my clothes. I thought two or three times that people would see me clothes walking about and nobody in them. We have finished Haymaking and begun Harvest but we are not so busy as we have been. So now Polly I think that I must draw to a close. I would have sent you a paper but there is nothing in it that I thought you would care to see.

Hoping this will find you in better spirits, I say goodbye, with fondest love believe me. Yours most affectionately

ALF

Remember me to all at home when you write.

Much Cowarne
Bromyard
July 30th 1878

Dearest Polly,

I think that I am making up for lost time in writing to you so quick. You blowed me up for not writing oftener. Now what are you going to do to me for writing very near by return of post. I think you ought to make some allowance. What do you think about it. I have got something to tell you this time which I expect you wont care to know. That is I have spoken to Captain Bourne about a house for us. He seemed quite delighted and asked me all the particulars: how you was and where you was and how soon I should want the house and if you were the same that I used to have and everything concerning the affair. I told him that I should want the house by this time next year, that is if you would agree to it. He told me that he would do everything he could to make us comfortable.

Dear Polly, I have well considered the course I am taking and I think that I am doing the thing that is right as regards you and myself so I hope you will agree with me. There might be a change in things before the time comes but it wont effect me in any way. I have calculated everything. I find that it will cost me about £25 or £30 to make a comfortable home and begin in the right way and I shall have that amount by next June if I have any sort of luck and then after that a house rent free with a good garden and other privileges besides with 16/- per week. I fancy that I shall be as well off as anybody about. So, dear Polly don't talk about waiting years for I almost lose myself when I hear anybody talking about years.

I am sorry you brought up that grievance for I don't care to remember it and perhaps it was for the best. So please let it drop for the future. Dear Polly you must excuse me for writing in this form to you but it is just to let you know how I intend doing. It is right that you should know so that you can improve my way if you can see anything that would be likely to be better for us for you know two heads are better than one and 12 months is ample time for us to think about it when you write next time.

Now for the news. I was at a fire at one of the farms on the Estate last Saturday. Nearly all the buildings were burnt down and it was a hard job to save the house at one time for the fire was got such a hold of the barns before it was discovered. It is not known how it was set on fire. The Captain was there and worked like a tinker. It is a good loss to him. It is the third fire that has been on the estate since he bought it. It was not insured. I will send you the paper this week so that you can see the news from about home. Herb is coming to see me next Saturday, then I shall hear all the news. I think all at home are quite well. Give my love to your mother and all the rest of the folks when you write.

    Now Polly I must say goodbye for the present
      With fondest love I am yours affectionately
                ALF

Much Cowarne

Bromyard

Sept. 1st 1878

Dearest Polly,

I did not receive your letter until Saturday afternoon, too late to write back again so I am writing on Sunday but you won't get it before Tuesday as there is no post out here on Sunday. When I first saw in your letter that you wanted to know the nearest station to Cowarne I thought you were coming. I very near shut up the letter without finishing it and am now answering it. All the stations are a long way from Cowarne but I think one called Stoke Edith is the nearest and the * gainest to get to. So Polly that is the one I shall go to to look for my parcel.

I think you are very good to think of me as you do. I must think of you some day in return but I hope the day will soon come when we can share what we have with one another. I shant say any more about you coming down here again situated as you are. I was not aware that you were in such an unlikely place. I should think Miss Knoderen is a perfect cure. Is she an old woman or a young one. A young one I should think, by her ways. You will very soon be the oldest servant on the ground. If they continue to leave as they have this last 12 month you will very soon be having a pension. I wrote to your Mother last week and told her all the news. I told her that I should come and see them at Christmas and try and get you there too but I must write and tell her that you are fixed at Cheadle until next Summer. Ted Vale told Herbert that Hanbury Harvest Home was next Thursday and Mother sent word by an old man that was coming to Cowarne that I was sure to be there but I shant.

Thursday is our first shooting day so we shall be busy but if you had been there I would have got someone to do my work that day. As it is I shant trouble. We have got next year if we live and have good luck.

I believe there was grand doings at Bromsgrove last week on account of Lord Windsor's coming of age. Two oxen were roasted and a grand display of fireworks. Herb is going to send me a paper with all the affair in it. I will send it to you. I did not get last week's paper until last Friday and then I did not think it worth sending, there was nothing in it. The Captain has been very ill with inflamation since he went away from here on Saturday week but I think he is better now. I don't think that I have much more to tell you this time for all things are about the same. We expect Hop picking to begin here this next week, there is a lot of pickers come. Now Polly I think I must say goodbye. I must write a longer letter next time.

So goodbye Polly, with fondest love,

I am ever yours

ALF

Note: * 'gainest' means most convenient.

COMING OF AGE OF LORD WINDSOR
(Later Earl of Plymouth)

Meeting convened

After receiving a requisition, the Bailiff (Dr. Wood) convened a meeting at Bromsgrove Town Hall, to consider the most fitting way to make public recognition of the event.

Mr Jefferies, Chairman, invited ideas. He also said that at a previous preliminary meeting of some gentlemen of the town, it had been suggested that an illuminated address signed by the Chairman, be presented to Lord Windsor.

The Vicar was not present because he "didn't care to attend public meetings" but his representative said he supported the proposition.

Mr Sanders suggested a whole ox roast. This was approved.

Mr Corbett proposed a committee of twelve persons.

Mr Prosser suggested planting New Road with trees and changing the name to Windsor Road.

Mr Jefferies said the meeting had no powers to change the name and mixing the two projects of ox roast and tree planting was deemed impracticable.

Mr Prosser then suggested that if any money was left over from the ox roast it could form the nucleus of a fund for tree planting and he recommended the Local Board change the name.

The Rev. Massey referred to the kindness of Lord Windsor in arranging the building of a parsonage for All Saints Church and suggested the roasting of two oxen instead of one. This was acclaimed.

A committee was formed and £35 subscriptions promised. By the weekend nearly £76 had been subscribed and two oxen had been purchased by the committee to be roasted on Wednesday. The oxen were of prime quality and weighed 40 pounds.

PROGRAMME FOR THE COMING WEEK

Tuesday - Address presented by tenants to Lord Windsor, emblazoned address presented by Bromsgrove inhabitants and address presented by Redditch inhabitants.
This to be followed by: Dinner for tenants and others in large marquee in park.

Wednesday - Labourers and school children will be regaled. The oxen will be roasted and there will be other refreshments for the poor. The afternoon will be a general holiday and businesses in the town will be closed.

Thursday - Garden party for tenants and tradespeople.

Friday - Cricket match and a number of sports for both men and women, and boys and girls. There will be a large number of prizes.

From: Bromsgrove, Droitwich and Redditch Weekly Messenger. 24th August 1878

Much Cowarne
Bromyard
September 24th 1878

Dearest Polly,

I am so sorry to have kept you so long without a letter, but I have been very unwell for this last fortnight and I have had a terrible lot of walking about to do, that it has kept me on very nearly night and day too. We have got people from all parts here hop picking and they are not the best of characters either and they are after everything that they can lay their hands on and some of them more. They will have all they can see if it is to be had. So having such a rough lot to deal with it has caused us a lot more work.

Dear Polly don't be alarmed at me being a little poorly. It is only a cold and it will soon be better. At least I hope so. I have had it a fortnight now and I feel a little better today. I have not had to give over work through it and I don't think that I shall have to. This is just the weather to catch cold. First a warm day then a wet, cold day. It is a very lucky man that don't get one. Dear Polly, Mrs Beard would be very pleased to have your photo if you don't mind sending her one. She asked about you today.

I don't think there is much news to tell you but I heard the other day that Jim Graves (Emily's chap) was married to a girl that he kept company with after he gave up Emily Eaton. I think Ted Vale won't be long. So I think our turn ought to come somewhere in amongst them. We have been in partnership longer than either of them. I hope we shant have to say, as Jim has said already. He told Mother the other day that he had been to church once too many now, so I suppose he repents the day already.

He should have stuck to his first the same as I did. You know I feel quite conceited about my choice and I am apt to tell people so sometimes. I am asked 2 or 3 times every day if it is true that I am going to be married. Sometimes I say yes and sometimes no. It is just according who asks me. I think the Captain told our Steward and then he jokes me about it when others are with me. That is how it gets about. I don't mind it. In fact I rather likes it for when it do come off they can't say I have been sly over it.

I think that my brother Fred is going home from Stafford on Saturday and he wants me to go and have a Sunday with him but I can't go this time, we are too busy. I must go next time. He is going to give me his dog so I must keep in with him. Have you heard from home lately? How are they all? I have not had an answer to my letter yet. Please give my best love to all when you write and tell them that I don't see any chance of coming to see them yet. My Mother and all at home (except Father) are quite well and send their love to you.

Now Polly, I must say goodbye, for it is post time.

    With fondest love, I am ever your loving

ALF

Much Cowarne
Bromyard
Oct 4th 1878

Dearest Polly,

I think that this is the only chance that I shall have to write to you before Sunday so I am taking it although it is late at night, and I am very glad to tell you that I am got quite well again. I was very middling for a week or so but I have got beyond it. I wish you could get all right as quick but then you will as soon as you get down here. This is a first rate place for curing people - if they can stand the pure fresh air. Everybody gets well as soon as they come to Cowarne. I hope it will have the same effect on you.

Mrs Beard wants you to come more than ever now. She is very pleased with the photo. She says that you are quite a different sort of person to what she thought you were. She is going to have her photo taken soon then she will send you one of hers. Beard says that photo of yours is not a good one or else you are altered very much from what you were when he saw you. Everybody about here thinks they know what sort of girl you are. I have a dozen different accounts of you in a day. Some say you are little, some say you are big and some one thing and some another. I had to tell one man what I thought about him on Monday for saying you were a poor little thing. He did not say it to me but told my landlady and she told me. If he had said it to me most likely I should have knocked him down - or tried at it, but anyhow I don't think he will say it again - at least not in my hearing. The people about here are good ones for knowing other people's business better than they do their own. That is the worst point they have and they are very cunning in getting hold of it.

If you should happen to stop and talk to anybody I'll bet that they asked where you was going to and what for, so you will know how to deal with them. We are got quite used to them now and are up to all their dodges. Now Polly, I don't think that I have got a lot of news to tell you for I never hear any now. Captain Bourne has been here all day today. He is going back tomorrow. He says that he is quite well but he don't look well. He looks very thin and bad.

Please give my love to your Mother and all at home when you write and tell them that I should like to hear how they all are and how they are getting on. Well Polly, I have not a lot more to say this time for it is getting late. I hope that you will soon be well again. If you continue to get worse at Cheadle it is better that you should go home. I would sooner you did but you can please yourself for I know the country air suits you the best. But Polly please yourself then you will please me for your head is as wise as mine I know.

Polly

Now goodbye dear Polly.
    With fondest love I am ever yours affectionately
ALF

That young man that I told you I knew in Manchester is coming to see you some day so look out for him. He is a littlish chap and he has got light hair and a little whiskers. He is not so tall as I am nor as stout. He wants to see you very bad.

Much Cowarne
Bromyard
Oct. 13th 1878

Dearest Polly,
    I am not half such a good one as you are at answering letters quick. I am rather longer this time than I have been lately but the Captain was down here all last week so I had not much time. He was in a deuce of a temper so we had to look out for ourselves. But now I am writing I must try and make up a good long letter just to make up for last time. First of all I must say that I am quite well and getting on as well as can be expected but the time of year is coming on now that we must expect some changes. I got wet about twice every day this last week but I have not caught a cold through it but I will tell you what we caught instead and that was some poachers. Last Sunday night they were pheasant catching so we happened to catch them. They are the first we have caught since we have been down here. I don't know what they are going to be done with, we have not had them before a magistrate yet. We caught two. There were more of them.
    Well Polly, I don't think there is anything else of importance happened here so I must go on with something else. Do you remember this night 12 months ago. It was that windy night. I don't suppose you have forgot it. We have had some very rough winds here all this last week but nothing like it was that night. It don't seem so long since that night but it is one more year added to our lot. I heard from Nance this last week, she told me that all was well at home. I must have a talk to her again when I see her. She wants me to go over about Christmas and perhaps I shall and perhaps preach her a sermon.
    Your Mother says that she likes the new parson very much so you see there is one in Hanbury parish that likes him, if Jessie Barber don't. You know Polly sometimes I think I should like to go and have a look at the whole lot of them. Just take them by surprise and I think I shall some of these days. Suppose you and I were to go some

Sunday night, wouldn't they stare, especially if there was a lot of them together. We had better do it but I don't see how quite. It is too far to get from Manchester to Hanbury on a Sunday afternoon. Have you had Mr Portman (the young man I knew in Manchester) to see you today. I sent him a note to tell him how to go and what time, and if he did go to write and let you know on Saturday. If you have seen him of course you can judge for yourself what sort of a chap he is but this is my opinion of him. He likes company but he is not a drunken sort. He is a chap that I like very well but he is not just my sort, but he is good company as long as you can keep him in your company. But he is never happy without he is in company with some girl. He is at home with any of them. All the girls about here have kept company with him so I have heard. So that is Mr Portman.

Now Polly, I don't think that I have got a lot more to say this time. I will send you the Worcester paper. There is a stabbing case in it which happened about here. I know the one man very well so I take a little interest in it. Dear Polly I forgot to tell you that I did not have anything to pay for the Mackintosh. Tom Green that used to go to Grafton after Louisa was married last week. Now Polly I really must say goodbye hoping this will find you quite well, hearty and strong as you were this time last year. Mother and all at home send their love to you. All are pretty well.

Now goodbye.

With fondest love I am ever yours affectionately
ALF

Much Cowarne
Bromyard
15th Nov. 1878

My dearest Polly,

You will I dare say think that I have quite forgotten all about you but you see it is not come to that yet although I am a long time about writing but I always manages to write some time or other; so I must ask to be forgiven this time for I don't offend very often and when I do it is not quite my own fault, for I, like you, am busy sometimes. We have been shooting the covers this week for of course, we have had something to do. We have shot all the preserves on Beard's beat but the Captain can't find time to shoot them on mine just yet for he can't get gentlemen to come just now. Cowarne is a fearful bad place to get at now - this time of year. You know it is 5 miles from any Railway Station so it makes it awkward for gentlemen to get backwards and forwards and the Captain has no place to ask them to stay the night, so we have to wait our chance of getting the covers shot.

The Captain is very well satisfied so far for what we have done for him this year and I hope he will always be. People think that gamekeepers have got a nice time of it but they wouldn't if they knew everything. If they saw us starving and standing about night after night as we have to do, they would not envy us our place. Today it has been raining hard all day and we have been out shooting some rough outside woods and I am just come in wet through. I don't think it is anything to be nice about. There is not many that would change with us if they had the chance.

Well Polly, that is enough about that sort of thing and it is a blessing to think that I am in good health through it all, and I trust that you are the same. It is now more than 12 months since we parted and tonight is just such another as that Sunday night was, cold and wet. There is a good many changes since then, some for the good and some for the worst but I think you and I are on the same old footing and I hope that we shall always have the same faith and trust in one another as we have tonight. I am often thinking of our future. In fact it is my only aim just now and there is many a thing that I should like to talk to you about concerning it. That is one reason I should like to see you, but don't put yourself about, it is no hurry just yet. My time will suit yours. I think about going home just for a day as soon as the woods are shot. I shant trouble about it being Christmas or any other time. I shall go as soon as I can but it may be a fortnight or 3 weeks yet.

Well Polly, I have not got much news to tell you for I don't hear much now but Mother told me the other day that Tom Green (Stoke) has got a SON so he is getting quite a family man. Jane has left Grafton at last. She has been gone about a month. I expect she is living independent now. She must have got a good stocking somewhere I know. I have heard that Wilde is going to leave Grafton but I don't know how true it is. Beard was at Grafton last week and he heard it there. If you and I go there again we shall see nobody but strangers there. I should like to know how our old chums gets on. I suppose you have not heard anything of Sarah Bradley lately. I should like to know how she is getting on. I expects Bill at Grafton knows.

Now my Polly, I think that I must draw to a close or I shall have nothing to say next time.

I hope by this time some of your company are gone and you are got quiet again and I hope they have left you in good health. That is the main thing. Please give my best love to your Mother and all at home when you write and tell them that I shall be taking a peep at them some of these days. My Mother sends her love to you and hopes to see you soon.

Now goodbye Polly, with fondest love
    I am ever your affectionate
        ALF

Much Cowarne
Bromyard
8th Dec. 1878

Mother and Father and all at home are quite well and all send their kind love to you and hope you are the same.

My dearest Polly,

I am like you this time. I have to wait until Sunday to get a chance to write. I have been very busy all the week so I could not write before. We shant have so much to do after this week for the Captain is going to shoot the remaining covers on Wednesday if all goes well. He is got a good deal better but he is not got well by a long way. It is worry and self neglect that has brought him to be so bad. If you were to see him now you would not think he was the same man that he was five years ago. He looks awful thin and white. If he don't soon alter and take better care of himself he will be a dead man for I think he looks worse than ever I saw any man look in his life. I think him and Mrs Bourne have been on bad terms lately and that worries me a good bit.

That was a rum job that happened at Grafton a week or two ago wasn't it, but it was a very sad affair for the poor girl. She must have been a foolish thing to have done it.* I believe there has been a regular turn out at Grafton this last week, 6 or 7 gone I believe but what for I can't tell. I expect Grafton is got a rum place to live at now. I have heard that Mrs B has got a regular tyrant to the servants and I have heard that Stubbs (the Butler) is the cause of it. None of the servants like him.

He has been trying to get poor old Wylde the sack but I don't think he will succeed in that. Mrs B would sack him but the Captain won't, so taking things as they appear Grafton is getting no very desirable place for anybody to live at. William (Sal's chap) was among the lot that left last week.

Now Polly, for something else. But first I must tell you how I am getting on. I am getting on alright and quite well thank God and I hope you are the same. We have had a lot of frost here this week and it makes the weather feel like winter. I find it rather cold out watching at night. I don't care how soon I have done. Two more nights after tonight then we have done for a bit. I think that I shall be able to go home on the 21st if nothing happens, so you can tell your mother that I expect to be home by then and I will let her know which day I shall go to see her. Please give my love to them all when you write.

Dear Polly we are getting farther behind then ever for Julia Long is married and so is Ted Vale so we must begin to look sharp and think about it. Ted Vale was very sly about it. Nobody knew anything of it until three weeks after, then my brother Fred happened to meet them both and they asked him to tea with them. You know Ted's wife was an old sweetheart of Fred's. She lived at the Moor Farm at Upton Warren. Ted wants me to go to tea with him when I go home but I don't know that I shall have time for I shall have a lot of folks to go and see and I shant have much time to do it in.

Dear Polly I have heard from that young man at Manchester last week. He has been very ill. That is the reason he has not been to see you but he is better now and he says that he shall try to come to Cheadle about Christmas.

So look out for him. I wish I could get to see you for I have got such a lot to tell you that I can't write. When I do see you I shant be able to leave off talking for weeks, I shall have such a lot to say. Well Polly Christmas is drawing on apace but I think it won't be a happy one or a merry one to many poor creatures for trouble is so bad that people must starve if it don't alter. I hope and trust that things will soon mend for it is a dreadful thing to read in the papers week after week about the great distress that prevails in almost every part of England. This will be the worst winter that our country has encountered for a long time.

Now, my Polly, hoping things will take a turn for the better for all, I say good night and God Bless my darling Polly.

> With fondest love I am ever yours,
> affectionately
> ALF

* A servant was thought to be stealing money. A trap was set and she was caught and dismissed.

Much Cowarne
Bromyard
19th Dec. 1878

My dearest Polly,

I am rather quick in answering your letter this week but as I have not a lot to say this time it will be short and sweet for I am going home on Saturday 21st then I shall write and tell you a lot about everybody and everything. Please tell your Mother if you write to her before I do that I shall go and see her either Sunday afternoon or Monday. If I go on Sunday I should be there by teatime. If I go on Monday I shall have my dinner early and be there by 2 o'clock. I shall call at the Firs for Nance so she had better stay 'till I call for her on Sunday or Monday. I think it would be as well to let Nance know for perhaps she wont be able to get off both days. So you write to Nance and I will write to Mother. Then everything will be right on that score.

I shall write to you again when I get home so you must please excuse this short scribble. If you write to me between Saturday and Tuesday please write home. I shall be back here on Tuesday night.

Now goodbye for the present
      With fondest love, I am yours affectionately
              ALF

Please excuse bad writing for I have written it in a hurry. I don't expect that you will have that young man to see you this Christmas now for he is stopping work and we expect him here.

LOOSE CONTINUATION SHEET.

Reference to Polly being at Clewer two years ago. Polly was in hospital in Clewer at Christmas 1876. So this gives the date for this page as:-
Christmas 1878

.....on such a day. It has been terrible hard weather here for this last month. I expect it has been a bitter hard Christmas for a good many poor creatures. It has begun to thaw a bit today and I hope it will keep on.
    Well Polly, I don't think that I have got a lot more news to tell you this time. Father and Mother send their best love to you and wishes you a Merry Christmas and a happy New Year. Looey has got quite a big girl now. They are a grown out of knowledge nearly. Albert is Telegraph Messenger now and he is grown quite a big lad, nearly as big as me. Now Polly I think I must say goodbye for the present, hoping you are enjoying yourself and making the best of your leisure time. This time two years ago you were at Clewer and I came to see you there, but I haven't the luck to see you this time. There has been a good many changes since then but still you and I are as we used to be and may we ever be the same.

Hoping this will find you quite well. I once more say goodbye and God's Blessing on you my only Polly.
    With fondest love I still remain
           Yours most affectionately
               ALF
Write soon.

1879

Alf moves to South Wales in an effort to secure a gamekeeper's cottage. Polly remains in Cheadle. Nothing is going right. Polly visits Alf with some advice and things finally come to a head when Alf is sacked. He is angry at being let down once too often but he returns home with a new strategy.

Little Elms
Much Cowarne

Much Cowarne
Bromyard
5th Feb. 1879

My dearest Polly,

I was very glad to see a letter from you. I was rather surprised to hear that you thought of leaving Manchester, but I quite agree with you in the course you think of taking. If I were in your place I would not stand any of their nonsense especially if I could not please them. It is always the best way, to leave if you can't please a Master or Mistress or else they are always picking at one. Perhaps Miss Knoderen wont let you leave. Perhaps she will make it worth your while to stay. You will hear what she says when you give her warning. I would sooner you leave though and come somewhere here just for another few months.

If you come home I should like you to come to Hereford, it is just as near and I could meet you at Barr's Court (Hereford) Station. I think there is a train that leaves the London Road Station at Manchester about 9.15 in the morning and runs via Crewe and Shrewsbury and gets to Hereford about 2.30. That will be as good a way as any. You could get to know the station. If you come, try and come either on a Wednesday or a Saturday then you could come and stay a night at Cowarne for there is a carrier goes to and from Cowarne on them days. I should be very glad to see you. I dare say you wont leave before your month is up. Then you see that will be March so there is plenty of time to make arrangements about that. I thought I would just mention it so that you could think about it. Whether you come to Cowarne or not I think Hereford is your best way for you wont have to change but above once. Well Polly, think about it and let me know the next time you write.

I have had a dreadful cold for these last 3 weeks but it is a little better now. We had a dreadful accident happen here on Wednesday fortnight. One of our farmers was coming home from Hereford market at night when just below our house the cart was pitched over and the man and his wife was thrown out. The man was killed on the spot and the woman was so badly hurt that her life was despaired of for about a week but now she has got the turn and is going on first rate. They are young folks and there is 2 little children. It cast quite a gloom over the place. I had just done writing my last letter to you and got to bed when my landlady was fetched to them. I sent Herb a paper with an account of it in. I will ask him to send it to you.

It is 12 months on Thursday since we came to Cowarne so we begin to know something about it now. It is not a very choice place to come to just now for this last lot of snow is just going and the dirt is pretty plentiful about. I hope by March it will have dried up a bit. I don't think the Captain is going to build here for a time yet for I have heard that he has taken a fine mansion not far from here called Cheyne Court but how true it is I don't know but I think it is most likely he means to give up Grafton anyhow. I have not heard from any of the Grafton folks since I was there at Christmas. I never by any chance hear of Sarah Bradley. I suppose she is gone off our list. Do you ever hear of little Lizzy that used to be at Wimbledon. I should like to know how she is getting on. I suppose the other Lizzy is married long since. Well Polly I dont think there is any more news this time. All our folks at home are much about the same. Please remember me to your Mother and Nance when you write. I was glad to hear that they were well. Has Nance left the Firs yet? Please write soon and tell me how you are getting on and all the news. Now Polly, goodbye, hoping this will find you quite well.

With fondest love,
      I am ever yours affectionately
           ALF

Much Cowarne
Bromyard
5th March 1879

Please give my love to your mother and Nance when you write.

My dear Polly,

As you thought I had forgotten you last time I wrote, I am writing directly after reading yours so that you may think that I am just remembering you again but Polly I thought we had known one another long enough for you to know better. If we had intended quarreling we should have done it long ago, not now. We ought to be better friends than ever and believe me Polly I think more of you now than ever I did since I have known you because of your untiring and unselfish love for me. Perhaps if we were nearer one another things would seem far more pleasanter. I don't know of any girl that would have kept up the undying love for the man that she loved for so long a time without seeing him as you have done for which I shall be ever indebted to you.

To be nearer to me is one thing why I want you to leave Manchester and come down this way. So Polly I hope that you wont think that I have forgotten you again without you wish to forget me for I don't think that I am worthy of love such as yours, yet it would grieve me much to lose it for it is to attain your love that I have been working these last two years. Was I to lose it, my course would be altered quite different to what it is now. In fact I don't know what I should do. I am just beginning to see the end of the journey that you and I have so long been looking for although not very plain just at the moment but with a little patience I shall succeed in reaching it.

As I told you last time I wrote that Captain Bourne had promised me a house, but it cant be got ready just at present. Well what I intended to do was make it a comfortable home then ask you to share it with me. You know Polly, if you were anywhere

where I could reach you easily I could tell you more and explain things better to you and that is why I want you to come here. I shant make any arrangements with Captain Bourne until I have seen you and you see the place, for it concerns you as much as it does me. So that is how things rest at present.

Dear Polly, you would not have thought that I was going to write again if you had known the reason of me not writing oftener. Although I did not tell you I have not been well for a long time and many a night after I have come in I have not known what to do with myself and when I have wrote I have been that bad that I did not hardly know what I did write. There is not, nor has there been anything very serious the matter with me. Only one cold on the top of another ever since Christmas but now I think I have got nearly rid of them all. I have felt better this last week than I have for some time. This has been such a hard winter that it has tried a lot of us out door folks. I have had a deal of trouble with a lot of the folks round our manor for, in the frost and snow, they would persist in shooting the partridges. I have watched them day after day in the cold. That is where I have cought my colds. I took one of the chaps to Ledbury today but I did not do much with him, made him pay all the expenses. So Polly that is the reason I have not wrote oftener. I may be able to write oftener now but things are so unsettled that it is impossible to say. I hope that I shall see you down here before long then I shant get into any more rows about writing.

I was glad to hear that you had given notice to leave but I wanted to see you before the middle of May and I wanted you to come here on your way home but if you think via Birmingham is the best way I don't mind, and another thing, perhaps by the middle of May things will be a little more settled and some of the dirt dried up for it is fearful dirty here now. So Polly I have not got a lot more to tell you this time but never think me so mean as to give you up without first asking you to release me and giving good reasons for so doing. If I don't write just when you expect me to, wait a day or two before you begin to get such silly thoughts into your head. I shall be busy gardening all my leisure time now for a month so if I don't write you will know what has become of me.

Now Polly I must say goodbye for the night is getting late and I hope this letter will find you quite well and with better feelings towards me.

With fondest love, believe me
              yours affectionately
                  ALF

Addressed to:
  Miss Weaver, Cringle House, Cheadle, Manchester.
Postmarked:
  Bromyard   MR 6 7?
  Manchester MR 7 7?

Much Cowarne
Bromyard
March 16th 1879

My dearest Polly,

Sunday evening is come and for once for a long time I have got a quiet one. I think I can't do better than write a few lines to you. I was very glad to receive your letter on Monday and to see that you were only scolding me and not in earnest the week before. I was glad to hear that you were coming home earlier than May. I think I have better hope of seeing you sooner. I want to see you rather particular and you must look out ready for a long speech when I do see you. I must tell you that I have got to live a batchelors life for a bit all by myself after Beard leaves the shooting box. For the Captain wont hear of me staying where I am as we shall be both on one side of the estate and the workmen on the place have such a lot to do that they can't get the places ready for people to go into. There is four people waiting for their places to be done now, which ought to have been done by the 2nd February and I don't think they will be done before midsummer. So our house will have to stay for a bit, but when you come over you will see more about it.

Dear Polly, the distance from Droitwich to Hereford is about 35 miles but you wont have to go on so far as Hereford. When you come here you will get out at Stoke Edith station. If you get to Droitwich by 1 o'clock you will be able to catch the train that gets to Stoke Edith at 3 o'clock. I shall be able to manage to meet you I dare say with a horse and trap for it is nearly 5 miles away. But I shall be able to see you about that when the time comes.

I have been thinking lately that it would be best for you to go home first before coming here, as I wanted you to at first. For when you leave Manchester you will have all your kit with you and perhaps it would inconvenience you to get it about in a country place like this. So if you go home first and then bring what few things you will want for immediate use with you it will be much better, don't you think so? I do hope you wont be long before you come for I have such a lot to tell you and lots of things to arrange about.

Mrs Beard was asking me today when you were coming. I think she is as anxious to see you as I am. She will spin you a fine yarn when you get here. She says she don't care how soon she gets away for she is tired of the Captain coming bothering her. He has been here all this last week and is going back on Monday. We had a fine week last week and part of this until the Captain came, then it began to snow and rain and has done so ever since. It always snows or rains when he comes. He has never had a fine time of it down here since he bought the place. He looks much better now than he did in the first part of the winter but he does not look like he used to do.

Well Polly, I have not got a lot more to tell you this time. There is no news to tell you and as I hope to see you soon I shall refrain from writing long letters and I hope I shant have to write many more before I see you. I keep on counting the weeks until

Easter. I hope I shant be disappointed in seeing you about then. I can't hardly believe now that I am going to see you again. It seems like a thing of the past or a dream but I hope for a reality. When you write again I hope you will be able to tell me about what day you will be able to come then I must rest contented until the time arrives.

I saw in the paper this week that Lady G.Vernon had made a start at a new Nurses home at Worcester but it will be on a different principle to the one at Hanbury. It will have a good many supporters in the shape of all the leading men of the city and county of Worcester and keep from 12 to 20 nurses. So there will be a tidy lot for somebody to look after. I should think Nance wont tackle that lot. They would polish her off clean in less than a week. Give my love to her and your Mother when you write and tell them that I am quite well. I hope they are the same. Now Polly I must say goodbye for this time. Hoping this will find you quite well as it leaves me at present. No more this time.

    With fondest love
             from your ever loving
                    ALF
Write soon.

Note: This journey was delayed until May 1879 and Polly used slightly later times. See letter of May 7th.

                    Much Cowarne
                    Bromyard
                    April 10th 1879

My dearest Polly,

You will, I dare say, wonder why I am writing back so quick. It is to tell you about my last letter for I was so mad when I read your letter and saw that my last letter was not stamped that I could have broke everybody about their neck and my own too. I would not have had it happened for any money. Not for the value of the postage but for the look of the thing. It looks so bad a letter going into a gentleman's house unstamped. It looks though as if one was too niggedly to pay the postage. I should not have minded so much if it had been anybody but you. I can't hardly write I am in such a passion but Polly I must tell you that it was not my fault and the worst of it is I don't know whose it was but I will find out before I am many days older.

I wrote my last letter to you on a Sunday evening and took it down to the house (what we have to take our letters to and fetch them from) on Monday morning and left a penny for the stamp with the letter and I suppose someone took the penny and the letter was sent off without a stamp. The house where our letters are left is a blacksmith's shop where the postman comes to. There is no delivery at any of the houses on the estate so we all have to fetch and take our letters to and from the blacksmith's without it is sometimes when the postman takes it in his head to bring them but he is not compelled to. The postman always carries stamps with him so if anybody takes their penny down to the blacksmith's he will put the stamp on for them. That is what I did so either the folks at the shop had my penny or the postman, and then forgot to put the stamp on.

But I will see into it and if I can find out which have got it they will hear something, perhaps something that they don't like. So Polly that is how your letter got away from here without being stamped, at least I think so. Please tell me in your next letter if you have received any more letters from me unstamped for if folks will do a thing one time they will do it another.

Dear Polly next Sunday is Easter. I should so much like to be out with you. Most of the folks about here go to see their friends at Easter but I shant be quite alone for my brother Fred is coming down to see me tomorrow (Friday) so I shall be alright I suppose. I must hope to see you about a month from Easter. It will soon slip away. Mrs Beard often says to me "It will soon be May, Alfred!" I think she wants to see you as bad as I do. She is always on about you. She wants it to be fine weather while you are here for she wants to show you about. You will have a job to get away from here. There is lots of folks eager to see you but no one more than I. You must try and get 3 weeks holiday or else I shant hardly see you. I don't care if I can just get a glimpse of you for then I shall have some hopes of seeing you after a bit. You say shall we see any difference in one another. Well I think there wont be much. I can't see any difference in myself and I don't care if I can see you looking as well as you did when you went to Cheadle. But if you look better I shall be all the more pleased, but we shall see if all goes well, I hope ere long.

Dear Polly the Zulu war is a dreadful thing. I read all the accounts that come about. I am much interested in it. I heard today that the Zulus had killed another company of English soldiers about 100 strong. I don't know how true it is. I hope it is not.

Now Polly I must say goodbye for it is getting late. I hope this will find its way to Manchester stamped and find you quite well.

Goodbye, with fondest love
        from your affectionate
                ALF
Write soon

The Little Elms
Much Cowarne
Bromyard
20th April 1879

My dearest Polly,

Just a few more lines to let you know that I am in the land of the living and I am glad to say, quite well and in a better temper than when I wrote last for I have found out who made the mistake in the postage of your letter. It was the postman. He had the penny and forgot to stamp it. So it is alright now and I don't think it will happen again.

Dear Polly, I was glad to see that you had fixed a time when you thought of coming home. If you get away on the 3rd or 5th of May I should like you to come down here on about the 9th and stay over Sunday (that will be the second Sunday in May) I should like you to be here on that day for we are trying to get up a Forester's procession to Cowarne church. I should like you to be here to see it. If it is fine it will be a very nice thing but if it is wet it will be very awkward for us. We are not quite sure that we can get it on that day but we are trying our best for it. We have been to one today at a place called Lugwardine about 8 miles from Cowarne but it was so wet that we could not do much. But we had a very nice sermon preached to us in support of the principles of Forestry which we hope to get at Cowarne on the 11th May. So Polly if you can manage to be here about the time to go to church with me I shall be so pleased and I hope, please God, that we shall have some fine weather for the occasion. If Captain Bourne is here it wont matter in the least about your coming. I know he would be glad to see you here. I am going to see him tomorrow to have a bit of talk with him for he is down here now.

Most likely I shall tell him about it so all that will be put straight. All that I want is to get you here. I will look after you while you are here. Everything will be put right for you as regards comfort, but Polly you must try and get 3 weeks holiday or else you wont have any time to see about yourself and as Miss Knoderen proposed that you should have a holiday she can't have any objection to you having a week over the fortnight. And you have not had a holiday since you have been there. If you ask her she can only say 'no'.

Well Polly, I have not much more to say this time so I shall leave all the news till I see you but before I shut up I must tell you that I received a mysterious letter from Manchester on Saturday week and I could see that two persons had had a hand in it. The letter and my name in full was wrote by one hand and the other part of the address was written by another. The letter was not a very long one. 'I love you' in big letters was all the letter. Then signed A.B.C. So it was not a very long one. So if you know who it was who wrote it, you can tell them that I have guessed who wrote it, and tell them: I am glad they love me and I love them in return.

Now Polly I must say goodbye. Please give my love to your mother and all at home when you write and tell them that I am quite well and I hope they are too. Now

Goodnight and bye my dear Polly

> With fondest love I am, most affectionately
> ALF

Fred came down to see me last week and stayed 3 days but it snowed all the time so he did not have much pleasure. All are quite well at home.

> Much Cowarne
> Bromyard
> 7th May 1879

My dearest Polly,

Just a line or two in answer to yours of yesterday and to tell you the way to Cowarne. I am glad that you got home safe, and glad to hear that you found all at home quite well. I should like to have been there to meet you but at this time of year I can't get off. But it is a good job I was not, as you had so many to see you on Sunday, or else between us all you would have been worried to death. But never mind it is nice to have friends to flock around one. It shows that you are loved and respected by them. I should like to have seen them all when I was over at Christmas but it was such a day that nobody could get out of doors - only old Nance and I. Please give my love to them all and tell them that I hope to see them the next time I come.

Well Polly, I don't want to write a long letter this time as I hope to see you on Saturday. I must now tell you the particulars: The train that it will be best for you to come by, leaves Bromsgrove at 1.14 (and don't stop at Stoke) and gets to Droitwich at 1.28 and gets to Worcester at 1.45. Then the train for Hereford leaves Worcester at 2.05. You can book from Droitwich to Barr's Court. I will be there to meet you. There is an earlier train that stops at Stoke (11.02) but you would have to stay in Worcester until the 2.05 train for Hereford.

I don't think that I shall say much more this time, only that you will find us in a muddle when you get here for we all are busy shifting. Beard is going to his fresh home on Thursday.

I hope it will be fine on Sunday for our walk to church. It has been very cold yesterday and today and looks likely for wet but I hope not. Did you go to Bromsgrove on Tuesday? I hope you found all my people quite well. You must bring me all the news when you come. Don't trouble to bring any parcel for me if you have to walk to the station for it will only tire you.

Now Polly, goodbye. Please give my best love to your mother and tell her she must take great care of you this time or you wont come home again.

Goodbye and look out for me on Saturday

With fondest love, I am ever

Yours affectionately

ALF

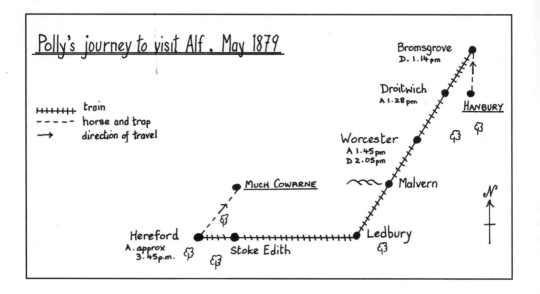

Polly's journey to visit Alf. May 1879

Much Cowarne
Bromyard
May 27th 1879

My darling Polly,

I was so glad to see a letter from you and to see that your cold had got nearly well and I hope this will find you quite well again as I am glad to say it leaves me at present. I quite agree with you Polly in what you say about me staying at Cowarne. I am sorry to leave it but I will not be trodden under foot by anyone. Since the Captain gave me notice he has been remarkably civil to me. I asked Mrs Beard to tell him that I wanted to see him on Saturday, so she did and he asked her what I wanted to see him about so she told him something about him taking to my garden stuff. He was rather surprised and sent out for me but I was away somewhere and did not see him. I think he is in a bit of a stew. He thinks I ain't going to leave but he is sucked in.

He thought when he gave me notice that I should be surprised and make a fuss about it, but he was disappointed for it just suited me. He wants me to think better of it. For I asked him today to spare me a few minutes to speak to him but he would not. He said that he should be coming over again on 6th June and by that time I should have time to think over it but I got nothing to think over for my mind has been made up a long time. For I don't mean to stay here after I get another place. I shall go if it is before the 6th. I shant wait for him. I mean to be as independent as him. I thought when he told me that he should not part the cottage it was only his nastiness but I have found out since that it is a fact. I was talking to our foreman builder about it today.

He told me that the Captain told him not to do anything at all at it except pull the W.C. down and make that other little room next to it into one. That is being done today so I suppose that will be a finish. It is a good job Polly old girl, that things have turned out as they have for I should never have gone there 'till the house was properly divided. I shall soon get hold of another place as good I dare say and then I shall be able to wash my hands of them all. I know Beard is mad about me going and what makes him worse is because the Captain did not tell him to give me notice. For he has been telling everybody about that he was my master. Now he is sold and it makes him so crabbed. I believe nearly everyone on the estate, both workmen and masters, wants me to stay. They have asked me to try and make it up but I tell them that I shall look out for a better master in a better place. Old Pennent is come over here from Grafton and he says that all the servants there are on my side and that I am to stick to my guns and face it out and they will let me know how things stand at Grafton, but I shant trouble. I shall look out for another place and go to it and show them that I am independent of them and their place. I am glad that I have the most on my side for it let one or two know that I am thought as much of as them.

Dear Polly, don't think that I am down spirited about it for I am not. In fact I am rather pleased and if I could only have you near me I should be all right. I seem to miss you more now than I did before you came down here. If I could get a place where we could be both together for a few months we could do nicely but I suppose we must stay apart until we are married as it has always been our lot. But when we do come together we must pray to God to grant us a long, happy and useful life together. Which I hope will be granted us and then we shall be able to make out for all this long parting.

Polly I have tried to make a comfortable home for us in future and although I am frustrated just now, I am in no way going back or losing ground. As soon as I get settled again we must try our luck together, for the summer never failed us yet, no nor never will.

Now Polly my girl, I must say goodbye for the present. We Foresters are not going to the local church on Whit Sunday but to Stoke Lacy - that is the next parish to Cowarne on the Bromyard road. I think Herb is coming to see me then so he will have a good outing. I will send you all the particulars about it next time. I will send you the sermon that you heard preached at Cowarne church. Please give my best love to your mother and all at home and tell them that most likely I shall come and see them towards the end of June.

Now goodbye and God bless you.
       With fondest love I am ever yours.
                                    ALF

Much Cowarne
Bromyard
June 2nd 1879

My darling Polly,

Just a few lines to let you know how I am getting on and to tell you the news if there is any. Well Polly, I am still at Cowarne and I expect I shall be for another fortnight. I have not heard of anything yet that would be likely to suit me. I think of putting an advertisement in the Worcester paper this week for I don't care to go a long way from home and the Worcester paper would be the most likely to suit my purpose. But the Captain is trying to get me a place but I don't know if he has succeeded. Just after I had finished my last letter to you I went out and by chance met the Captain. So he asked me what I meant doing after I went from here, so I told him that I should try and get an under gardener's or a groom and gardener's place. He looked at me rather old and asked if I intended giving up the keepering. I told him that if I could get a single handed place or head over a beat I should try it again but I should not take an under keeper's place again. He told me he would try and get me a place and do all he could for me and he would be most happy to give me a good character and I was to go and see him when he came down here again on 6th June and he would talk the matter over with me. So I shall wait until I have seen him before I do much for myself.

I shall like to have a week at home to go and see all the folks about Hanbury, so I shant be in too big a hurry but if I should see anything that would be likely to suit my interests and yours of course, I shall take it. I am not bound to stay my month if I see a chance to get another place but I think most likely I shall for it is a dreadful busy time with keepers just now.

We have got over a hundred young pheasants and the weather is so much against them that it makes us a lot to do and if there was a fresh hand to come amongst them perhaps it would be the cause of killing most of them. I don't think they want me to go now they have given me notice but I have not been asked to stop. Well, my Polly, how are you getting on by this time. I hope you are quite well and got settled again. Don't be fidgety about me Polly, for I shall soon be settled again at something and I shall always have one thing in sight to guide me and that is Right and not might. Although things look rather black at first, something bright always turns up out of it and I mean to be always pushing forward. It is no use nowadays waiting for something to come to you. We must look after it and we shall be most sure to find.

Dear Polly, we had our walk to Stoke Lacy church on Sunday and a very nice one it was, and the sermon that we had preached to us was capital. I will send you the paper on Thursday with it in. There was only 40 of us this time, just the Foresters from about Cowarne. Herbert was down here and him and I led the Foresters to church and back. Mr Meredith, my former chum, was a little behind so Herb took his place. After we came back from church we all had tea at Mrs Palmer's but Polly we did not have you to pour out for us. I missed you I can tell you. Mr Lane and Mr Prosser were the only two that came from Hereford and we spent a very happy evening together.

Dear Polly I got the paper alright with the letter. It was a shocking thing to see so dreadful an end of a drunken life but it is generally the case but Polly is it not a warning to us. It shows us what drink does for us.

It makes us a miserable life on earth and cuts off all hopes of a happy life hereafter. Well Polly, now I must say goodbye for the present. I will write again at the end of the week after I have seen the Captain. Then I shall be better able to tell you what I mean doing.

So Polly, goodnight and God's blessing on you.

> With fondest love,
> I am ever yours affectionately
> ALF

Much Cowarne
Bromyard
June 10th 1879

My darling Polly,

I know you have been expecting to hear from me to know how I am getting on. I ought to have wrote before but I thought if I waited a bit I would be able to tell you what I am going to do but at present I am unable to say. I saw the Captain on the 6th as he promised he would but I did not get much out of him. He said that he should be most happy to give me a first rate character and he would do all he could for me. He told me he had been to Lord Windsor's at Hewell to try and get me in there as keeper and he said I stand a very good chance of getting in there, but Polly, I won't have it. It is not the sort of place that I want for it is another underkeeper's place. I want either a beat to myself or else head over a beat, while I should get neither at Hewell. So I told him that he need not trouble about getting me in there. So then he asked me how I should like to go to Hanbury Hall. At that name I began to think that I was getting on first rate for I have been wanting to get to Hanbury for a long time. I have heard that it is a capital place for a keeper and Mr Vernon is a good master as you know.

Well Polly, the Captain told me that I should have a very good chance of getting there. He had seen Mr Vernon and talked to him about me and told him why I was leaving and everything about me and I suppose I am got into pretty good graces with him for he told the Captain that when he had an opening he should be very glad to have me. The Captain says that I should be most sure to get there directly and he will let me know more about it on Monday, so until then I am uncertain what I am going to do.

Should you like me to go to Hanbury or do you think it too near home? My heart is with it, my Polly, as I know I have got some fast friends there and people that I know I could do well with. So if I can get a keeper's place there I shall take it but I don't think I shall try for one anywhere else. I mean to try the gardening. I have written an answer to the advertisement you sent me but I have not had an answer yet but I expect one tomorrow (Wednesday) I hope I shall get it for I think it is a place I should like and I know I can do the work for I have done it all lots of times. The beans are easy enough except when they are forced which I don't suppose is done there. It is only done where there is a lot of sorts grown and a lot of people kept to look after them. Perhaps there is some done at Mr Sykes (Polly's employer) but of course that place advertised is not so grand as his or else the gardener would not have to look after cows and a pony, he would find plenty to do in the garden. Anyhow I hope I shall get it and then I will try and do the work.

You know Polly I don't mind going a long way from home. The reason I should like to get a place near home was because I thought you would like to be near home. I can be happy anywhere with you Polly whether near home or not. All I want now is a home for you and I, and the sooner I get it the happier I shall be. If it is at Doncaster I don't care or anywhere else, it will be the same, but I am very glad it is not at Cowarne under Captain Bourne. I am very glad you came to see it for if I had brought you here before you knew what it was and things had turned out as they have done I should never have forgiven myself. I can see now that I should never have done what I wanted to have done and I am very glad that I am leaving it. I have found out lately that one or two wanted me gone long ago so now I hope they are satisfied.

I know Beard is for one, although he says he is sorry I am going but one of his croneys is coming from out of Staffordshire in my place so you can see how things have been working. I hope they will do well but I never saw a Staffordshire man do long for the Captain yet. If Beard don't mind he will find that he is playing a wrong tune. He is telling every little tattle to the Captain that he can get hold of not only one but of everybody he comes in contact with and a good many are waiting their chance to land him one. There is not a man on the estate that likes him and I know that if a keeper is not liked he can't keep game, for everybody is against him. I hope he will see his folly in time for I don't wish him any harm although he has done his best to do me all the harm he can. But I don't think I am any the worse off for it and I shall soon be out of his way.

Well Polly, I have not much more to say this time only we are very busy amongst the Foresters. We have made about 20 since you were here and we expect as many more shortly. I am going to a Forester's Fete at Saltmarsh Castle near Bromyard on the 18th. That will be the last before I leave here as I leave here on that day. I must now say goodbye for it is getting late. I will write again on Sunday and perhaps by then I shall be able to tell you more. I shall go home for a day or two if I get that place at Doncaster for I want to see your mother. I hope she is quite well. Please give my love to her and to all the folks there and tell them that I hope to see them on Sunday week if all goes well. My mother and all at home send their best love to you and are anxious to know how you are getting on.

Now Polly my dear, goodbye. Hoping this will find you quite well.

With fondest love, I am yours affectionately

ALF

Much Cowarne
Bromyard
June 19th 1879

My darling Polly,

I am so sorry to have kept you so long without a letter for I know that you have been anxious to hear how I am getting on and all the rest about me. I have had a lot to do this week as regards the Foresters. I have been out every day this week. That is how it is that I have not written before. Well Polly, I was very glad to receive your letter and to hear your advice which I thought is sound and good. I have given up going to Hanbury Hall as I think, with you, that we are better away. I have told the Capt. not to think any more about it as I do not intend to take another keeper's place, so I think I shall hear no more about it. I think you are quite right in saying what you did as regards Hanbury. Of course you know more about Hanbury than I do. That is why I asked you what you thought about it. I thought at the time that you would not care to live at Hanbury, then I thought you would be near your friends and perhaps you would like to be near them for a bit.

You know Polly, I don't care to be too near home as there is always some unpleasantness going on either one way or the other. Yet I don't care to be quite out of the reach of home for after all there is no friend like a mother and I know your mother don't like you going so far away from her and we all know we can't live for ever and I think that if children are to be comforts to their parents it ought to be in their old age. So Polly you see how it was. I thought you would like to be near home. When I think of taking a place I think of everything belonging to it. I study your comfort more than I do my own.

I should never forgive myself if I took you to a place where you could not be happy. It would break my heart to see you miserable and that is one reason that I shant take another keeper's place. I can do very well without it and I am getting tired of trudging about nights and days, Sundays and all the time that is sent. I begin to see that I have been doing a wrong thing for myself and now I will try and set it right. While I have been a keeper I have not been able to get to church on a Sunday or go out like others of an evening; always trudging about in the dirt and all for nothing. I am heartily glad that I can see my way to give it up. I know that you would not like to be penned up in the house all day. You would like to go out for a bit sometimes, while if you were a keeper's wife you would have no chance of getting out anywhere especially in the summer time for they are always expected to be at home. So Polly it is better for you and I to give it up.

I never used to think what you would have to do as a keeper's wife but now the time is near that we are to be married it makes me think of our future comforts as well as the present. So from now Polly, I shall cease to think of being a keeper and try for something else - a gardeners if possible. I did not hear any more about that place in Doncaster. I should have liked it very much but never mind I shall be at Liberty next week to go where I like and then I can apply personally to an advertisement. It is always the best way. I am going home on Saturday so this will be the last letter I shall write to you from Cowarne, and the next you will write to my home. All the people about here except Capt. and Beard say they are sorry I am going but tells me it is the best thing I can do under the circumstances. They say I would never be properly settled under the Captain as long as Beard is here. They all say that Beard is the snake in the grass.

I don't think there is a man or a woman in the place that cares a turn about him. We have got him fast though now. He put some poison down in amongst Mr Meredith's sheep and poisoned his sheepdog. Of course Mr Meredith went to the Captain to ask him to buy him another which would cost £5. The Captain was very sharp with him (Mr Meredith) and told him that he should do no such thing. So Mr Meredith told him he should have to make him then. When the Captain heard that he asked him to prove that Beard had put the poison down as he knew Beard would not do such a thing. So after a lot of sharp talking Mr Meredith said that Alfred would prove that he put it down. That shut the Captain's mouth and he is to buy another dog or make Beard, just to stop further proceedings. It is a heavy penalty for laying poison about. So we have got the Captain and Beard for once. That will let them know that they can't have it all their own way.

Now Polly, I must say goodbye for the present. I was at a Forester's dinner at Saltmarsh Castle yesterday. That is about 10 miles away from here towards Tenbury.

I will tell you all about it next time I write if I can't get a paper with it in to send you. I am going to Hanbury on Sunday if all is well then I shall be able to write a long letter next time.

Now goodbye, with fondest love,
I am ever yours affectionately
ALF

Rock Hill
Bromsgrove
July 4th 1879

My darling Polly,

Just a few lines in haste to answer yours if I can. I waited until today thinking that I should be able to tell you more about the place I told you of at Macclesfield but I have not heard any more since I told the gentleman to apply to the Captain for my character but there is plenty of time yet as I did not hear from the place 'til last Saturday, then I have wrote back since then so I may have a letter tomorrow. I don't think the Capt. would recommend me for it as there is a lot of fishing belonging to it and I have not had much practice at it, none at all at river fishing as I never lived near a river. The man's address is: P.Dale in Macclesfield. If I hear any more about it I will tell you when I write next time.

Dear Polly, if the Capt. will give me a good recommendation I shall get a very good place near Milford Haven but I shant be able to go until September. I think of the two, this is the best. The wages are £1 a week, house and garden and clothes. It is a single handed place, at least I should have a boy to help me. So if the Captain's recommendation is satisfactory I shall get it and know it in a week. If I get it I shall want you to come with me or else very soon after I have got the place a bit straight, for I don't think I could go all that way off without taking you along or else having a good understanding when I should fetch you. But as the time draws on we must make up our minds which will be the best thing to do. I will talk to your mother about it when I go to Hanbury again.

Milford Haven is in Pembrokeshire, South Wales. It is a watering place. The gentleman's name is Stokes and he wrote a very nice letter to me so I think he is a nice sort of a man. I have been at work all this week at gardening and I expect I shall be at the same place next week so I am not idle yet. If I can get a bit of work until September I don't mind for I feel confident that I shall get the place for I know that my character will bear the strictest investigation. Well Polly, I am in a hurry tonight so please excuse mistakes and bad writing. I will write again on Monday.

Dear Polly, it is a rather singular thing to see a human being with two odd eyes but it often happens among dogs, sheep and cattle. Sheep dogs are very apt to have odd eyes but they are none the worse for it, so perhaps your fellow servant is no worse for it.

Now Polly, goodbye for now, hoping this will find you quite well as it leaves me at present. Fred comes home tomorrow for a day or two. Fanny as been rather middling since Dogday come in and her thumb pains her a bit. So it makes us rather frightened. She is better today.

> Now goodbye Polly, with fondest love
> I remain yours affectionately
> ALF

Rock Hill
Bromsgrove
July 21st 1879

My darling Polly,

You will see by the address that I am still at home but I don't know how long it will be, for I am not at work today because of the wet. The ground is so wet that no one can get on it. I don't like losing wet days so tomorrow I am going to see if I can't alter it. I am going to try to get into the Railway Police for abit until I can see something that will be likely to suit me. Everything that I have applied for has always been taken up before I get at it except Col. Stokes and that, I believe, I shall get yet. I don't care about him advertising in 'The Field' for I expected he would do that for he is trying to get the best man he can. He told me he was in no hurry for a man as it was a long time until the 29th September. He told me he had received a first rate character from the Capt. and he thought I should suit him but he would let me know. As long as he keeps advertising it shows he has not found one.

But, my Polly, never mind. I did say I shall be alright again after a bit. I don't put myself about now like at first. I have had some work. Although it is not regular, it has kept me going. Wet days make me a bit downhearted for a time but I bears it. I thinks of the hymn that says "Oh Lord how happy we should be if we could cast our cares on thee." I am going to Derby tomorrow to see what can be done. I don't intend to take no porters place. I mean to try for the Police as I shall have a chance of getting about then. How I get on I will let you know one of these days. I might see a chance of doing well in the Railway Police.

If I do I don't see why I should not stick to it. Of course I shall know more about it after I have been in it a bit, then I can let you know and seek your advice. For I never regretted taking your advice yet. Dear Polly, you will think me a 'rum un' for taking to fresh whims but it is something that has propended* my head these last few days. I don't see any harm in trying it, do you? I might see a chance of getting a gardener's place as I get about. I liked the idea of your gardener's, in writing to Nurserys. I have done it before now but sometimes you have to wait a long time - 6 months sometimes. If I don't do what I want to at Derby tomorrow I will write to some of them. The Nursery people don't get much places for outsiders. All the best places are taken by their own men so it is not much use after all but I will write. I mean to by and by and get settled into something before the week is out. I am tired of all chance work.

Dear Polly, I did not go to Hanbury last Sunday nor yesterday, for last Sunday it was so wet and yesterday it rained sharp just as I thought about starting. I shall most likely go one day this week. I shall be sure to if I do any good at Derby tomorrow. The Rifle Corps goes to camp at Hewell this week and Friday (the field day) the gardens are going to be thrown open to visitors. I would sooner see the gardens and sham fights than plays of any sort. There is a lot of people going from Stoke, Droitwich and Hanbury.

There is no news from about here worth telling but I walked home with Ellen White from church last night. She told me that Grafton was nothing like it used to be. They are always at loggerheads with one another and everything goes on very unpleasantly. She says she shall leave the first chance she has. So you can guess how comfortable they all are.

She and Albutt wishes to be remembered to you, and Mr Stubbs. They all ask after you. Now Polly I must say goodbye for this time. Hoping to be able to tell you better news next time and that this will find you quite well.

With fondest love,

I am still your old affectionate

ALF

Note: *'Propended' means inclined

Rock Hill
Bromsgrove
August 1st 1879

My darling Polly,

At last I have got some favourable things or news to tell you of. At least my troubles are come to an end for a bit I hope. I have got a place in South Wales, a keeper's (in Glamorganshire). I can't tell you much about it yet for it is come about so sudden that I have not had time to learn many of the particulars. I know this, that it is much a better place than Cowarne was to me - at least as far as my work goes. The master told me that it is a beautiful and healthy part of the country and if I take care of myself I shall have a good place, which I shall be sure to do. I always try to do my duty where ever I go - and Polly, this place I want to make my home so I shall try and do my best.

There is no works any where near the place I am going to. It is a very hilly place and the name of it is Penllyn Castle, near Cowbridge. I must tell you all the particulars when I get there and have seen the place. I shall be there all being well by Tuesday evening. I am to be second keeper but I don't know how many there are kept. I must leave all that 'till another time. What I know of the place as yet, I think I shall like it very much. The Head Keeper have wrote to me and by his letter I should judge he is a very nice man. He gives me all sorts of good advice and he wants me to take him some fowls from about here. I am going today to look for some. I am going to Hanbury after dinner to see if there is any about there of the sort that I want. I should have went to Hanbury yesterday but I waited to see how the affair would turn up. Now everything is settled.

I go there to say goodbye once more. I shall have to go and see all the folks for I shant have another chance. I have been writing a letter to the Bromsgrove Paper of Forestry. If it is put in I will send you the paper tomorrow. I am nearly tired of writing this week for I have done such a lot of it. I have not got any news to tell you for all is about the same about here, but Polly, be of good cheer. I hope to have better news for you from now and that our troubles are come to an end for a bit and I hope the next we have we shall be able to share them together.

Never think that you did wrong in trying to persuade me to leave Cowarne for I did quite well in leaving. I can see now that I could never have done any good for myself as long as Beard was there and you could see farther than me to see as you did. So if it should please God that I should do well hereafter I shall always think that you were the means of helping me to do it. Ever since I have known you I have taken your advice and I have always found it to be good and sound and been the means of bettering myself in many respects. If I don't happen to see the drift at the time it always comes to me in time. So Polly, I shall always take your advice for the future.

Now Polly, my darling, goodbye. If you write on Sunday write here. If you don't you had better wait until I write to you from Wales. Now goodbye.

With fondest love

I am your affectionate

ALF   Please excuse mistakes.

From: Bromsgrove, Droitwich and Redditch Messenger. Saturday August 9th 1879

Friendly Societies and Hospital Sunday
To the Editor of the Messenger,

Sir,

Will you kindly allow me to make a few remarks, through your valuable paper on the Friendly Societies in Bromsgrove. No one, I know, can feel more pleasure than I do to see the noble way in which they are trying to benefit the working classes. I saw it announced in the Messenger of Saturday week that the whole of the friendly societies in the town were trying to make a hospital Sunday of their own, and that a committee had been formed to carry the object into effect; the proceeds to go towards defraying the expenses of the cottage hospital.

This sir, is a grand work. The societies themselves are gatherings of respectable working men, to aid each other in sickness or distress, and to provide something for the benefit of their families should it please God to take them away by death. Therefore each society in itself is a great relief to the ratepayer; because, if a man provides for himself and family when he is strong and in good health, should sickness overtake him he would not have cause to apply to the parish authorities for relief; therefore every shilling saved in that way is a shilling in the ratepayers' pockets. Now, if all the working men in Bromsgrove were in some friendly society, how much lighter the poor's rate would have been last winter; but I am sorry to see that not more than one-twentieth are enrolled in any society.

There are three Foresters' Courts in or near the town, but they barely average a hundred members each; and I believe there are two or three Odd Fellows' lodges, and one of Druids: they may muster three hundred more; but what are six hundred men to the whole population of the parish of Bromsgrove?* I may here mention that any respectable man, in good health, who is over eighteen years of age and under forty can become a member. If the gentry and tradesmen in the neighbourhood were to take the matter up, and enrol themselves as honorary members, they could do a good deal towards influencing working men to join some society. I don't think that either of the Foresters' courts in the town can boast of an honorary member, while some courts possess as many as twenty or thirty, and I know of one that possesses over sixty.

But how is this Sir? It is because the different societies don't keep themselves sufficiently before the public. I would suggest a Sunday parade now and then; that is, let the different courts or lodges meet at a certain time at their respective club-rooms, or any convenient place and then walk in procession to church, first getting the consent of the clergyman, and I am sure that no clergyman, if he rightly understood the object in view, would refuse. The whole thing would be made surer if the clergyman would consent to hold a special service for the occasion. The good Vicar of Bromsgrove, who is ever ready to assist in any good work, would, I am sure, be the first person of whom to seek advice on the subject. Perhaps there would be a difficulty in getting all the members into one church at once; if so, half might go one Sunday, and the other half when convenient for the clergyman. Friendly societies would thus come more before the public, and would be the means of getting more members, and making their objects more fully known.

In conclusion, I would ask the gentry and tradesmen to give the local friendly societies a helping hand. Any respectable man over the age of twenty one years of age can become an honorary member by paying one guinea per year to the funds, or if they don't care to become members they can be subscribers, and subscribe what they like; but I can assure any gentleman who becomes an honorary member that his guinea will be a guinea well spent, and I am sure he will never regret the day he became a Forester, or an Odd Fellow, as the case may be.

A FORESTER

Rock Hill, Bromsgrove, Aug. 4th 1879

*This assertion is incorrect. "Forester" must be ignorant of the fact that the Wolverhampton Order of Odd Fellows and the Bromsgrove Order of Odd Fellows, have a number of lodges in the parish; there are also several other friendly societies in the town and neighbourhood. Ed.

Penllyn Castle
Nr. Cowbridge
Glamorganshire
August 7th 1879

My darling Polly,

You will see by the address that I am in Wales. I got here safe and sound on Tuesday evening but Polly I can't say I like this place at present. This part of the country is very pretty and healthy but the people are a thorough Welsh and they don't like Englishmen a bit. I have spoke to several but I don't like them. If the people were English instead of Welsh I should like the place very much. I believe the Master is a very nice man. His name is Humphrey and he lives at the castle. I am lodging at the Head Keeper's now. I am to have 18/- per week and lodgings found. I dare say that I shall be able to get a cottage after a bit, after I get to know the people more, but Polly I don't think that you will like it but I shall tell you all about the place as I learn it and then you can judge for yourself.

The servants seem to stay for a long time. They are all old ones but I think I would sooner live in England now than Wales. I don't like lodging at the Head Keeper's for I shant have a minute to call my own. I shall try and alter it when I have been here a short time. By the time I have been here a month I shall know more about it. There is 4 men kept here as keepers but 2 of them does anything that is wanted besides. I have nothing whatever to do besides, just my keepering. The Master has only just begun to preserve so I don't know how he is going on. Perhaps he will give it up again directly but I can't say. There is no game on the place now so we have got our work cut out. If I stay here I shall try and get a beat to myself.

The Head Keeper is an Englishman and as yet he seems a very nice man and does his share of the work, different to old Beard. There is only 1 room to this house to live in and of course everybody is here, youngsters (3) and all so please excuse mistakes and bad writing. Dear Polly, perhaps I shant be able to write very regular but I will write as often as I get a chance, if it is twice a week, but don't be disappointed if I am a little longer than usual sometimes. If I don't think that this place will do to make a home in I shall chuck it directly. I shall try and get another first. I can't understand the Welsh people. If they were English here I know I could do very well. We are about 4 miles from the sea so we can often get a sea breeze and we are about 12 miles from Cardiff and 6 from Bridgend. I don't know much about either place yet but I hope in course of time to know all about everywhere. I do want to get a settled place. I can't have changing so much. There is not much night work here for we are a long way from any factories of any sort so we are free from poachers.

Well Polly, I have not got much more to say this time but I hope to be able to tell you a better account of the place when I write next. When you address my letters please put Game Keeper on them for all the letters go up to the castle, then the letter carrier will know who it is for. Now Polly, my darling, I must say goodbye for the present hoping this will find you quite well as I am glad to say it leaves me at present.

I went to see Aunt Barley and Polly and Jessie the night I was at Hanbury. I did not see William Barber but I saw Jessie. Tell Nellie I can get lots of nuts about here. Please tell your mother how I am getting on when you write. Please give my love to them. Now Polly goodbye, with fondest love

I am ever yours affectionately   ALF

Penllyn Castle
Nr Cowbridge
August 12th 1879

My darling Polly,

I was very glad to see a letter from you this morning and as the place is pretty quiet just now I thought I would write a line or two to you. I have been here a week today and I have seen a lot of the place and I like it very much. Penllyn Castle is a very nice place but it is not very old fashioned. It has been built in modern times. The master and missus, I believe are very good people, especially her. She is something like Lady Vernon in her ways: She has a Sunday School of her own and superintends it on Sunday and she has sewing classes and all sorts of things. Everybody about here gives them both a very good name. Most of the servants have been here a very long time. The coachman has been here 26 years and the gardeners and labourers about the place have been here 8 or 10 years. They don't get very great wages but I believe they get other things instead. The chaps on the place tell me if I were married and lived in one of the master's cottages I should only get 16/per week. They say that is the standing wage for everybody.

I am told that all the servants on the place get all sorts of treats and a seaside trip once a year and at Christmas something else is getting forward. There is several English people here, 3 or 4 of the servants are and 1 or 2 of the tradesmen in the town is, but the Welsh don't like them. The old coach man's wife told me today that the best way was to leave all the Welsh people alone and not offend them, then all would be right. She is English.

The Head Keeper and his wife are the rumest folks I have seen for some time. They have both been married twice. She was a cotton merchant's wife in Liverpool at first and have seen better days and she doesn't forget to tell me so sometimes. She is about 40 and her husband is about 50. They have both got a large family by their first marriage but only 3 of them are at home. I get on pretty well with them. I am near enough my own master and I dare say that if I could get a cottage on the estate I should do very well, that is if I can get nicely settled. I should so much like you to come to me and see what you think of the place. If the people were English I should like it better than any place I have been to. One bad thing belonging to the place is there is nothing but soft water to drink. I don't think there is a well in the parish.

Living is very reasonable and coals are 10/- per ton. Clothes are much about the same as about our part of the country. I shall see in the course of a month or two how I shall be likely to do. I have seen the master two or three times but not to say much to him. I shall have a better chance to talk to him when the shooting season comes in but I think I can get a cottage, for there is several on the estate now. I must get more used to the place before I say anything about it. The churches about here are most of them English and we have got one, and a very nice one it is too, close to the castle and Mr and Mrs Humphrey are head and chief in it. As I learn more about the place I will keep telling you how I like it. I don't think any servant leaves here unless he or she want particularly to leave. They think a good deal of their servants. If I see a chance of settling soon I think we could do very well here at least as far as I can see now.

There is a Forester's Court in the town but I have not had anything to do with them yet. I must know them a bit first. My letter was published in last Saturday's paper. I send it with this. Nance said she should like to see it so when you have done with it you can let her have it. Please give my love to all at home when you write and tell them that I am getting on pretty well and that I like it better than I did at first.

Now Polly my darling, I must say goodbye for the present. Hoping to write to you again soon. I am quite well and I hope, please God, you are.

Now goodbye, with fondest love

I am ever your affectionate

ALF

Goodbye and God Bless you.

Penllyn Castle
Cowbridge
August 19th 1879

My darling Polly,

Just a few lines to let you know how I am getting on, and to let you know all the news but the news are very scarce. I am getting on much about the same as when I wrote last. I seem to like the country better than I did at first. In fact if I can get some fresh lodgings I shall be all right but I don't like the lodgings here. I can't have a minutes quietness at all. This is the second letter I have written to you today for the youngsters knocked the ink all over the first one, so I am writing this one in its place. I saw my master yesterday and had a little talk with him but I had no chance to ask him about a cottage. I shall have to stop until I get more used to the place but I shall certainly seek for some fresh lodgings. That is, if the master is agreeable for me to lodge with anyone else.

I cannot bear the keeper's wife. She is nearly master here but I have told her that I won't have any of her masterful ways. She is always on and expects me to do everything for her but I have to tell her that as soon as I have done my own work I want my time for myself, but if I do come into the house I don't get any peace for she is on the whole time. I only wish I could get a cottage at once and on the place. I wont stay here but I think I can get one. The master seems such a nice man that I think if I ask him he wont refuse. All the other servants seem to get on very well but I don't think they like the head keeper. He makes himself too fast with them. I am very good with them all and they will do anything for me.

I and the head gardener are very great friends. He often gives me things out of the garden. There are 5 gardeners kept but most of their work is to look after the shrubberies for there is such a lot of it and a great deal of grassland, pleasure grounds etc. It is not much of a garden. Something like Grafton but the place is 10 times as large as Grafton.

There was an accident near Cowbridge on Saturday evening. The passenger train from Llantrisant to Cowbridge ran off the rails and down an embankment but no one was killed although several was injured and all are going on all right as I heard today.

Dear Polly, I know it is far too far for you to come down here to look at the place. I only wish it was not. I seem to get more and more out of the way. The railway fare from Bromsgrove to Cowbridge is 9/5 so it is considerably over 100 miles but Polly, let us hope that our long separation will soon come to a close. I hope to go home at Christmas if I stay here and I want you to be at home too. Perhaps before then I shall have come to some settlement. At least if I stay here I shall know what I am going to do by 1st October then I shall be giving you a chance.

Now Polly, I must say goodbye. I can't write while I have such a noise to contend with. So Polly my darling I say goodbye and God Bless you.

With fondest love, I am ever yours affectionately

ALF

Mother and all at home send their love to you.

Addressed to:

Miss Weaver, Cringle House, Cheadle, Manchester.

Postmarked:

Cowbridge	19	Au	79
Cheadle		Au	20	79
Manchester	20	Au	79

Penllyn Castle
Cowbridge
26th August 1879

My darling Polly,

I am trying to let you have a letter before you go into Wales just to let you know how I am getting on. I am writing this at 4 o'clock in the morning before anybody is up. For there is no peace after they get about. None of them can bear to see me writing. The woman is as bad as the children. I had a regular blow up with them yesterday morning. The headkeeper and his wife went out visiting on Sunday evening not letting me know where they were going to or what time they would be back. They left the children at home, a lad of 15 and a girl of 12 and a little one. Well, I went to church. It is about 150 yards from our house. After I came from church I waited up until after 10 o'clock and the folks did not come back so I went to bed and they came home about 1 o'clock. I heard some loud talking but they said nothing to me until I got to breakfast in the morning.

Then they both began to blow me up like one o'clock for going to church in the evening and for not stopping up for them. I very soon told them I would not sit up all night for nobody and as for going to church, it was the first time that I had been blown up for going to church and I should go to church when I thought proper. When they heard that the man said that I could not stay there so I said that I would get some fresh lodgings. Then he said that Mr Humphrey would not allow me to lodge anywhere else so I mean to see what can be done. Mr Humphrey is from home now and when he comes back I mean to ask him for a house to myself or I wont stay. I will do anything sooner than I will be trod on by people no better than myself.

Oh Polly, if only I had got a comfortable home here I should be as happy as anybody could wish to be for the work is not hard and I believe Mr Humphrey is a first rate master and the place is very healthy and pleasant. The sea comes within 4 miles of us in lots of places. A place called Dunnaven is a noted place for the people about here. There is a beautiful oldfashioned castle there and many people go there in the summer time. Then there is Swansea not far from us and several other places that I don't know the names of. We are situated near the turnpike road leading from Cardiff to Swansea. We are about 14 miles from Cardiff and 2 miles from Cowbridge and 4 from a nice little town called Bridgend. The roads are capital so it is easy to get to town and back. This is a noted place for limestone and most of the roads are made with it so when it is wet weather the roads are like wet mortar but they dry directly and then they are capital travelling roads. There is a great annual cattle fair held close to here today at a place called St Mary Hill. It is supposed to be the largest in Wales. It is held on the top of a mountain far away from any town. It is a queer place to hold a fair.

I think it is very cold and windy here this morning so if it don't get better the people will all be blown away. It has been very bad weather here for the haymaking. There is lots not carted and some not cut. The corn harvest here is very late. There wont be any cut about here before 1st September. I hope when it is ready there will be some fine weather to get it up together with.

Dear Polly, I was glad to hear that Nance was going on alright and liked her place. I hope she will be well and able to stay. Do her thumb ever pain her now. Give my love to her when you write.

It is a bad job about Mrs Cole. It was the best thing they could do with her was to send her to the asylum. She will be well looked after there. Give my love to your mother and Nelly when you write and tell her I don't hardly know what I am going to do about stopping here but I shant leave until I have another place. Now Polly, my darling, I think I have told you all for this time. Mother, father and all at home sends their love to you. And now goodbye old girl and God Bless you .

With fondest love I am ever yours affectionately

ALF

I may try to get some sort of a situation in or near Worcester. I am going to see about it this week. I shall try it just for a bit to see how I like it because you will like to live near Worcester.

No. 1 Barbourne Terrace, Worcester
(Autumn 1879)

My dear Mother,

I hope this will find you and my dear Nellie quite well. You will be glad to hear I am getting on alright. We have got enuf to do to get the house straight, as the people are so long bringing the things. We have got two nurses. They came on Tuesday so I hope they will soon have something to do. I saw Dick on Wednesday night. Miss Topping told me to have him in so I told him to come in again and then I could send this by him and the biskits for Nellie. I shall be very pleased to hear from you and Jessie for it seems a long time since I came hear. Miss Topping is very kind and trys to save me in many ways for she sais she is sure I am not so strong as I ought to be so she wont let me do no more than she can help. There is so many stairs and my kitchen is at the bottom. She gets the nurses from the top so that helps a bit, and take them to there room and bring them back again so I think I shall get on alright when we get straight.

What dose my darling say about my being away. I wish I could see her sometimes but I suppose I shant for a long time. I hope she is good. I have sent the biskits for her to have one or two when she is a good girl. Tell her if she is very good I will send her some more soon. How is she getting on with her work. Is Aunt Mary's quilt done yet? Let me know all about it and how Nellie gets on at school. How is Mrs Cole? Is she better or gone away? Please send me word if you have heard from Pollie since I came hear and if she has sent you word how Alfred is getting on in Wales. I suppose Jessie has not missed me much because she has had her aunt and Miss Blisard with her. I suppose Bill is come back by this time.

Give my love to Jessie and ask her to write and let me know all about how she has got on and give my love to all the rest. I have not had time to write to anybody else but I will write to Pollie after I have heard from you again.

Hoping you and my darling are quite well.
I remain your ever loving child
ANN W.

Penllyn Castle
Cowbridge
Sept.12th 1879

My darling Polly.

I am afraid you will think that I am not going to write in time to catch you while you are in Wales but I hope this will. I could not write before for I can tell you that I can't get a minute to myself now. I don't intend to stay here for I can see that I shant do any good with this keeper. I saw Mr Humphrey this week and spoke to him about the way I was going on. He was quite willing for me to change my lodgings but he did not see his way clear to let me have a cottage. He said that he had not got one that would do for me, so Polly, of course I shant stay.

I will try and see what I can do in the Police. The place is always sure there and this is not. For I don't believe our master cares a fig for game. We have been out 4 days shooting and only killed 4 head of game. You know Polly that is too brown (dull) after preserving for years. If I get fresh lodgings, the head keeper will always be at me for we get worse friends every day. He wont be here long for the master and the farmers are beginning to complain about him, and not one of the servants on the place likes him. If I was here by myself as keeper I could stay here all my life for I believe our master is as good a master as ever was and a very straight forward man.

I shall look out for a gardener's place while I am here and if I don't hear of one I shall try the Police when I get to Worcester. The wages of the Police are 21/-, 23/8 and 25/- per week with a bit extra for books.

The above sums are for constables in the 1st, 2nd and 3rd Class. It don't state what a sergeant's pay is, but about 28/- I think. So Polly if you come home in November I will try and be there to make some arrangements. I will write to your Mother in a day or two. Our people at home will be very glad to see you when you get home. They all send their love to you. I am sending the paper to you with this letter. You will see about the Hanbury Show in it.

Dear Polly, you must please excuse a short letter this time for the folks are bothering me. I will write a longer one when you get back to Cheadle. I don't think there is any more news to tell you as I have not heard any. My brothers Frank and Albert have joined the Foresters. Fred has been at home bad. The doctor's tell him he must leave Birmingham for he can't stand the foul air. Now Polly, my dear, I must say goodbye for this time. Hoping your visit to Wales has done you good and that you have enjoyed yourself. It has been wet here every day this week - makes sad work with the Harvest.

Now goodbye, with fondest love
I am your ever affectionate
ALF
Please remember me to Polly Barley and all the rest of the Hanbury folks.

Penllyn Castle
Cowbridge
Oct 6th 1879

My darling Polly,
You will think that I am a long time in answering your letter, but I am often away from home when I ought to be writing. Sunday is generally my day since I have been here but yesterday we had a general job to do. We were at it nearly all day. We were trying to catch an infuriated bull that had got away and it took nearly a score of us all day to do it but we mastered him at last. It belonged to our master. So Polly that is the reason I did not write yesterday. You will get this as soon as you got my last if you did not get it until Wednesday. I wrote it on Sunday afternoon and posted it at night for I thought then that you would get it on Monday night. I wrote in answer to an advertisement at the same time. I have not heard any more about it so I expect it did not get to its journey's end till Wednesday like yours, then it would be too late.

Well Polly, I must tell you that I am getting on much better here than when I wrote last. I think that the people that I lodge with can see their mistake. They find that I

am as good as they and can take my own part as well. They are got exceedingly obliging but I think they were labouring under a mistake from the first. They thought I was
their servant and they my master but they have found out a different thing. They don't
want me to leave now but I think they are afraid, for I heard that the steward said that
if I left the head keeper would have to go too. I am going to see the steward one of
these next days and know what the master means to do.

I want to see him before next Saturday if I can for I want to give notice on that day
or else you will be home first. I am rather in a fix just now. My Hereford friends want
me to go into the Hereford force and my friends at Penllyn are trying to persuade me
to stay here a bit longer, and Father and Mother and all at home want me to stay here
a bit longer too but I want to know which will be the best for you and I. That is what
I am looking out for. If I can find out what all the civility is about I shall be better able
to judge. I expect a letter from Hereford every day. What I want to do is to get something without troubling Capt. Bourne. I mean to cut him altogether if I can.

Dear Polly, I and the other keeper had a very narrow escape from a dreadful death
on Friday afternoon. How we escaped I don't know. We were out rabbit shooting and
we came to a heap of dead hedge trimmings when we saw a rabbit go in. So we sent
two dogs into the heap to fetch him out. Well, we missed one dog at once and could
not tell where he was gone to. So we got onto this heap of trimmings to tread the rabbit out when the old rotten rubbish gave way under our feet and the dog that had stayed
with us was thrown down into an old lead mine about 70 feet deep. How we saved
ourselves I don't know but thank God, we did, but the poor dog was knocked all to
pieces in the bottom of the mine. Then we found out where the first dog had gone to.
It had fell into the bottom of the pit at the first. We got a lot of men together and pro-
cured ropes and a pulley and let a man down to see if either of the dogs were alive.
One was, but badly hurt and we don't expect him to live. The other was nowhere to be
found, he must have been killed then sank to the bottom of the water which was in the
bottom of the pit. I will tell you more about it when I see you. It makes me shudder
to think about it.

Dear Polly, I should be home as soon as you for I long for a quiet Sunday at home
with you. It will be 2 years next Sunday since that very windy night, do you remember, just before you went to Manchester. Now Polly, old girl, I must say goodbye for
this time, as it is getting late. I am surprised to hear that there is to be no Harvest
Home at Hanbury this year. I shant write to your mother until I have seen our Steward
or heard from Hereford for then I shall know better what I am going to do. There was
a grand Forester's Church Parade at Ashperton on Sunday week. John Palmer was
there. I will send you the account of it when I get it. I heard from Mrs Meredith last
week, she is quite well and all her family send their kind regards to you.

Now goodbye, Polly, with best love
          I am yours affectionately
              ALF

Addressed to:
   Miss Weaver, Cringle House, Cheadle, Manchester.
Postmarked:
   Cowbridge   7   Oct 79
   Manchester   8   Oc   79
   Cheadle   Oc 8   79
   Cheshire

Penllyn Castle
Cowbridge
October 23rd 1879

My darling Polly,

   I am so sorry that I have kept you so long without a letter but I was in hopes to have told you when I should be at home, but I can't yet as my master has been out for some time until yesterday and I have not had a chance to see him, but I shall most sure to be at home about the 22nd of Nov, 3 weeks after you. I should be glad if I could be at the station to meet you but I don't see a chance of that now. I am getting on about the same with these people. They don't want me to leave. I have not told them that I intend to give notice. He thinks I have made up my mind to stay but I would not now, after what has passed, for any money. They have begun to find out that I have seen as much as they. I am on exceedingly good terms with them.

   Our Master is out hare hunting today so perhaps I might see him tonight. When I have seen him I will let you know what he says but I expect he wont say much for he will soon be able to get another to suit him, for there is not wanted a first rate man here, only a rabbit catcher. For there is nothing else to do. When I came here there was 4 men on as sort of keepers. As soon as I came they began to leave the keepering and go to work at something else for the Master, so I am the only one left now. If I had known before I came that it was such a place as it is I would not have come. The farmers are grumbling every time I meet them about the rabbits so I shall be glad to get away and leave my worthy companions to it.

   Well Polly, old girl, I suppose this will be the last letter I write to you at Manchester. If all goes well I suppose by this time next week you will be thinking about packing up. I only wish that I was there to meet you. I long to see your face again and I hope after this that we shall be able to see each other oftener. There is nobody I know longs more a nice quiet Sunday that I do. I hope for a good many after I get away from here. I have not been to church since that time I told you I got blowed

186

up about it. I have often stood outside the door of the church and listened to them singing the hymns. When I get home we must have a turn down to that chapel that we used to go to. I have been almost buried alive since I have been here. I have not had a minute to call my own. I have been out (at work) nearly every night since September came in, yet when I came here I was told there was no night work hardly. There is more here than I had a Grafton or Cowarne. I cought them Poachers that I was after when I wrote last to you and took them to Bridgend and fined them 15/- a piece.

Well Polly, I don't think that I have much more to say this time. There is no news to tell you and I must write short letters now or else I shant have anything to tell you when I see you. If you are too busy next week to write to me, which I expect you will be, I shant mind if you don't write till you get home. If you don't write I shall con-clude that you will get home on Saturday the 1st Nov. I shall most likely write to you for, that day too, old Jane is going back to Grafton as House Keeper. Now Polly, my darling, goodbye for this time and please give my love to your Mother and Nance and remember me kindly to all enquiring friends when you get home. I have wrote this in a hurry so please excuse bad writing and all mistakes.

With fondest love, goodbye from your ever affectionate

ALF

Penllyn Castle
Cowbridge
Nov 1st 1879

My darling Polly,

Just a few lines in haste, hoping you are got home quite safe and sound and Mother and little Nelly quite well, who I know would be glad to see you. I only wish I could have been at the station to meet you but you are there by this time. It is half past 6. I shall be home to meet you before long but I can't hardly tell you yet which day it will be. I am going to leave as soon as our people can get someone else in my place. I don't care how soon they do for I want to be away from here. I hope to be away by this day fortnight that will be the 15th. Our people here rather stared when I gave them notice, they did not think I meant it. I was unable to see the Master the day I wrote to you last but I saw him this next. He was in a hurry so I had not much time with him. I have got to see him again before I go. I shall be able to get a very good recommen-dation from him. That is all I want. He is a jolly sort of fellow but he don't like ser-vants leaving him. He always wants a very good reason. I have got mine to give yet but it is a very good one.

Well, Polly old girl, I dare say you will have plenty of company for a day or two now, for I know there will be a lot glad to see you again, Aunt Barley amongst the rest. You must remember me to her and ask her if their new Cider is made yet for I shall be sure to call and look for some. I wish I could be with you for a Sunday or two - which I hope to be when I get home. We must go and have a look at Stoke Church one Sunday morning just to keep up old times. I have not been there for some time now. We shall find people altered, especially the young ones.

I can't stay much longer now Polly to write more for I have to go out watching. This makes the 12th night running. I don't get much rest. The Police can't be no worse. But before I finish, I wish you Polly, many happy returns of your birthday. Last year I was in hope that we should have been in a position to spend it together this year but it was so willed that we should not. Let us look forward to another with faith, and trust in God, and I know all will be right.

Now Polly I must conclude this short scribble. I will write again in the course of 2 or 3 days. I was in hopes to have been able to have wrote so as you could have had this as soon as you got home but I was out all day on Friday and till 4 o'clock this morning.

Now goodbye for this time. Give my love to your Mother and little Nelly and remember me to all enquiring friends.

> With fondest love, I am ever
> your affectionate
> ALF

Addressed to:
> Miss M. Weaver, Nr. the Vernon Arms,
> Hanbury, Bromsgrove, Worcs.

Postmarked:
> Cowbridge   No 3   79
> Bromsgrove   No 4   79

Rock Hill
Bromsgrove
Nov 21st 1879

Dearest Polly,

Just a line to say we all hope to see you here, before dinnertime on Sunday. Never mind about going to Stoke for you would have to start so soon. If you start about half past 10 I will do the same and meet you. I have asked about a bed for you, so please ask your Mother if she will mind if you stay all night. Fred and Fanny are coming and Fanny will sleep with you if you don't mind, at Mrs Butler's just below our house on the opposite side of the road. Come if possible for all will be glad to see you. Come by all means to dinner for we shall all be at home, Fanny, Fred and all for they are coming on purpose to see you. Now goodbye. Hoping this will find you and your Mother quite well.

With fondest love,
I remain yours affectionately
ALF

My Police papers is filled up and sent off.

Alfred

County Police Station
Worcester
Nov 29th 1879

Dearest Polly,

Just a few lines in accordance with my promise and to let you know how I am getting on. You will see by this that I am at the Police Station and all letters that is addressed to me here will find me. I shall be very glad to see you next Sunday. If you come please let me know what time you will be likely to be here then I will get leave and come with you. I have to ask leave to go anywhere but I have no trouble to get it. We are expected to go to some place of worship at least once every Sunday so it will be no problem for me to come with you.

I know the place where Nance lives and I will try and see her before this day week then she can arrange a place to meet at. If you come on Saturday I will try and go as far as Barbourne and see you, but I shall be able to tell you more about it before then. Well Polly, I don't think I shall write very long letters as I hope to see you very often. After I have learnt my drill I shall be able to get off oftener. I like this place very much and the work. The more I see of it, the better I like it. I saw Herbert today. He told me he had been to Hanbury and seen you. I hope you are alright and your Mother. I shall have lots to say to you when I see you. Now I must say goodbye for now. I will write again in a few days. I might see Nance tomorrow.

Now goodbye, with fondest love, I am your ever affectionate
ALF

Fred is bad at Birmingham.

County Police
Worcester
Dec 4th 1879

Dearest Polly,

I received your letter alright today and was glad to hear that you are coming to Worcester on Saturday. If you can be up at the Cross at Worcester, or the Market Hall about 4 o'clock on Saturday afternoon I shall be sure to meet you. If I don't see you on Saturday I shall be sure to on Sunday evening. I don't think I shall be able to come and meet you in the afternoon and evening too but I will if I can. I shall like very much to go with you to St. Paul's. I will try and see Nance before then. I shant want my shirts but if you have done with the coloured one I should like you to bring that. I am getting on first rate here. I don't expect I shall be here long.

Now I must say goodbye for the present. Hoping to see you on Saturday. Give my love to your Mother and all the Hanbury people. Hoping they are all quite well.

With fondest love,
        I am you ever affectionate
                        ALF
Wrote in a hurry, not much time. I shall be in plain clothes.

Addressed to:
    Miss Weaver, Nr The Vernon Arms, Hanbury, Bromsgrove.
Postmarked:
    Worcester   DE 4   79
    Bromsgrove DE 4   79

County Police Station
Worcester
Dec 13th 1879

My dearest Polly,

I know you will like to know how I am getting on so I will write a few lines to you instead of going to church. You will see by the address that I am not shifted yet. I have not heard anything more about it since I saw you, only I have heard that I shall most likely have to go to Whitley this next week for a few days. It is Lord Dudley's shooting week and the Policeman that is stationed there fell down last week and broke his leg so I expect to have to go and do his duty while the shooting is going on. I have been once just to learn the way about a bit but I have not been ordered to go there. The man stationed around his beat is doing his work now. I expect before this day week that I shall know where I am going to for good and as soon as I know, you shall know.

I have not got any news for you this time but don't be surprised to hear some any day. I hope I shall be able to know by this day week. If I do I will try and get off and come and see you. I shall be able to tell you more than I could if I wrote. I am glad to say that I am getting on first rate. The more I know about it, the better I like it. Sometime when you are talking to Polly Barley ask if she knows a chap by the name of Clark. He used to be a miller at Mr Jackson's at Wychbold and Polly used to talk to him a bit on the sly. He is in the Station along with me now. Well Polly, old girl, I shant write long letters for I hope to have you with me soon. So until then I will write short and often, just letting you know how I am getting on. Give my love to your Mother and remember me kindly to all enquiring friends.

I hope to see you in a few days, so goodbye my Polly, for the present
With fondest love
I remain yours ever affectionately
ALF

If I go to Whitley this week I will write to you from there but any letters directed here will be forwarded to me.

1880

Alf takes to his new life. Polly stays at home nearby. This time promises are kept and at last the long wait seems to be over.

Hanbury from Jinny Ring
June 94 and May 99
E.M Hoyes

County Police Station
Worcester
January 1st 1880

My own dearest Polly,

It is with a heavy heart that I have to write to you again without telling you the news that we both so much want to hear. I am very anxious to hear them and before another week is over our heads, I will know. I may know by tomorrow for I intend to ask the Colonel tomorrow, if he is here. I was going to ask him today if he had come. He will be sure to come tomorrow if he is well enough. He has been ill for this last week. If I see him tomorrow you will most likely have a letter from me on Sunday morning. I quite understand how you feel and that you want to be knowing what to be at. I did not think for a moment when I joined the Police that I should be at Worcester more than a month or I would have made a different arrangement; but it is owing to the Quarter Sessions and the Assizes being so near. I shall be sure to be off after they are over.

So Nance and I have been talking it over and I think, with her, that it will be best for you and I to be asked in Church while I am at Worcester and then be married as soon as I leave here. So I am going to ask the Colonel's permission and get it done as early as possible. I am almost afraid it will be too late to be asked for the first time on Sunday next but I will write to Mr Ogilvy tomorrow as soon as I have seen the Colonel. I think it will be best to be asked for at Hanbury and Bromsgrove, and be married at Bromsgrove. We will arrange that after a bit. I am getting quite out of patience. I did not think that I should have been half as long as this but this is very uncertain.

I was at Whitley 3 days last week but had to walk there in the morning and back at night so I did not have time to write. I began this letter on New Year's Day after I had seen Nance but I was called to go on duty at a moment's notice so I could not finish it. I don't care how soon I get away from here now. I am getting on first rate and go away at any time.

Dearest Polly, if you think what I have had said in this letter is right and that you agree to the plan please let me know. I think it will be better for us to be married at Bromsgrove than at Worcester for I am not certain where I am going to and Bromsgrove is handy for anywhere. Please tie a piece of string round your finger and send it to me in your next letter so that I may see the size of your finger. Now dearest Polly, I will say goodbye for this time and please expect a letter from me either Sunday or Monday.

Wishing you a Happy New Year. With fondest love
In haste, most affectionately
ALF

County Police Station
Worcester
Jan 4th 1880

My own dearest Polly,

Just a few lines in haste in answer to your kind and welcome letter. I dare say that you had mine at the same time that I got yours. In my last I said what I thought would be best but yours is the better plan, only that we shall have to be married at Hanbury but it will be quiet enough if we like. I can't stop to explain much now as I am tied for time. We shall be very busy till Thursday morning for it is Quarter Sessions. After that I will write again. I have spoken to my Superintendent and he will see the Colonel before I can see him. I shall be able to tell you all in my next.

I have just seen Nance and brought your parcel away but I have not had time to open it yet. Very many thanks for it. The P.C.Hayes you saw in the Worcester paper meant your poor old Alf. I dropped on them in St. John on Christmas Eve. You will see it in again before long. I can't stay to say much more this time or else I shant post this in time. Nance is all right and sends her love to all. I am glad to say I am quite well and getting on first rate so far. I was at a fire last night at Norton and these next four days I shall be on duty in the City of Worcester at the Quarter Sessions. Now Polly, old girl, I must say goodbye this time. Remember me to all inquiring friends and give my love to your mother and Nell.

Now goodbye again, with fondest love
I remain yours affectionately
ALF

County Police Station
Worcester
January 17th 1880

My darling Polly,

I am afraid I shant be able to come to see you tomorrow as I have got to go with the judge to church at 10 o'clock tomorrow morning. I have written to Mr Ogilvy and to the Vicar of Bromsgrove so look out for squalls! You will hear of something, sure to, before evening.

Yours faithfully ALF

I may be able to get off towards evening. If I can I will come.

Mount Cottage
Hanbury

WEDDING ANNOUNCEMENT

from: Bromsgrove, Droitwich and Redditch Weekly Messenger
        Saturday 7th February 1880

HAYES - WEAVER February 5th at the Parish Church, Hanbury, by
the Rev. Norman Ogilvy. Alfred William Budd, second son of Mr
Joseph Hayes, Rock Hill, Bromsgrove, to Mary, youngest daughter of
the late William Weaver of Mount Cottage, Hanbury.

CERTIFIED COPY OF AN ENTRY OF MARRIAGE   GIVEN AT THE GENERAL REGISTER OFFICE, LONDON

Application Number Y71320.

1880. Marriage solemnized *after Banns*			in the *Parish* of *Hanbury*			. in the County of *Worcester*		
No.	When Married.	Name and Surname.	Age.	Condition.	Rank or Profession.	Residence at the time of Marriage.	Father's Name and Surname.	Rank or Profession of Father.
279	Feby 5th 1880	Alfred William Hayes	23	Bachelor	Policeman	Great Malvern	Joseph Hayes	Gardener
		Mary Weaver	26	Spinster	Domestic Servant	Hanbury	William Weaver	Bricklayer

Married in the *Parish Church* according to the Rites and Ceremonies of the Established Church, by _____ or after _____ by me, C.W. Norman Offly

This Marriage was solemnized between us, { Alfred William Hayes / Mary Weaver } in the Presence of us, { Frederick Joseph Hayes / Ann Weaver }

CERTIFIED to be a true copy of an entry in the certified copy of a register of Marriages in the Registration District of **Droitwich.**
Given at the GENERAL REGISTER OFFICE, LONDON, under the Seal of the said Office, the 9th day of May 19 89.

MX 257649

This certificate is issued in pursuance of section 65 of the Marriage Act 1949. Sub-section 3 of that section provides that any certified copy of an entry purporting to be sealed or stamped with the seal of the General Register Office shall be received as evidence of the marriage to which it relates without any further or other proof of the entry, and no certified copy purporting to have been given in the said Office shall be of any force or effect unless it is sealed or stamped as aforesaid.

CAUTION:—It is an offence to falsify a certificate or to make or knowingly use a false certificate or a copy of a false certificate intending it to be accepted as genuine to the prejudice of any person, or to possess a certificate knowing it to be false without lawful authority.

County Police Station
Great Malvern
Feby 10th 1880

My own dearest Polly

I received your very welcome letter this morning and very glad I was to see it, for I, like you, are not contented. I feel quite lost and I don't care how soon these people find me a house. If there is not something said about it before my Superintendent visits this station again, which will be about Monday, I shall ask him about it. I don't want to bother too much for fear they should shift me from Malvern. I think if I don't bother them much I shall stay here but if I get on to them too much they will put me to any sort of a place - the first they have got on their hands. I don't care what sort of a place for my part they put me to so that I can have you with me but I should like for you to come here. It is a nice place and I know you would like it.

I can tell you that I am regular lost since I left you. Sometimes I think I will find a house for myself and chance displeasing them, then I keep on hoping and thinking it wont be long. I think it will be like all the rest of the affair - all come right in the end if let go on its own way but I can't stay very long without saying something about it. I miss you more now than ever I did in my life. I don't seem to be able to do anything in my old way. I seem to be something short and so I am, for I am short of my wife and until I have got her with me I shant be right and I shant rest until I have started something to get her with me. Dearest Polly, I was so glad to hear that you had not had to stand any sneers from anyone. I was so afraid you would but I suppose they know better. Then we are never sure what people are.

It was the hardest thing, Polly, I ever did in my life to leave you behind. I don't think I could do it again. If I had not been obliged to go I would not have gone on Friday night.* I might have stopped until the first train on Saturday morning but I knew if I had stayed any longer it would have been harder for me to have left you. I hope it will never be my lot to have to part from you again. Oh Polly it is hard! I can't tell how you stand it but at times I can't hardly bear it. I thought I should be able to stand it better as I had my work to do but I can't forget. I seem that miserable sometimes I don't know what to do. I will try and bear with it. It can't be for long, then with God's help we will try to do the things that is right. Then we shall be happy in the true light of married life. Until then we must do our best to be happy, if not content, with our lot.

Dearest Polly, I was sorry to hear that poor little Nell was poorly and with the measles too but I hope they will come out well, then there is no fear of danger if she don't get cold. I hope she will soon be better for I know your mother is anxious about her. I shall most likely be in Worcester on Saturday morning. If I am, I will call and see Nance. Well Polly my darling, I suppose I must soon say goodbye again for it is time to go on duty again. I should like you to send some wedding cake to Mrs Beard and Mrs Meredith for I know they would think a deal of it. I should like all our old friends to know about it. I think it was put in the paper very well. No one can make a mistake as to who it is. We must keep one paper ourselves. I have got mine so if you like you can send off all yours. Now Polly, I really must say goodbye. Give my best love to Mother and tell her I am getting pretty well under the circumstances. I hope she is quite got over the wedding party. Tell her we wont have another wedding if she got knocked up at it.

I will write again in a day or two - perhaps before if I hear anything. Now I must say goodbye with fondest love.

Goodbye, goodbye and God Bless you my darling wife

Believe me, your ever affectionate husband

ALF

As I was going home on Friday I met Polly Barley.

Note: *Alf and Polly were married on Thursday 5th February and Alf had to leave Polly and return to work on the evening of the following day, Friday 6th February. They did not get their long desired home for a further two weeks when Alf was transferred to Broad Heath near Worcester where they lived for the next four and a half years.

The Police House
Broad Heath

8, Market Street
W'hampton
May 27th 1880

Dearest Alf,

I think it is time I sent you a few lines just to let you know I am in the land of the living and quite well I am pleased to say and I hope you and Mary (Polly) are the same. I hope she has got sound again. This nice weather will do a good deal towards it. I should have very much liked to have seen you at Whitsuntide but I was obliged to return on Monday so I thought it was hardly worth while coming for so short a time as an hour or two but it is only a pleasure deferred.

I must tell you how I am getting on in the first place. I like W'hampton very much. I am quite agreeably surprised I can assure you. It is as pleasant a town as I have been in for some time and I am in hopes of being settled here before long. My masters are very good ones, both young men not much older than myself, both under 30. They were both apprenticed at this shop together and when their master gave up the business they took to it. It is a wholesale and retail place. There are 6 in the shop, 4 in the tin shop and 3 in the Smith's shop, myself and another smith who has been there 26 years, and a youth that helps us both. The oldest tinman has been there 30 years, so you may guess it is not a very bad place. I am pleased I took it. I go out of town sometimes but very seldom stay over night and I am glad of it for I had enough of it. Fanny sends her love to you and Mary and says she has nearly finished that thing she is doing for her and will send it in a few days. She is staying with me for a few days and she likes the place as well as I do and she will very likely stay.

Dear Alf, I have very little more to say this time so I must now conclude. Hoping you are well.

I am ever your aff-ate brother
FRED

P.S. Please excuse this scribble as I have written in haste.

I dare say you have heard that Herb is corresponding with his schoolmate, and playmate sweetheart and she is a very nice girl got, I can tell you. I saw her in Droitwich on Whit Monday.

* W'hampton is short for Wolverhampton.

Alfred W.B.Hayes

Alfred Hayes joined the Worcestershire Constabulary on November 25th 1879. He was retained in the reserve until January 1880, when he was posted for one month to Malvern. His first permanent posting was to the Worcester Division of Broad Heath, where he served from February 1880 until September 1884. He appears to have progressed well, and attained his P.C. 1st class by September 1881. (There were at that time three classes of P.C.) He was transferred in October 1884 to Fernhill Heath where he remained until 1892. During this period four children were born - Harold in 1884, Gilbert in 1886, Alfred in 1888, and Eleanor in 1891.

In August 1892, he was promoted to Sergeant, and stationed at Worcester. His period in this posting was marred by the death of his second son Gilbert, who was found drowned in 1895. In 1897, while still at Worcester, he was promoted to Inspector, and his last child, Albert, was born.

He moved to Redditch in 1901, and became Superintendent there in July 1902. He remained in Redditch until his death in 1913.

Mary (Polly) continued to live in Redditch and died at the home of her son Alfred in 1930.

Source: Police Headquarters, Hindlip Hall.

Alfred W.B. Hayes

Alfred and Polly attend the wedding of their son Harold to Nancy Linton.

Back Row: 2nd from left - Alfred W.B. Hayes   3rd from left - Mary (Polly) Hayes
5th from left - Mrs. Linton   6th from left - Mr. Linton
Middle Row: 3rd from left - Harold Hayes   4th from left - Nancy Linton
5th from left - Alfred K. Hayes   6th from left - Eleanor (Daisy) Hayes
Front Row: right - Albert Hayes

WHO'S WHO

A

Mr. & Miss Ainge	Friends of Polly, and Mary Douglas.
Albert	Alf's younger brother.
Albutt	Worked at Grafton Manor, near Bromsgrove.
Rev. Aldham	Priest at Bromsgrove.
Alf	Alfred William Budd Hayes. Polly's fiance. A gamekeeper based at Grafton Manor. Born 1856 in York Town, Surrey.
Alf's brothers	Herbert, Frederick, Frank, Walter, Albert.
Alf's father	Joseph Hayes, a gardener. Born in Rydal, Lake District, next door to the poet Wordsworth. Joseph left Rydal the year Wordsworth died. He moved to Royal Military College, Sandhurst and then to Bromsgrove in Worcestershire where he lived until his death.
Alf's mother	Harriet Maria nee Budd. Married Joseph in Slough, Bucks.
Alf's sister	Youngest sibling. Harriet Louise, known as Louie.
Alf's uncle	Fred Budd, a lamplighter at R.M.C. Sandhurst.
Alf's grandfather	Jonathan Budd, a warehouseman at R.M.C. Probably a former soldier, hence his military funeral.
Alice	Kitchen maid at Grafton Manor.
Miss Amiss	Attended Grafton Manor Ball with Joe Carwell.
Mr Amphlett	Visiting speaker at Hanbury Harvest Home.
Annie Turner	Lived in Hanbury, had a trick played on her.
Ann/Annie/Nance	Polly's sister. Married Bill Weaver, one daughter at the time of the letters, (Little Nell). Cook in Hanbury and at Worcester.

B

Sir Samuel Baker	Provided surety for Col. Baker.
Col. Vaughan Baker	Apparently brother of Mrs Bourne. Accused of misconduct.
Miss Banner	Lady's maid at Grafton Manor, lived in Bromsgrove.
Jessie Barber	Friend of Mary Douglas and Polly in Hanbury. Needlewoman. Later married John Stanton. Related to Sarah.
Sarah Barber	Friend of Mary Douglas and Polly. Needlewoman.
Aunt Barley	Polly's aunt.
Jessie Barley	Polly's cousin.
Polly Barley	Polly's cousin.
Richard Barley	Polly's cousin. Also known as Dick.
Mr Bayliss	Farmer at Howning's farm, Hanbury.
Mr E.Bearcroft	Mere Hall, Hanbury. Supported local causes around Hanbury.
Miss Bearcroft	Broughton Court, Hanbury.
Mr H.Bearcroft	The Mount, Hanbury.

Mr & Mrs Beard	Worked with Alf at Grafton Manor and Much Cowarne.
Mr Bedman	Under gamekeeper at Grafton Manor.
Billy Best	Attended Hanbury Sunday School Treat.
Clement Best	Newly married. Visited his relatives in Hanbury.
Jemima Bicknell	Cook at Hanbury Rectory. Court Case - concealed birth.
Mr Birch	Gamekeeper with Alf at Grafton Manor, died in Kansas, USA.
Mr Blunn/son John	Friends of Alf, lived in Charford, a district of Bromsgrove
Mr & Mrs Bodwell	Newly married, visited Bromsgrove.
Mr Botley	Had a butler and nurse. Involved in search for Mr Smith.
Cptn. Bough	Employed Alf's brother Albert.
Cptn. Bourne	Later Colonel Bourne. Owner of Grafton Manor and Cowarne Court. Employed Alf.
Robert Bourne	Known as Bertie, son of Cptn. Bourne. Died at the age of nineteen after catching Typhoid at Army Camp. Visited Alf at R.M.C. shortly before his death.
Sarah/Sal Bradley	Friend of Alf and Polly, servant at Grafton Manor.
Mrs Butler	Neighbour of Alf's at Rock Hill, Bromsgrove.

C

Father Campbell	Roman Catholic priest attached to Grafton Manor. Died 1874
"Carrots"	Under housemaid at Grafton Manor.
Joe Carwell	Attended Grafton Manor Ball with Miss Amiss.
Mrs Caustin	A widow. Polly's employer at Richmond, Surrey.
Charley	A gardener at Grafton Manor.
Col. Chesney	His funeral was held at Royal Military College.
Jessie Cole	Friend of Polly's, Hanbury. Married William Griffin in 1878. Daughter Annie born 1880.
Mrs Cole	Taken to an asylum.
Bessie Cottrill	Lived in Hanbury. Fell out of a wagon in 1876.
Mrs Creswell	Landlady of the Woodrow Inn, Hanbury.
Jane Crockett	A servant at Grafton Manor.
"The Colonel"	Alf had to get permission to marry from the Colonel when he joined the Worcester Police Force.

D

Dr. Davenport	Doctor in Bromsgrove. Probably died of erysipelas.
Mr. P.Dale	Alf considered working for him in Macclesfield.
Mr Day	An under gamekeeper at Grafton Manor.
Mrs & Miss Dixon	Lived at Stoke Grange, near Bromsgrove. Had a servant called Harriet.

The Rev. Henry Douglas	Rector of Hanbury Church. Later St. Pauls, Worcester. Registered blind 1881 Census. Father of Mary.
Mrs Douglas	Wife of Henry
Mary Douglas	Writer of letters to Polly. Polly's friend and confidante.
Douglas family	Relatives of Mary living in Dorset. He was also a priest.
Lord Dudley	Lived at Whitley Court 10 miles N.W. of Worcester.
Duke of Cambridge	Visited Royal Military College in 1876. Grandson of George III.

E

The Rev.J.Edwards	Priest visiting Hanbury from Prestbury in Gloucestershire.
Emily Eaton	Friend of Alf and Polly. Servant at Grafton Manor then moved to Birmingham.
Ellen (Little Nell)	Polly's niece
Emily Payter	Servant at Grafton Manor.
Emma	Servant at Grafton Manor.

F

Fanny	Girlfriend and later wife, of Fred, Alf's brother.
Rector at Farnborough	Suffered smallpox. Staff at R.M.C. Sandhurst concerned
Joseph Fisher	Ditcher injured while at work.
Mrs Forby	Cook/housekeeper at Grafton Manor, and at Stoke Grange.
Mr Fradley	Under gamekeeper at Grafton Manor. Replaced Mr Day. From Staffordshire.
Frank	Alf's brother
Fred	Alf's brother. Working as a whitesmith in Wolverhampton Married Fanny.
Ancient Order of Foresters. A Friendly Benefit Society. An association for the relief of sickness, old age or widowhood.	

G

Fanny Garratt	Recovering from illness.
Louise Garratt	Also known as Lou and Loo. Maid for Rev. Mildmay, Rector of Alvechurch, Worcestershire. Friend of Alf and Polly.
Mrs Gilder	Gave evidence at the inquest of Mr Smith.
Mrs Glidden	Housekeeper at Grafton Manor.
Bill,Jane,Jim Graves	Friends of Alf's
Hannah Grazier	Resident of Hanbury. Glovemaker.
Tom Green	Friend of Alf's.
Bertha Greenhill	Resident of Hanbury. Friend of Mary Douglas.
William Griffin	Later married Jessie Cole.
Joe Gwynne	Servant at Grafton Manor, Friend of Alf's.

H

Jessie Harber	Not to be confused with Jessie Barber. Both from Hanbury.
Harriet	Maid to Mrs Dixon at Stoke Grange.
Herbert	Alf's Brother. A legal clerk at Worcester.
Herbert	The 1881 census indicates Alfred had a son called Herbert in March 1881. He does not appear to have survived to maturity.
Tommy Honeybourne	Child at Hanbury Sunday School party.
Mr Horton	A gardener. Employed Alf's father - and Alf at times.
Mr Humphreys	Owner of Penllyn Castle, near Cardiff. Employed Alf.

J

Jack	Servant at Grafton Manor. Various girlfriends.
Jimmy	Alf's "chum" at R.M.C. Sandhurst
Miss Johnson	Girlfriend of Alf's brother Fred. Fanny?

K

Mrs Kelsey	Well off relatives who lived near London. Visited by Alf.
Miss Knoderen	Housekeeper at Cheadle where Polly worked.

L

Mr Lane	A Forester from Hereford.
Leah	Former servant at Hanbury Rectory. A dressmaker.
Little Lizzie	One of two Lizzies who worked at Wimbledon with Polly.
Little Nell	Polly's niece. Born 1874
'Old' Long	Gardener at Grafton Manor.
Long's son	Once Page for Mrs Caustin (Richmond) then a sailor.
Louie/Louise	Alf's little sister.
Louise Garratt	Also known as Lou and Loo. See G.
Mr Lowe	Helped with haymaking at Grafton. Interested in Polly.
Harry Loweman	A soldier friend of Alf's.

M

Matron of The Firs	A nursing home in Hanbury.
Mr Meredith	Forester friend of Alf.
Rev. & Mrs Mildmay	Rector of Alvechurch, Worcestershire. Employed Louise Garratt.
Liz Moore	Maid to Mrs Bourne. Replaced Polly.

N

Nellie	See L

O

Rev. Ogilvy	Rector of Hanbury, replaced Rev. Douglas. Officiated at the marriage of Alf and Polly.

P

Sir J. Packington	Speaker at Hanbury Harvest Home.
Mrs Palmer	Alf's landlady at Much Cowarne, Herefordshire.
Thomas Parkes	Resident of Hanbury.
Mr Pennent	Servant at Grafton Manor and Much Cowarne. Supported Alf.
William Phillips	Landlord of Bell Inn, Hanbury.
Polly	Mary (Polly) Weaver. Alfred's fiancee. A lady's maid. Born 1854 in Hanbury, Worcestershire. Met Alf at Grafton Manor.
Polly's Mother	Eleanor Weaver nee Barley. Second wife of William Weaver whom she married in Hanbury in 1850
Polly's Father	William Weaver. A bricklayer. Died 1865. First wife was Charlotte Griffiths by whom he had a son, John.
Mr Portman	An acquaintance of Alf.
Mr & Mrs Price	Residents of Hanbury. Mr Price died 1875
Mr Prosser	A Forester from Hereford.
Mrs Pugh's son	Injured when playing near a tree in Hanbury.

R

Mr Randan	Visited by Alf with Cptn. Bourne when at Grafton Manor.

S

William Smith	Drowned at Bowling Green Farm. Inquest.
James Stanton	Former servant at Hanbury Rectory.
Joe Stanton	Possibly a close friend of Jemima Bicknell.
John Stanton	Later married Jessie Barber.
Station Master	At Swadlincote, Derbyshire. Employed Alf briefly.
Mrs Steel	A landlady in Hanbury.
Mr Stokes	A farmer at Milford Haven. Interviewed Alf for a job.
Mr Stubbs	Servant at Grafton Manor.
Mr Sykes	Employed Polly in Cheadle. Connected to a large chemical company. Later knighted.

T

Theresa	Probably a servant at Hanbury Rectory.
Miss Topping	Head Nurse at new Worcester Nurses Training Centre. Employed Polly's sister Ann who worked there as a cook.
Mr Tustin	Worked at Bromsgrove Station Wagon Works. Also in Rifle Corps. Given a military funeral after an accident.

V

Ted Vale	Alf's closest friend. Supported him in a fight in Bromsgrove.
Mrs Vaughan	Polly's aunt.

Sir Harry Vernon	Family owned Hanbury Hall from 17th Century. Sir Harry and his wife were much admired by the local people.
Lady Georgina	Wife of Sir Harry Vernon. Much involved in pastoral care. Set up local nursing training. Paid for Polly's convalescence in Weston.
Rev. & Mrs Vevers	Curate at Hanbury church. His wife died leaving a young family.

W

Mr & Mrs Walker	Employed Polly in Wimbledon as a lady's maid.
Alf Ward	Originally a friend of the Weaver family but later a quarrel remained unresolved.
Lord Ward	Owner of an estate near Bromsgrove.
Fanny Weaver	A relative of Polly's. A house/parlour maid.
Mr Weaver	Fanny's father. A butcher in Hanbury injured by a bull.
Ellen White	A servant a Grafton Manor.
Ted White	A friend of Alf's in Bromsgrove.
Mr & Mrs Wilde	(Also Wylde) Servants working with Alf at Grafton Manor and also at Much Cowarne.
Mr J.Wilson	A speaker at Hanbury Harvest Home.
Robert Windsor - Clive	Lord Windsor, subsequently Earl of Plymouth, lived at Hewell Grange, near Redditch. A large land owner with estates in Wales and Shropshire.
Dr. Wood	A doctor in Bromsgrove. His cook was visited by Tom Green.